Searching for
MARY POPPINS

Searching for
MARY POPPINS

WOMEN WRITE ABOUT THE INTENSE RELATIONSHIP
BETWEEN MOTHERS AND NANNIES

EDITED BY
SUSAN DAVIS
AND GINA HYAMS

FOREWORD BY NATIONAL PUBLIC RADIO'S
MELISSA BLOCK

HUDSON
STREET
PRESS

HUDSON STREET PRESS
Published by Penguin Group
Penguin Group (USA) Inc., 375 Hudson Street, New York, New York 10014, U.S.A.
Penguin Group (Canada), 90 Eglinton Avenue East, Suite 700, Toronto, Ontario, Canada
M4P 2Y3 (a division of Pearson Penguin Canada Inc.) • Penguin Books Ltd., 80 Strand, London
WC2R 0RL, England • Penguin Ireland, 25 St. Stephen's Green, Dublin 2, Ireland
(a division of Penguin Books Ltd.) • Penguin Group (Australia), 250 Camberwell Road,
Camberwell, Victoria 3124, Australia (a division of Pearson Australia Group Pty. Ltd.)
Penguin Books India Pvt. Ltd., 11 Community Centre, Panchsheel Park,
New Delhi – 110 017, India • Penguin Books (NZ), cnr Airborne and Rosedale Roads,
Albany, Auckland 1310, New Zealand (a division of Pearson New Zealand Ltd.)
Penguin Books (South Africa) (Pty.) Ltd., 24 Sturdee Avenue, Rosebank,
Johannesburg 2196, South Africa

Penguin Books Ltd., Registered Offices: 80 Strand, London WC2R 0RL, England

First published by Hudson Street Press, a member of Penguin Group (USA) Inc.

First Printing, October 2006
1   3   5   7   9   10   8   6   4   2

HUDSON STREET PRESS   REGISTERED TRADEMARK—MARCA REGISTRADA

LIBRARY OF CONGRESS CATALOGING-IN-PUBLICATION DATA
Searching for Mary Poppins : women write about the intimate relationship between mothers and
nannies / edited by Susan Davis and Gina Hyams ; forward by Melissa Block.
     p. cm.
   ISBN 1-59463-023-2 (hardcover : alk. paper)
   1. Nannies—United States—Case studies. 2. Mothers—United States—Case studies. I. Davis,
Susan. II. Hyams, Gina
   HQ778.63.S43 2006
   649' .10973—dc22

2006011438

Printed in the United States of America
Set in Simoncini Garamond
Designed by Leonard Telesca

PUBLISHER'S NOTE
The names and identifying characteristics of many people described in this book have been changed
to protect the privacy of the individuals involved.

This book is printed on acid-free paper. ∞

For our children,
Annalena, Bella, and Milo.

Contents

Foreword
Melissa Block xiii

Introduction
Susan Davis and Gina Hyams xix

PART ONE
SEARCHING FOR MARY POPPINS: THE HUNT

The Natural
Marisa de los Santos 3

You, Ceci
Lauren Slater 12

The Story of Robbie and Velma
Jessica Neely 28

Mammy Poppins
Kymberly N. Pinder 39

My Nanny, My Self
Jane Meredith Adams 50

Finding Mary
Joyce Maynard 63

PART TWO

SISTER SUFFRAGETTE: IN IT TOGETHER

The Nanny Conundrum
Susan Cheever 73

The Unflappable Lina G.
Karen Shepard 80

Sisters
Marina Budhos 88

Something to Tell You
Elizabeth Graver 99

Till Faith Do Us Part
Jacquelyn Mitchard 113

The Best Laid Plans
Elissa Schappell 124

PART THREE

A SPOONFUL OF SUGAR: TAKING THE BAD WITH THE GOOD

Dumped
Pamela Kruger 145

Wildfires
Ann Hood 155

In His Memory
Andrea Nakayama 163

The Company of Strangers
Caroline Leavitt 177

The Forever of Remembering
Meg Waite Clayton 187

Nanny Dearest
Daphne Merkin 198

PART FOUR
TILL THE WIND BLOWS IN FROM THE WEST: DEPARTURES

Missing June
Suzanne Berne 215

Inflammitis of the Affluentitis
Rebecca Walker 227

Madame
Roxana Robinson 236

The Long Good Lullaby
Alice Elliott Dark 249

The Other Mother
Anne Burt 258

Tina
Katharine Weber 267

Acknowledgments 277

About the Contributors 279

About the Editors 289

FOREWORD

I start with a confession. Sometimes a whole week goes by in which I never see my nanny. Maybe I've taken my daughter, Chloe, to preschool before Maria arrives, and left work too late to see her before she goes home for the night. My husband, Stefan, has a more elastic schedule; he often handles the handoff. It's possible he should be writing this foreword.

I've also had jolting moments when I've realized that my mother has managed to learn more about my nanny's life in one conversation over tea than I have in an entire year of her employment.

And while I'm at it, I confess that I have, on occasion, found myself coveting my friends' nannies. We have friends whose nanny would leave long notes detailing the daily triumphs of their infant daughter ("Today Ava lifted her hat off her head and put it back on!"). I was green with envy. We know another couple whose au pair prepares sushi for them—sushi, I tell you!

With those disclosures out of the way, I'm happy to add my thoughts to these essays on mothering and nannying from writers who have learned well and, often, learned hard.

As particular as these essays are to their writers' own experiences, they also vibrate with themes familiar to those of us who outsource some of our parenting: gratitude, guilt, resentment, relief. And many of them highlight a common trait in this often-tricky relationship: giant vacuums in communication, in comprehending each other's lives.

In these essays, there are examples of nannies who become far more than children's caregivers, who truly integrate themselves into these writers' families. I also notice nanny misdemeanors that pop up again and again: chronic lateness, erratic behavior, depression, lies, hostility. And I see patterns of maternal response: fears of inadequacy, of asking too much, of underprotecting, of *over*protecting.

Stefan and I hired two nannies in our daughter's first two years. Chances are, you know the drill. An ad placed in the local paper outlining specific needs: Full-time. Live out. Must be legal. Must drive and speak fluent English.

Then, the phone jangling for days, each time bringing a whiff of raised expectation. And then, inevitably, the letdown. A string of inquiries from women who can't drive, who aren't legal, and who—whoops!—don't speak English.

We met a woman who had been extolled by a reference as "the Michael Jordan of nannies," but who spoke in a loud, nasal bray that I knew would drive us crazy. A woman who told us nonchalantly about a boy in her care who fell down a flight of stairs, and then, looking around our house, asked whether we were sure we didn't have enough room to have her live in.

Yet somehow, out of the chaos, a contender emerges. When Chloe was seven months old, we found Claudia, who had solid references and seemed unflappable. In our interview, she gently advised me that maybe the baby shouldn't be chewing on the metallic tag of my fleece jacket. That parenting tip seemed almost reason enough to hire her. And we did.

Chloe would refuse to take a bottle from Stefan or me, and I had nightmares about her withering away when I went back to work. But she took one from Claudia without fuss. Claudia easily navigated the steep stairs up to our house with Chloe and stroller in hand. She made friends with another nanny in the neighborhood, and discovered story time at the local library. Chloe was happy.

After a while, though, some mildly troubling signs emerged. A children's table completely covered with orange marker (not hard to clean, but how long did it take Chloe to complete that art project, and where was Claudia when she was doing so?). Bottles that hadn't been rinsed and bubbled with soap when Chloe drank. Nothing outrageous and perhaps there were perfectly good explanations in each case, but something seemed amiss.

And then, just as I was about to talk with Claudia to go over our concerns, she dropped a bombshell. A family member in Jamaica had died; she had to go home and would be back in a couple of weeks. We scrambled to cobble together childcare. Two weeks passed. No word from Claudia. Then, a vague, brief phone call from Claudia's sister: Her return would be delayed. More cobbling. More anxiety. More and more the suspicion she simply wasn't coming back. Finally, another call from the sister, this one abrupt and ending with a hang up, announcing that Claudia had quit. As much as we reassured ourselves that we were the ones who'd been taken advantage of, we were still stung by worry: Were we bad bosses? Did we ask too much? Pay too little?

When I called her house one evening, angry and ready for a confrontation, she finally answered the phone. "Claudia," I said. "It's Melissa." "Claudia's not here," I heard her say. Click. We've never seen or heard from her again.

So how comforting to find in these pages that we were not alone in our abandonment. Pamela Kruger writes about her nanny, Mary, who said she had to go home to Jamaica to care for her sick father, and then disappeared—also without so much as good-bye. Kruger discloses, "In talking to other mothers, I quickly found out that many of us had been dumped unexpectedly by our nannies. . . . I also discovered that 'going back to the home country' was an infamous exit line among nannies, the equivalent of 'Let's just be friends,' or 'I'm not ready for a commitment.'"

Suzanne Berne writes of her despair over her daughter's sadness after their nanny, June, similarly disappeared without warning: "This was a child so much more sensitive than most, who registered every disappointment, every deviation from routine the way a leaf registers a breeze. A child who also never gave up on her disappointments, but repeated her demands for whatever she'd lost over and over and over."

We heard through the nanny grapevine that Claudia had found another job not far away. (We're still wondering how she explained her lack of a reference for the prior year.) My heart ached when I heard that Claudia would show up at the library for story time and Chloe would run over and sit in her lap, unaware of her betrayal.

But we move on. Chloe has formed a fast bond with Maria, who joined us when Chloe was nearly two. Along with Maria, our daughter has acquired a happy coterie of other Filipina nannies who dote on her and twist her hair into elaborate braids. Not long ago, when we bought her the toy cell phone she'd been requesting for months, we heard her chatting away in the backseat in some singsong language we didn't recognize. "*Sabi na Maria. Sabi na Weng.*" She explained, "I'm talking like a nanny."

Many of the women included in this collection write about their guilt over assuming the role of a boss, with all of its attendant class complications. Elissa Schappell unflinchingly details her own blundering attempts to reach across that class divide, much to her nanny Jesamine's bemusement. Later, she comes to realize that "I wanted to know her and she wanted me to act like a boss."

Katharine Weber writes lovingly about her nanny, Tina, who lived in New Haven's housing projects, and who swept Katharine's daughters into the embrace of a large extended family: "I think she pitied us a little bit, too—prosperous white people who had to pay someone to love our babies because we didn't have sisters and aunts and grandmothers handy and eager to do it." But then Weber catches herself, hesitant about listing some of the many ways her family helped Tina's. "Is it too self-congratulatory to mention these things?" she wonders.

And Kymberly Pinder wrestles with the fact that her baby son is cared for by Teo, who left her own son behind in the former Soviet republic of Georgia. George "was only fifteen months old and still nursing on the day she left him for the United States," Pinder writes. She describes crying with Teo as her nanny tells of a phone call home: "Her hands were shaking and her voice became very high and thin . . . 'George refused to talk to me on the phone today. My mother-in-law kept calling to him but she said he would not come. She also told me that he asked for all of the pictures of me to be taken away.' My stomach turned."

There are stories here of uncommon grace in times of crisis. I marvel at the many-layered sweetness of Andrea Nakayama's "manny," Matthew, who enters their life as Nakayama's husband, Isamu, is on a downward slide with brain cancer. Matthew becomes Isamu's "last friend," Nakayama writes, engaging him in conversation about poetry, love, and Bob Dylan; concocting vegan desserts; and sheltering their son, Gilbert, from the worst of his father's illness.

Caroline Leavitt gets to know her newborn son only by photographs after she contracts a form of postpartum hemophilia and is confined to a long hospital stay. When she comes home, it's through the kind wisdom of nannies that she learns about mothering.

And Ann Hood writes from a chasm of pain about her former nanny's wedding day, shadowed by the grief that her own daughter did not live to be there, too.

Listen to Lauren Slater, who distances herself from her daughter, convinced she lacks maternal instinct, and only later realizes, "I gave my mothering away." Her lesson: "It is important to claim the tasks of motherhood, even when time or trauma makes it difficult. You must, of course, sign the permission slips, shop for shoes, cook when you can, do her hair, with or without the knack."

This can be a complicated dance, this nanny-mother tango. The women who write here have much to tell us both about how it's done, and about the missteps along the way.

Melissa Block
Washington, D.C.

INTRODUCTION

When we were growing up in the 1960s and '70s, the only nannies we knew of were English: storybook characters from worlds so far removed from our own as to be the stuff of fairy tales. Eloise had a nanny who lived with her at the Plaza Hotel in New York City. Jane and Michael Banks had Mary Poppins, who pulled lamps and mirrors out of her carpet bag and whisked the children up chimneys—and who had a remarkably similar singing voice to that of the Von Trapp children's nanny, Maria, in the mountains of Austria. We had babysitters, not nannies: teenaged girls who let us watch TV into the double-digit hours when our parents went out to dinner and the movies on Saturday nights.

When our generation started having babies the world looked like a completely different place. Although we held the same kind of jobs as our parents and their friends—lawyers, teachers, healthcare workers—we were unlike our mothers in that many of us had no choice but to work. Although we shared the same aspirations as our parents—home ownership, education funds, twice-yearly vacations—these aspirations were impossible to achieve on a single salary. Gone were the days of calling the next-door-neighbor's thirteen-year-old daughter to make paper-bag puppets with our children while we dashed out to the supermarket. Instead, we combed city playgrounds with our infants in their BabyBjörns looking not for friends or play-mates, but for nannies who seemed to genuinely like their charges so we could befriend them and learn if they had a sister or a cousin looking to leave Jamaica, the Dominican Republic, Brazil, or Puerto Rico for a chance to take care of our precious children as well as provide for their own.

And, of course, times had changed from when we were little: The feminist movement made us the first generation of American middle-class women who entered adulthood with the assumption that we would work as long and as hard and as seriously in our careers as our male counterparts. After more than four decades of feminism, many of the quandaries of women's lives had been worked out. We could go to any school we could get into; we could participate in combat; we didn't have to be ashamed of childbirth or menopause or other women's health issues; and we could work if we wanted (and often get paid what we were worth). Motherhood, however, remains a problem.

Feminism has not figured out how a woman can experience ful-filling work while being fully present in her marriage and to her children. Instead, we must pay other women to raise our children with us. Hiring a caretaker even makes economic sense, of a kind: Quality daycare is often available, but it can cost as much as a nanny—more, once siblings come into the picture. "Nanny" no longer sounds like the province of wealthy women in penthouse apartments; the word has become interchangeable with "babysit-ter," "au pair," even "housekeeper."

In general, however, most middle-class mothers find themselves unprepared to negotiate what is, to be blunt, a mistress-servant re-lationship. Eloise's mother was rich as sin. Ditto the Banks parents; ditto Captain Von Trapp. Staff was their birthright. If we imagine

Eloise today, all grown up, she is a Park Avenue Princess who attends charity balls, sits on the board of the Metropolitan Museum of Art, and has a succession of nannies for her own daughter along the lines of the fictional NYU student exploited by the New York upper crust in the bestselling novel *The Nanny Diaries*. Eloise would not sob in her pajamas on the kitchen floor if her daughter's nanny quit with no notice.

We would, though, because we didn't grow up in homes filled with servants. We don't have a bred-in-the-bone understanding of the difference between family and staff. We become emotionally involved—whether through deep dependence on our nannies to take care of us as well as our children, our sense of obligation to take care of them, lend them money, and help them navigate the American governmental systems, or through the jealousy we feel when, at the end of our work days, we come home to find our babies clinging to their nanny, crying "Don't go, I don't want Mommy!" It's this raw emotion, the kind that keeps us up nights crying or fuming, that is the pitfall of every mother-nanny-child relationship we know.

These relationships are so perplexing because it's nearly impossible to make peace with them. There is guilt, yes, about working rather than being home and guilt about enjoying our work. But there is also anger: anger at not being able to have it all; anger at having to be an employer; anger at having to be, God forbid, "the man" and negotiate another personality—someone who isn't a member of our family, but trusted with the care of our most beloved family members. We're also angry at having to navigate the exhausting terrain of race and class while trying to earn a living and care for our families.

In the throes of our own nanny troubles, we turned to our local bookstores for answers and found several novels that use nanny characters as an opportunity to poke fun at rich women and an array of scholarly titles that analyze the politics of exploited childcare workers. Books from the mother's point of view tended to fall into two camps: how-to books that deny the complexity of the nanny-mother relationship by claiming that angst and anxiety vanish if one simply follows logical, step-by-step procedures in relating to one's employee; and books supportive of working mothers that note how indispensable nannies are to achieving any semblance of work-life balance, but sidestep the emotional and moral implications of this choice.

Among all of the nanny books, from honorable to humorous, nothing existed that presented the emotional issues that mothers experience when they turn the care of their children, and, to a large extent, themselves, over to a stranger. This is because, among professional and middle-class mothers, emotional loss of control over childcare is almost impossible to talk about.

We were hungry for more: more honesty, more candor, and more company from women like ourselves who struggle with our identities as mothers, working women, housewives, feminists, or any of the above. *Searching for Mary Poppins* grew out of our desire to figure out why having nannies in our homes made us think so hard about who we are and what we want.

The topic of mother-nanny relationships is an emotional minefield. The contributors to this collection overwhelmed and amazed us with their eagerness to write about the powerful feelings they have about the women who have cared for their children. They explore the issues that come hand in hand with the inevitable intimacy of the mother-nanny relationship: discomfort with the role of employer; fear of another woman invading the home and marriage; conflicts about religion; the complexity of women of color hiring other women of color; and much more. The nannies they write about are a far cry from the British governesses of old in their starched aprons pushing perambulators. These women are African American, Central American, South American, Indian, Eastern European, Asian, Caribbean, and Caucasian American, and they bring a vast range of personal and cultural gifts and challenges to the women who hire them.

For the writers in this collection as well as for professional women across the country, employing a nanny is beyond a necessity: It becomes a question of identity. Political rhetoric, how-to advisors, and guilt-assuaging or -reinforcing books don't come close to capturing the true emotional complexity of the relationship. In the context of the single-employee business these mothers are running in their homes, they are CEOs and CFOs and chairwomen of the board on top of their other lives. Some of them are heroes; some of them are rotten bosses. Nearly all of them have learned lessons about love, family, identity, and forgiveness—either of themselves or their nannies or the inevitable American predicament that forces women into these relationships.

This is why the essays in *Searching for Mary Poppins* matter to the world we live in today. The nanny conundrum raises questions for women that must be addressed—questions that go beyond money, race, class, gender, immigration, legality, and exploitation into the darkest areas of love and fear that a mother can feel.

Susan Davis and Gina Hyams

Part One

SEARCHING FOR MARY POPPINS: THE HUNT

THE NATURAL

Marisa de los Santos

*I*n a Pull-up and a pair of plastic mules, my daughter
Annabel is wolfing Goldfish crackers and feeding them to
her doll, while mercilessly stabbing her LeapPad book
with her LeapPad pencil, causing it to wearily cry out the same
three words again and again and again, and all the while, with a sub-
lime combination of absentmindedness and volume, she belts out a
pretty decent rendition of "Night and Day." Typical morning fare.
If there is anything unusual about this scene, it is that Annabel is not
wearing her tiara. Her tiara must be lost.

For months now, my children have been crazy for Cole Porter,
crazy for Cole in the way only small children can be crazy for things,
which means that their entire beings have opened up and curved
themselves around the Ella Fitzgerald two-CD set like amoebas, de-
vouring it whole, so that it is now part of everything they do. They
sing. They draw pictures of Ella singing. Charles has choreographed
hand gestures to "Don't Fence Me In" and "I'm Always True to
You in My Fashion" that would make Jerome Robbins proud. And

the notion of a car ride without Cole and Ella strikes both kids as the most depraved kind of madness.

The previously unissued version of "Let's Do It (Let's Fall in Love)" (which Charles will quickly point out is cue number 19 on disc two), includes verses I'd never heard before. The version I knew starts with birds doing it and ends with goldfish; this one goes on to include all sorts of higher mammals: bears, chimpanzees, guinea pigs, giraffes, all doing it and doing it and doing it. "Ella doesn't like this one!" cries Annabel. "She thinks it's too long!" shrieks Charles. "She yells!" yells Annabel. And they both clap their hands over their ears.

And it's true. Ella breaks off during the recording session to voice her doubts about the song, and, of course, she's right on target. It's long, too long. Each verse is as brilliantly clever as the one before, but there are just too many. What's clear to me as I listen, though, is that the song could've been so much longer. Cole Porter could've written those jewel-like verses all day long, could've dished them up like scoops of ice cream blindfolded or in his sleep or while eating Goldfish crackers and torturing a LeapPad. He was that good.

Which brings me to this: The world loves a natural. Even the world of two- and five-year-olds. *Especially* the world of two- and five-year-olds.

Which brings me to Diane.

∽

I AM IN THE KITCHEN getting a glass of water to bring up to my office. In the next room, Diane, Charles, and Annabel are playing Harry Potter. Annabel is Ron. Charles is Hermione and is also, as always, the godlike, supremely bossy third-person narrator. Diane shifts back and forth between Professor Dumbledore, Professor Trelawney, and Sirius Black, apparently without effort, although the transitions require her whole person to reconfigure itself: Each character has a different voice, posture, set of facial expressions and gestures.

I know this story. Potter Three. I can never remember the actual titles, which exasperates my son, but I definitely know the story, having read it twice. Once to myself and a second time aloud to Charles during at least a month's worth of bedtimes.

Except that, as I stand there listening, I realize the story I know was just the tiniest seed of the one being enacted with tremendous verve in my living room. That seed has grown into a plant of such complex and immense proportions, it is more planet than plant, a planet on which my children and their nanny tread with surefooted glee.

In this version, mild, silly Professor Trelawney is the villain, viciously tormenting distractible, tutu-clad Ron and brave Hermione, until Hermione, shielding Ron with one arm, points her wand and lets out a string of sounds that bears more than a passing resemblance to an African harvest song from Charles's holiday concert. Professor Trelawney falls back, vanquished. Or . . . not? Is her eyelid moving? Her eyelid's moving! Screams.

At least, this is what I think is going on. It's what's going on, as far as I can follow it, but, honestly, that isn't very far. The story twists and loops and zips around as quickly and weirdly as my son's mind can twist, loop, and zip. This doesn't surprise me. He's five; his brain is a SuperBall.

What surprises me is Diane. She's two decades removed from five years old, but each time Charles throws out a wild line ("And suddenly they're not in the Whomping Willow anymore; they slid down a chute into a pile of disgusting dirt!"), she snags the end of it in one hand, deft as anything, and takes off like a shot. "Hold on! This dirt is moving! It's not disgusting dirt, it's disgusting spiders!" It's a relay race, a tango, a game of jai alai, a jazz trio riffing and jamming and creating music such as the world has never heard, dazzling music, electrifying.

Like all virtuosos, Diane makes it look easy. A snap. A cinch. Child's play.

*   *   *

ANNABEL AND I are sitting in Brew Ha Ha eating orange pound cake. She has just emerged from a morning at her Spanish-immersion preschool. I have just emerged from working out at the gym. She tells me that she played in the kitchen area with Olivia and didn't sit in circle time (a chronic problem) and that she missed me. "I didn't cry," she tells me, "but I got tears in my eyes." The woman at the next table says, "Isn't she sweet?" And she is.

Then Annabel says, "You have a ponytail, Mommy. You be Hermione's mommy, and I'll be Hermione."

The logic of this eludes me completely. To buy time, I pop a lump of cake into Annabel's mouth and wrack my brain, shuffling through chapters and movie scenes. Does Hermione's mother have a ponytail? Have we ever actually *met* Hermione's parents? Hermione's parents are Muggles, right?

"Hermione's parents are Muggles, right?" I ask.

Through a mouthful of cake, Annabel gives an impatient grunt.

"Um, so, what kinds of things do you think Hermione's mother does?" I ask.

"Mommy!" protests Annabel, forgetting her coffee shop voice, "Don't ask me questions! You're Hermione's mother! Be Hermione's mother!"

I look at Annabel.

"Hermione, darling," I say in a truly lame British accent, "why don't we go to the bathroom and brush your hair? It's really *ratha* tangly."

My daughter picks up her milk cup and turns her adorable face away in disgust. The woman at the next table gives us both a look of sympathy. Don't worry, I want to tell the woman, I'm not all she has. She has Diane.

*   *   *

DIANE SHEEHAN STANDS a shade under six feet tall, sports intricate tattoos, including a lovely one of Thumbelina on her lower back, and has a true city girl's adventurous, ever-changing hair. She's the kind of woman who can glean treasure from the most unpromising thrift store rack and who has the right balance of aplomb and playfulness to wear argyle knee-highs with a short skirt and look marvelous. She rides her bike through all manner of weather, marches on Washington for all the right reasons, and listened to bands like Modest Mouse before their own mothers had heard of them. She is cool, hip, au courant or whatever word currently stands in for these that I'm too old and un-whatever-the-word-is to know.

In short, she's the kind of woman you'd expect to see through a cloud of smoke at a nightclub or a gallery opening, not taking the train five days a week from Philadelphia to my semi-stuffy, nearly suburban Wilmington, Delaware, neighborhood to weave grand tapestries of agony, ecstasy, and sorcery with two children under the age of six. But if it's an incongruous sight, it should be. What happens when Diane is with Charles and Annabel is magic and magic isn't congruous with anything. Magic never makes any ordinary kind of sense.

Moreover, this magic is shot through with delight. It takes about two seconds of watching Diane in action to know that she loves this. She loves playing these games with my children. I have to admit that, to me, the delight is even more remarkable than how good she is at it. Because I've done the games, of course I have. I've been Professor Snape, the storekeeper, the sick patient, the dancing princess, Charlotte the spider; I've put in my time with the dollhouse dolls and the plastic animals. But I have never found it fun. Never.

This is not the real problem, though. The problem is that, no matter how boisterously I speak, how fast I dance, my kids can spot a fake a mile away. "That's okay, Mommy," Charles has said more than once with a fond but pitying smile, "You can read us a book now."

Diane is the real deal; she brings to the enterprise a bottom-less joy.

ONLY, AFTER YEARS of knowing her, I know that her joy is not bottomless. If she has any imperfection as a nanny, it is that she has, on rare occasions, simply failed to show up and failed to call, and sometimes, when she finally did call, she would have an excuse that didn't quite ring true.

Finally, in a long, heartbreaking letter to my husband David and me, she revealed that she has struggled with depression her entire adult life, a bleak immobilizing despair that could come out of nowhere to devastate her, particularly during the winter months. It is at least partly the reason her college career has been a series of false starts, even though she's a tremendous reader and as bright and creative as anyone I've ever known. It is at least partly the reason she has stayed in unfulfilling relationships for far too long.

We struck a deal: If she couldn't make it, we agreed that she'd call us, so that Charles didn't sit by the door waiting, literally, for hours, but we also agreed that she never had to give a reason. Who could explain inexplicable sorrow?

But these absences are still few and far between. Certainly, Diane gets herself to work on plenty of days when she'd rather be in her apartment with the shades drawn. "How do you do it?" I want to know, "Where does the buoyancy come from?" She doesn't even pause to think. "From the kids," she says, and begins to explain a process that sounds a lot like photosynthesis: She soaks up the kids' imaginative energy and converts it to her own. She says it as though it were perfectly natural, as though everyone felt this way about children. When she's at her lowest, the kids don't wear her out; they lift her up.

This moves me, truly. But while it strikes me as an inarguably beautiful way to experience children, especially *my* children, it also strikes me as an inarguably inadequate way to deal with depression. My father is a physician. My mother has battled manic depression for over two decades, battled it quite successfully, thanks to lithium. I am my parents' child.

"What about drugs?" I ask Diane.

I can tell the question makes her uncomfortable. Her always-direct gaze becomes indirect, slides to the side and down.

"I tried them years ago," she tells me, "I didn't like the side effects."

I must look like I'm about to say something else, ask another question, because she says, firmly, "I'm okay, though. I'm handling it."

And I have to admit that there's a fairly substantial part of me that wants to say, "Let's *really* handle it though. Let's solve it. You tried—what—Prozac? Paxil? So we'll forget SSRIs, then. But there are a lot of options. How about Wellbutrin?" Part of me is dying to take this problem in hand and whip it. Part of me is already sitting down at the computer with Diane to Google Wellbutrin.

I've had a headache at Diane's apartment. I know the woman doesn't even keep aspirin in her house. Green tea, yes. Aspirin, no. More to the point, she didn't ask me for help. Diane is an intelligent adult living her life her way. Diane is not my child. Diane and I are different people.

That I have to keep reminding myself of this is a source of surprise and shame.

MORE SHAMEFUL STILL is the fact that this impulse to "help" Diane, to shape her life according to my values and priorities extends even to her chosen profession. In this essay, I've mentioned Diane's attempts at college, and I see that even now, even here, I'm spinning the story the way I want it spun.

Yes, Diane's depression has interfered with college, but that isn't the whole story. It may not even be the real story. "Interfered with college," for example, is a poor choice of words. Those words are not only inaccurate but are also loaded with judgment. The fact is that Diane isn't sure and has never been sure that college is something she wants to do. It may be more accurate to say that, for Diane, college has interfered with life.

Not long ago, my husband and I offered to pay for some college courses, if Diane was interested. She was, and for three semesters or so, Diane emerged from her classes with A's or F's, leaving a trail of professors either breathless with enthusiasm for her smarts and energy and skill with language or confused and disappointed by her mid-semester disappearance. While David and I pretty much kept to our resolution not to ask her about her grades, Diane was quite comfortable discussing her academic experience. A picture emerged: She stayed with the courses that interested her; she dropped out of those that didn't.

"But your GPA!" I wanted to wail at her, "What about your academic record? What about graduating?"

In my parents' house, the one I'd grown up in, it was as much a given that I'd go to college as it was that I'd go to kindergarten. I never considered not going, not getting good grades once there, or not graduating in four years. All of this was automatic. But Diane didn't grow up in my parents' house. For Diane, college provides one of many ways to learn about new ideas and to read new books, to uncover the lovely, the mind-blowing, the difficult, the odd. When you think about it, this view makes plenty of sense.

"But she's so smart," I say to myself. "She's so creative and insightful and open-minded and curious. She's so *gifted*. She should *use* those gifts!"

To my everlasting relief, even as I think this, this thought born of years of programming, my answer to myself—my retort—is right there: "She *is*."

God, of course, she is. Who knows this better than I?

*   *   *

My children are being raised by three parents, rather than two. If, when Charles was a newborn, you had told me this would be the case, I would have found the idea deeply troubling, bearing a freight-load of failure. But two children later, it's perfectly clear that kids are as soul-hungry and as intricately put together as any adult. Like adults, they have needs they can name and needs they cannot, and what I understand now is that no one person can even hope to uncover, much less satisfy, them all.

Charles and Annabel need the fabulous, otherworldly world Diane opens to them, the world in which they can fly, rage, grieve, and commit acts of cruelty and bravery and kindness inside their own living room.

They need David to make them laugh, and to hang solar systems from their ceilings, and to turn up the Pixies and the Talking Heads on the iPod every evening before bed, so they can dance like a pack of maniacs around the house.

What do I give? I read Dr. Seuss's *The Sleep Book* like I was born to the task. I teach them every song I know. And I do whatever it is that makes them, when they're hurt, or sick, or scared in the middle of the night, want only me to hold them.

But I've decided that my main role might be to put them in the way of good things, things that make me fall in love with the world again and again. I strew their paths with beauties, and while they might not go for them all, they've got an abundance to choose from: Cole and Ella, Potter Three, George and Ira, C. S. Lewis, E. B. White, Dr. Seuss, Balanchine's *Nutcracker*, Beethoven's *Pathetique Sonata*, Randall Jarrell's *The Bat Poet*, Roald Dahl, Van Gogh, Chet Baker, Mary Poppins, *Schoolhouse Rock*.

And Diane, brave and true, who reminds us that there are many ways to inhabit a life with grace. Countless ways. Diane tops the list.

YOU, CECI

Lauren Slater

I had my first child against my better judgment. Then I had my second child. That was also against my better judgment. My husband was the one who wanted kids. For various reasons, I believed I lacked maternal instinct. And instinct, being what it is, cannot be learned. Therefore, it made good sense to hire a nanny. It was a decision based at once on necessity—both my husband and I work full-time—and also a sense of my own inadequacy. I was sure that whoever took the job would be so superior to me that I would step to the sidelines while she took center stage. In a sense, I would be the other mother, offering help, holding out tissues, while the real drama went on without me.

This did not seem strange to me then, and, frankly, even though so much has changed, it still does not seem strange to me now. I was one of those kids raised by babysitters; Corita taught me to sew; Jane nursed me through my illnesses; Angela, the Irish nanny, taught me to ride a bike, to pray (*Our father, who art in heaven, hallowed be thy name*), and to name the wildflowers, something I still do today, by instinct, or rather, by habit: echinacea, columbine, chive, strawflower. Yesterday, I went to the woods with my daughter, and we named the wildflowers, studying their leaves, and it was Angela who was there, in spirit, my own mother nowhere near. And I was my mother's daughter, of course, similarly stunted and rageful. My father had told us that before my mother had children she was "a different woman, really," but that the pressures and conflicts of motherhood had done her in, changed her irrevocably and for the worse. Indeed, early photographs show my mother smiling on a Cape Cod beach with a red scarf in her hair; by the time my sister, her first, came along, her face has narrowed, her eyes small and fierce, screwed into her skull. I never knew exactly why having children caused her undoing, her mad chatter and intense anger, but not knowing made it all the more potent, more possible.

"You are the most like your mother," my aunts always told me, ominous indeed. In order to avoid her female fate, I got a doctoral degree, acquired prizes. I studiously avoided anything maternal, claiming a mannish incompetence, an inability to do baby talk and all of its equivalents. On the other hand, I held on to a sliver of hope, and my babies were born on this sliver.

∽

CECI CAME TO US from a friend of a friend of a friend of a friend. She was thirty-six—an excellent age, we thought—from Mexico, with shiny black hair and a beautiful face. She spoke little English. Not long after she started, our newborn, Clara, got sick. She corkscrewed her body and screamed. We stretched her, thumped her, cycled her little legs, but still she screamed, her tiny tongue extended.

I remember one night when I was up with her. Ceci was living with us, in a room down the hall. The baby howled. I turned on the fan to block the sound so Ceci could get some sleep. The baby's howls were one long skein of sound, it just went on and on. There is really nothing like being with a screaming baby dead in the middle of the night. Her room was lit by one small bulb, shedding shadows over the room, so my hand looked huge held up against the wall. I held the baby up against the wall and she, too, looked huge, her jaw flapping, her arms like wings, going nowhere. At five in the morning, it started to get light outside. The air got grainy and gray, the lawns visible, and far in the distance was a radio tower blinking its red light on and off. I started to cry right along with my daughter. Perhaps I cried even louder than she, for Ceci heard, and came to get us. "Here," and held out her arms. I gave her the baby. She said, "Go get me some lettuce leaves," which I did. She then ran a warm bath, and told me to drop the lettuce leaves in. "In our country," she said, "we know if you put lettuce leaves in a warm bath, it calms the child down." Our child calmed down. A cynic would say it was the water, not the lettuce leaves. Who cares? From that day on, Ceci made our colicky daughter a bath of lettuce leaves, and from that day on that other mother, she took my baby in, and always knew exactly what to do. She had a gift.

It DID NOT TAKE LONG for Ceci to become famous in our neighborhood. Everyone wanted to hire her. She was too good to be true, but let me tell you, she was true, the real deal, the best. It was not so much what she did—although she did a lot—but more who she was, her competence mixed with kindness, her energy. She never once was late for work. She never took a sick day. But perhaps she is best described by what she did outside of her working hours. Ceci took kickboxing, English as a second language, cooking classes. She was a gifted photographer and painter. She had her bachelor's degree in marketing from the University of Mexico, but her interests leaned more toward the arts. She knit elaborate blankets, used a loom, could crochet a piece of intricate filmy lace. She found a beaten-up bike in the trash and single-handedly restored it to working order. She loved jigsaw puzzles, huge four-footers with thousands of scrambled pieces, and she had the patience to put it all together, day after day, until a coherent scene emerged. Once she was finished, she would spray her creation with clear glue, hang it whole on the wall. It always delighted my daughter, the image at once cracked and solid, a seeming impossibility, but there it was.

MONTHS PASSED. The presence of Ceci in our family was like a light but firm hand arranging our shape in ways we could see only in retrospect. She was shocked to find out my husband and I celebrated neither Christmas nor Chanukah. My husband had been raised rigorously atheistic. I am Jewish by birth, but lapsed. "No tree?" Ceci said that first year she was with us. "No presents? *El niños*. What about *el niños*?"

"Clara doesn't care," I remember saying. "She's only one."

"Clara cares," Ceci said. And that afternoon she came home with a tree, tinsel, a plastic star, all those silk globes. My husband looked uncomfortable, but then after a moment he smiled. By the week's end we were all zooming around town, buying up toys and trinkets. "I'm Jewish," I kept saying to my husband; "I'm a communist," he kept saying to me, and then we shrugged. On Christmas Eve Ceci took us all to mass. The priest was bedecked in some kind of crown, waving his incense stick so the whole church filled with the smell of frankincense and myrrh. Music started playing, something salsa-ish, and then a clip-clop hip-hop version of "Deck the Halls," and before we knew it the whole congregation was skipping after the priest. We skipped too. The air was so thick and cloying I could barely breathe. I felt I would choke. On the other hand, it was a lot of fun.

It was for reasons like these that I felt grateful to Ceci, and continually lucky to have her; she brought humor into our tight little lives. However, I also know that her confidence and kindness, the charm she had for children, her easy engagement with them and her steadfast love of the things I did not love—the dressing, the hair combing, Chuck E. Cheese's, and swimming pools—only deepened my belief in my own inadequacies. I allowed it to.

Here is a scene. It is early morning and Ceci is brushing my daughter's hair. She draws the bristles through in a single sweep, hefts up a swath and braids it, her fingers flying. Moments later, Clara is ready for school, immaculate, her clothes matching, her hair a complex series of plaits and twists all miraculously held to her head with only a single bright barrette. Later on, after school, I find Clara in her room and tentatively approach her. My own hair I have always worn in a porous mop, too busy for conditioners, just a quick scrub, a brisk, businesslike rinse. "Let me do your hair," I say. I say it softly, shyly, almost like I am in seventh grade asking a boy to dance. "Why?" she says. She doesn't look up. She's playing with a doll. "Because," I say, and I don't know how to go on. I pick up the brush with its flat paddle handle and, standing over my daughter's head, I see the pink seam of her scalp where Ceci has perfectly parted her hair; I bring the brush to it, drag down, and my daughter screams. She gives a loud, dramatic murderous yell and operatic tears fill her eyes. All I did was one tiny tug. I know, I *know* I haven't hurt her. I stand there with the brush, frozen. She eyes me warily. I eye her right back. Then I cautiously slip from her room.

IT IS WINTER in ski country, snow falling everywhere, muffling the mountains. I am twelve, and full of holes. From across the kitchen, my mother snarls at me for reasons I cannot understand. Suddenly, she throws a spoon in my direction; it bounces off my cheek and lands, clattering, on the tiled floor.

Two years later we will sit together, my mother, father, and I, in a social worker's office on the second floor of a psychiatric unit, where I have been temporarily placed. My mother's left hand is badly bruised from where she put it through a wall. Over the years,

fury had become more and more her default response to the difficulties of raising children. I was mostly, although not exclusively,
her target. The irony of all this is that the psychiatric hospitalization
is for self-inflicted injuries, but years later I will come to understand
how those injuries were openings, each one, allowing me to tell the
tale of my home, the fear, the sideways swipes, the stung cheek, the
glass shattering.

Now, the social worker informs me I will not be going home.
This is in part a huge relief, in part a rupture of which it will take me
years to make sense, with only partial success. I left my home at the
cusp of adolescence and never went back. One day my family was
there; the next day they were gone, and I was living in a new home
with a musty smell and Civil War guns hanging above the fireplace.
It was so abrupt, and total.

It is perhaps for this reason that I have never understood sepa-
rations. I have never really understood how two beings can cast off
on their own without great grief. To avoid this grief, one has two
choices. Do not cast off, ever. Or, do not come close.

CHILDREN ARE NOT SUBTLE. They throw their arms around you, or
haughtily turn away. They answer you, or don't. My daughter is a
child, no different. At the end of every day, during Ceci's tenure
with us, I would come home from work. My briefcase was always
full. I was, at that point in my life, working full-time as both a psychologist and a writer. I sometimes worked sixty hours a week, trying to outrun my history, building walls with words.

I remember one homecoming in particular, not because it was
better or worse, but simply because a single memory becomes em-
blematic, standing in for all the rest. It was winter and when I
opened the door a cold gust of air blew in. Ceci and Clara were absorbed in a book, Clara on Ceci's lap, Ceci rocking the chair back
and forth in time with the Spanish sentences. I could hear the

words: *leche*, *arriva*, *tio*, but I did not understand. I saw my daughter's sleepy eyes, how Ceci held her. "Hi," I said, an interruption. Ceci smiled, beckoned me forward. "Clara," I said, holding out my arms. Clara looked at me. "Go," Ceci whispered, giving her a little push. *"Besito por Mamma."* Obediently, my daughter came forward and gave me a quick kiss.

Lest it be misunderstood, I loved my daughter. I loved her with my whole heart. Her face has always delighted me; she is fair-skinned, green-eyed. She seems the expression of all that could be good in me, all that I am that is healthy.

YEARS PASSED THIS WAY. Clara spoke Spanish before she spoke English, and when Ceci's friends came over they laughed and remarked, "She sounds just like a little Mexican." Even so, I had moments with Clara, many moments, that were easy and unfettered, moments writing poetry together, a story called "Ick I'm Sick," discussions about stars and God, Linnaeus and reptiles. We bought a vinegar-propelled rocket and shot it off together, our heads tipped back as it nosed straight into space. But her first love was not for me, and while, on the one hand, I really grieved over that, I also understood I had set it up that way, a safe distance, space between mother and daughter, this dyad dangerous, rife with rejection.

And yet, it hurt my heart. It hurt my chest, my breasts. When Clara was three years old, they found my ducts were crammed with misshapen cells. I had both my breasts removed, tiny squishy saline bags slid into the spaces left. Ceci brought me flowers, helped me with my bandages. In clothes, now, I looked fine but naked I looked maimed. Ceci, on the other hand, was whole and healthy. I know my daughter knew that. Sometimes she would come to me, pull down my shirt, peer in. "Ceci has nipples," she would say. "And you don't." I'm sure this was just a statement of fact, but I could not help but hear it as something more.

And so we went on. My husband, I hesitate to say, did not help the situation. He sided with Ceci, unconsciously, subtly, giving her his credence and confidence. Of course I am largely to blame, for I had impressed upon him my image of myself, the ratty foster child, the progeny of insanity, the work-driven defense against it all. At one point my child developed a pustule-like rash on the tongue and palms. Ceci hypothesized an immune response due to a recent fever. My husband agreed. They stood in the kitchen talking together while I watched, and they decided that if it got any worse, they would call the doctor tomorrow. *Give it a day*, they said. "Are you kidding me?" I said. "It's on the *tongue*." I called the doctor immediately. "My child has white oozing spots in the mouth," I said. *My child.* The pediatrician diagnosed foot-and-mouth disease. For me, this was a twisted triumph.

Clara started preschool. Here is where things took a distinctly downward turn. At the end of each day, while I was still at work, Ceci would pick her up, take Clara to a museum or to Chuck E. Cheese's and eventually this became common enough that Ceci no longer needed to tell us her plans ahead of time. Autumn passed into winter. Then, one day, their usual arrival time of four o'clock passed, and they didn't come home. Ceci had been with us nearly four years then. The afternoon ticked on into evening. Where were they? Cars rumbled by on the road outside my study, but none of them stopped. The day grew dark. Worried, I called my husband at work. "Clara and Ceci aren't here," I said, and I think I heard just the tiniest pause before he said, "They're fine." I called the school. It was closed. The church bells gonged. I thought crazy thoughts. *How do I know who she really is? Would she kidnap my girl? Of course not, dummy! But how can I know?* And, indeed, how could I? We had hired her years ago, based on a reference check and gut. It suddenly seemed careless, negligent; I pictured telling detectives, "She comes from Mexico," but not being able to say more. Hometown. "Cool-ya can?" something like that. Address, copy of passport, visa, we had none of it. At a deeper level, I realized we knew almost none of her. Her plans, her hopes, her fears, her lovers, her enemies, nothing. We knew Ceci intimately, day after day, year after year, we knew her laugh, her voice, her hands, her hair, and yet we knew her not at all. This, I believe, is common.

At six o'clock I heard a key in the lock, the dogs barking, and when I raced downstairs I saw them standing together, mittened hand in mittened hand. "Where were you guys?" I said.

"Field trip," Ceci said.

"Field trip?" I said.

"To Foss Park. I chaperoned. It was fun, wasn't it Clara?" and Clara looked up, smiled, nodded. "Fun," she said.

"But I didn't, you didn't tell . . ." and then I stopped. I held tight to the banister. "Wait a minute," I said. "Aren't parents supposed to sign a permission slip before their kids go on a field trip?"

"Yes," said Ceci, and if she thought her next comment was strange, she betrayed it not a bit. "I signed that slip weeks ago," she said.

I DID WHAT any woman at once indebted and enmeshed would do. I said not a word to Ceci. The next day I called the school. "All permission slips," I said to the teacher, "must be signed by me. Not Ceci. Me." I paused. The teacher didn't say anything. Her silence sounded accusing.

I BECAME PREGNANT with my second. Ceci, who had been living with us for four years, moved out. She found a fantastic apartment in Harvard Square, just minutes away. It was not a big change. She left behind most of her clothes, her bed made, her pictures up on the walls. "What are we," I said to my husband, "a storage facility?"

"You're just jealous," he said.

"Picture it," I said. Suddenly, I was speaking slowly. "Picture it. You and I have a child. We hire another man to move into the house and be the nanny. Your child falls in love with the man-nanny, this other father. I come to love the other father too, and I listen to all his childrearing advice."

"I don't listen to all her childrearing advice," he said.

"If I think she has an ear infection and has to go to the doctor and Ceci doesn't, you always agree with Ceci."

"I'm just being polite," he said. "She's still a guest. You're my wife."

"Exactly," I said. "That's exactly my point. I'm your wife. I'm Clara's mother."

"Clara loves you a lot," he said.

"Of course she does," I said.

"You have to have more confidence," he said.

"You tell me," I said—and I was surprised by the depths of my anger—"you tell me how you would feel having another father around for your kid."

"I would hate it," he said slowly. "It is something I would never allow."

ON JANUARY 20, 2004, I had a son. When I looked into his newborn face I saw nothing of my mother and nothing of myself. In part because of gender, in part because of experience, I approached my second child with more confidence, and he felt it. He stopped crying whenever I picked him up. I picked him up as often as I could. Ceci seemed to like him less. "Boys," she'd say, and sigh. "Girls are fun," she'd say. "The clothes. Boys are . . ." and then she wouldn't finish. From his earliest days she dressed him in little baseball shirts and high-tops. She called Clara "*mi amore*," and Lucas, "*señor*." "It's a cultural thing," my husband said. "It's Latino machismo."

Sometimes, she let Lucas cry and cry. "Oh," Ceci said to me one day. "Oh, he is a big bad boy. He has a terrible temper." At the time, Lucas was two months old.

I see this gender bias as one of Ceci's unintentional gifts to me, for it left a space, and I slipped in. I held the baby. I called him "*mi amore.*" He grabbed my nose, felt my face. I know he saw me standing over him, someone safe. And I learned, from him, that I was safe, that I was not my mother, that I could never hurt a child, my children, never, girl or boy no matter, these were indeed my children. The best I had to offer.

Every child changes you in different ways. Clara curved me toward my past and in doing so forced me to consider its complex intersection with my present curving toward my future. Lucas revealed for me the beauty of the single dimension. As a writer, one-dimensionality is something I had always avoided. The worst thing that could be said about one's work was that it lacked facets, was flat. Clara and I are two pieces of a single prism that keeps catching the light at an infinite number of angles. With Lucas, the surface is smooth. I could float here, catch my breath.

A YEAR AFTER Lucas's birth, Ceci's visa expired. In order to renew it, she needed to return to Mexico, submit an application, and wait for a response from the embassy there. Her chances of getting a new visa were fifty-fifty. My husband and I did whatever we could, sought legal aid, attempted sponsorship, suggested she marry her American boyfriend. In the end there was no choice but for her to leave us for many months, maybe forever. I cried, mostly for Clara, such a huge loss, so early on, and I cried for the girl I once was, standing in front of my house on a hot summer day, waving good-bye to my own mother as the car drove me away to a foster home, and who knew when, if ever, we would see each other again. I cried in relief and fear, the sense of something opening, something ending. Clara cried, too. That night, she slept with me, in my bed. In a dream she moved toward me. "We are finally finding each other," I thought.

CECI HAD LEFT BEHIND her clothes, her shoes, her artwork, she was everywhere in our home, her plan to return obvious. But a few days after she left, I found myself packing up her clothes, slowly at first, and then picking up speed, boxing the dresses and skirts and shirts, moving her toothbrush and cosmetics into storage, taking down the puzzle pictures, the lacquer still shiny, the cracks everywhere. "What are you doing?" my daughter asked.

I knelt down, took her chin in my hand. "I know Ceci is your very best friend," I said.

She nodded.

"But she is not your actual family," I said. "Ceci has her own family, in Mexico."

"I know," she said. She looked straight at me. "I know you're my mother," she said. "And Ceci is my stepmother."

"No," I said. "Ceci is your nanny. She loves you with her whole heart. But nannies do not stay forever, even though they love you forever."

"Do mothers stay forever?" she asked.

"Most mothers do," I said. "Some don't. But this mother," and I pointed to myself, "this mother will stay with you for as long as you want."

"Until you die," she said.

"Yes," I said. "Until I die."

"When will you die?" she asked.

"I hope not for a long time."

"I know you will die before Papa," she said.

"How do you know that?" I asked.

"You're forty-one," she said. "And he's only forty."

"You never know," I said. "But don't worry."

"I'm not worried," she said. "I'm not the worrier. You are."

"You're right," I said. "I worry."

"Someday," she said, "Ceci will have her own baby."

"I hope so," I said.

"And you know what I'm going to be when I grow up?" she said.

"No," I said.

"That baby's nanny," she said. "I'm going to be Ceci's baby's nanny and a mama, too."

"That's a great plan," I said.

"My plan," she said, "is to have four babies of my own, plus take care of Ceci's. So that's five," she said. "That's my limit."

WE HIRED SOMEONE ELSE to take Ceci's place during the months she was in Mexico. Although I knew Helen was competent in the care of my daughter, she seemed to me to lack Ceci's spark and humor, and her unique affection. She lacked the love Ceci had to give, and this, too, was in its own way fine with me, for I felt I had more room, more say-so, more authority and simple space. There were small tasks Ceci had always done without ever being asked, like making Clara's lunch for school each day. Now that fell to me. It is important, I think, to make your child's lunch. It is important to cut the bread, wrap it, arrange the lunchbox, tuck in a snack. It is important to know that when, the next day, she opens it, she will briefly see that in the arrangement and choice of foods, you have loved her, and always will.

It is important to claim the tasks of motherhood, even when time or trauma makes it difficult. You must, of course, sign the permission slips, shop for shoes, cook when you can, do her hair, with or without the knack. How one balances this with the competing demands of career or longstanding insecurities I really have no idea.

No advice. Only that it must be done, here and there, wherever you can. Motherhood is at once a sentimental abstraction and, in its true nature, a series of tiny tasks, not a lifetime but a day, which brings you to another day, which brings you to a third, and so you go. It is all dirty work, full of germs and life.

I gave my mothering away, and for too long a time. I did it one-eighth out of busyness and seven-eighths out of fear. I did it because I had the great good luck and simultaneous misfortune to find another mother so willing and skillful, so comfortably maternal, that I could not quite find my way, my voice, so to speak, the silly songs, the lettuce leaves. I did it, also, and paradoxically, out of a keen desire to protect my girl from the badness I believed was in me. My daughter and son have given me more than anyone could ask for. They have proven, by their very ruddy and vigorous existences, that even though my own mother gave me up and found me flawed, I had at least two good eggs to give the world, and I gave them.

CECI WAS, AFTER SEVERAL MONTHS, granted a new visa and wanted to return to work. But I knew it could not be. I knew I had stepped into some new space and wanted not to step back, but forward, enlarging my maternal role, helped but not *too* helped. To say we "fired" Ceci would be wrong, but we did let her go, the perfect nanny, Mary Poppins who in the end drifts upward on an umbrella, leaving the children to their parents' care. Ceci had no umbrella and the rupture was painful, her sense of betrayal enormous and understandable. "No," I told her over the phone, "no, Ceci, we love you absolutely but we just don't need . . ."

"It is up to you," she said.

"We will find you another job," I said. "We will find you a rich family who can pay you more."

"I can take care of myself," she said. We both hung up, in tears.

∽

Every once in a while Ceci visits us. She is, indeed, working for a far wealthier family, earning much better money, so all's well that ends well. Sort of. "You know," Ceci said to me a few weeks ago, when she was visiting. "You know, Helen is not keeping up Clara's Spanish. Since I've been gone, Clara's Spanish has really degraded."

"I will talk to Helen," I said.

"Clara doesn't like Helen," Ceci said.

"Clara will never love another nanny the way she loves you," I said.

But the strange thing is, while that is true, it is also too dramatic. For Clara, the transition was terrible but she has moved on. When Ceci comes to visit, she spends less and less time with her, wanting to leave after only a minute now, to play with her best friend next door. So Ceci and I are left together, sitting in the kitchen, watching the girl we both love best through the window, playing on the grass of our neighbor's yard. Upstairs, Lucas, the boy I love best, churns in his sleep, the monitor crackling, full of the sound of him. "I have always wanted to ask you," she said to me one day, "why did you fire me?"

"I didn't fire you," I said. "I didn't need as many hours . . . we were . . . the money . . . expensive . . . I didn't want to work so much—"

"Were you jealous?" Ceci interrupted.

Brief pause. "Yes," I said. "You were always the better mother."

"That is not so," she said. Her eyes filled with tears. "I am thirty-eight," she said. "Clara may be the closest I ever get to having my own daughter."

"She belongs to both of us," I said.

But it was clear, looking out the window, that Clara belonged to no one but herself. There she was with Maya, her best friend. I tapped on the window. Clara looked up, briefly waved at us, went back to the business of her life. Ceci and I sat together in the kitchen. It was so quiet. We could hear the heat turn on, the furnace tick and fire. We boiled water on the stove. We filled our mugs with chamomile. In the end, the most resilient bond perhaps may not be between Ceci and Clara or Clara and me, but between me and Ceci, two women, two mothers, knowing without words how hard and fierce and fabulous mothering can be, understanding the inherent losses of it all, soothing ourselves together, here, in the kitchen, at the very end of what is left: two women taking tea.

THE STORY OF
ROBBIE AND VELMA

Jessica Neely

One day last spring, I received a frantic call from a colleague, a new mother whose maternity leave was about to end. Would I meet her for coffee? We agreed on a café near the school where we both worked. And at the arranged time, I saw her striding up the sunlit sidewalk, bobbed hair a smart dash across her chin, linen dress, sandals—great-looking for two months out, I thought. It was interesting to me that she'd left the baby with her mother, a sign, I thought, that she was beginning the psychological transition back to work. When she sat down, though, my colleague began to frown. With little preamble, she asked me how I had managed to keep working full-time through three babies. How in God's name did I swing it? What luck had I had with childcare? Wasn't it horrible? This woman and I were not close friends; no doubt she knew, like everyone else at work, not only that I'm the mother of three, but that my oldest son has cerebral palsy. I had assumed, in agreeing to meet for coffee, that she wanted reassurance, a pragmatic assessment of her options from a fellow working mom, one whose own home life posed big challenges. I hoped for camaraderie, or at least respect. So I paused a few beats, waiting for the ironic laugh or exaggerated glance, something to bond us across the word "horrible"; it didn't come.

My friend leaned back in her chair. "There's no way I could keep it all going," she said, "like you. It doesn't seem human." Or maybe what she said was "humanly possible." This was that sort of "funny" compliment that I'd begun to find threatening. Usually, I relegated such praise *("Ms. Indefatigable, e-mailing at one A.M. again,"* or *"You're really modeling the whole thing for your kids")* to the slightly mean-spirited social chatter that pervaded our workplace.

My colleague had a terrific option—a daycare center at her husband's firm where he could check on the baby often, have lunch with the baby in his lap. And the family could use her income.

"But *I* won't be with my baby," she said.

I continued to string together the usual platitudes I myself relied upon, feeling with each my confidence deflate and then crumple. Yes, it was hard, but she'd do research, check references, trust her instincts; she had the reliable structure of her husband's workplace to count on, after all. Everything would be okay. "It is really awful at first, but you'll make it work," I told her. And then, "I have."

She frowned again. It was clear this woman wanted something different from me: a reason to reject the very options she'd seemingly asked me to confirm. In other words, her gaze said to me: You are who I'll become if I make your choices.

Walking home, I heard myself pipe up "I have" once again. In my imagination I watched those two cheerful words sprout wings and flap off into the stratosphere with no honest destination. Because, of course, I haven't always made it work. There is another story, wanting to be told, fragile with the prospect of exposure.

There is this story—at the center is a one-month-old baby boy, "Robbie," our first babysitter, "Velma," and me. Though we would not gather from his doctors the full picture of brain damage for some time, Robbie suffered a stroke at birth, an embolism in the left mid-cerebral artery of his brain with resultant encephalomalacia, or atrophy of tissue, in the frontal parietal lobes, which translates to the loss of functional use of his right hand, generalized right-side weakness, and a number of emotional and learning dysfunctions that would surface in time, along with a seizure disorder. But at this moment, he is a one-month-old baby who is alternately alert and in-consolable, blessedly robust, and attached by a soft electrode belt that he wears around his chest to an apnea monitor, which I refer to as a "millstone" and a "harpy" because one cannot carry Robbie (who weighs about ten pounds) without also shouldering the SmartMonitor, which also weighs ten pounds and screeches at a nerve-shearing sonic pitch in the event of an apnea event, or false alarm.

My first true memory of Velma begins on the first day she comes to babysit. She is twenty-five or twenty-six and petite with a heart-shaped face and dark, expressive eyes. A political refugee from Nicaragua, she has come to work with us through close family friends who helped her gain political asylum in the United States. I make her orange tea and put chocolate cookies on a plate. I en-courage her to sit down, and she takes a cozy chair by the window and reaches for the baby. I hand her Robbie. In that moment of transfer, both of us reaching toward each other, the baby a focal point, a fulcrum, Velma's right sleeve slides back to reveal a ten- or eleven-inch scar, thick with keloid tissue, a bad healing. I know the outline of her story in Nicaragua, that she worked for the Contras, that someone wanted her killed.

Velma settles with Robbie. I have slept an average of three hours in twenty-four since my son was born, fixated as I am on his health and feeding, on the possibility of another apnea event and my readi-ness to administer CPR. Periodically, bright explosions of fatigue network across my vision. I unshoulder the monitor and place it on the floor beside the chair. I thank Velma. I say thank you about four times in five minutes, then ask her whether she's okay. If the alarm accidentally goes off—because sometimes he bumps off one of the leads—I'll just be upstairs. "Try not to freak out. It's so loud."

Velma says everything is really fine and just go rest.

I walk up the stairs, watching the two of them, as Velma starts talking to Robbie in Spanish. What I feel is almost indescribable: My hands are free; I'm weightless without that machine. Velma looks up; we smile at one another. I trust her, implicitly.

IF YOU WERE TO LOOK AT HIM, lying in the middle of the bed or on a blanket, you'd see my infant son curved like the letter C to the right. The misfiring of neurons in the left side of his brain—all these electrical impulses with no place to go—resulted in muscular contracture. His diagnosis: right-hemiparesis, with spasticity in the upper extremities, neck, and trunk, mild in the lower body, required that Velma and I load up Robbie, the monitor, diaper bag, car seat/stroller, and go twice a week to Robbie's physical therapy appointments at Children's Medical Center. Gwen, our talented and extremely groovy therapist, taught us the series of holds and stretches that would straighten out the roped muscles, help his bones grow in strong lines. What you would watch were Gwen's hands, and particularly her thumbs, which she'd use to knead his neck and arm and right hand, each of the fingers. Thumbing then holding the muscle taut in elongation, deep into the fascia.

"*Blanca, blanca, blanca,*" Gwen would tell Velma. "And then you release and it's *roza.*"

"*Rojo.*"

"Exactly."

My belief in any sort of divinity, a force organizing benevolence in the larger world, has never progressed to the transcendent, by which I mean that my faith, if you can call it that, embraces but ends with the goodness men and women can bring one another or with the beautiful things they create, like a string quintet or a villanelle.

Each day, dozens of times, my mind would phrase the question, Why did my baby have this stroke? That this was the typical question of anyone who's experienced a catastrophe only made its asking all the more guilt-laden. My self-consciousness prevented open access to my grief. (How could I cry while feeling bad about crying?) Instead, the better release came when I listened to music. For example, I'd bought a CD of choral lullabies for children. Rocking in the bedroom chair with Robbie, listening to a four-part rendition of "All the Pretty Little Ponies," the resolution of a minor seventh chord, provided resonant catharsis. These were occasional, private moments, though. My husband blamed Robbie's stroke on the botched efforts of our obstetrician, who'd applied, he felt, undue force for a protracted period of time with a vacuum extractor meant to birth the baby. At the urging of his doctor-parents, my husband pursued this line as far as the door of litigation, but there were so many variables and inconclusivities among the medical records during and after Robbie's birth—Why had we been advised to wait six months to have an MRI, and why weren't there corroborated reports, post birth, of a subdural hematoma on the baby's scalp?—that in time, believing the medical community had covered for itself, he accepted the advice of malpractice attorneys who explained that without sufficient evidence, no one would prosecute a case that was at best fifty-fifty. In time he stopped pursuing the thought of legal action. For my part, the question was less one of legal obligation than of feeling enormously let down. I liked my OB. I'd trusted her. She'd had a reputation for quick thinking in emergencies. In difficult moments I blamed myself too, though I'd taken excellent care of my health during pregnancy. No point in the self-punishment, but it was hard to shake off.

So it's easy to see why a physical therapist like Gwen appealed enormously to me. Gwen believed in Robbie's powers of regeneration, praised both Velma and me for the good work we were doing.

She wore colorful cotton pants and pretty, dangly earrings that caught Robbie's attention. During PT sessions, we'd discuss her husband's restaurant business, joke about Velma's flunking cooking school. "If you ask me to cook you oatmeal, I'm going to find a way to burn it!"

Gwen's husband cooked with all fresh ingredients—lemongrass, cilantro, arugula—she loved arugula—fresh mint. They did serve meat, but only free-range. Velma lamented her new boyfriend's love of red meat—steak every day! Gwen said, "Throw a little soy product into a chili or casserole. He won't notice." Velma wanted to know what a soy product was, and where to buy it.

Gwen placed one palm behind Robbie's head, the other at his tailbone to connect, she explained, the cranial and sacral poles of the spine. There was no hard evidence, she said, but she believed this had a healing effect and calmed the baby's nervous system. Velma nodded. "I'm going to do this one, too, Gwen. You know I will."

With utter seriousness, Velma approached the unpleasant but essential task of stretching Robbie's muscles several times a day. To relieve the neck and trunk contracture, Gwen taught us, you had to hold him long across your chest in a stretch—head to the left, body to the right—that "unwound the rubber band" for five minutes every hour. Robbie screamed. Robbie screamed a lot. He was a "hypertonic" baby, the neurologist told us, which meant too much of everything—those firing neurons, those tight muscles, that neurological disorganization.

If the screaming wore on Velma, she never told me. In each of my memories, she is smiling, enormous dark eyes shining as she speaks to Robbie in the most animated voice. Responsible, intent about her work. "Jesus," my husband said once, "she's pretty military with the stretches." Queasy about inflicting necessary or even imagined pain on anyone, he was grateful to Velma and the stopwatch punctuality of her routine. We never said this, but it was the subtext, of course: The stretches are hard, but how many other parents can say they have a former guerrilla doing them?

You could not ask Velma directly to launch into a story of her past. There was always the sense of an unspeakable trauma I had no right to broach. But from time to time, I'd ask about a particular thing, her parents' names, the scar on her arm, or the smaller one, about the width of a steak-knife blade, that bisected her upper lip.

"Jessica," she would look directly into my eyes, "Nicaragua is a very different kind of life. And that's *my* past. I'm here now."

What I knew from our friend who'd expedited her political asylum was that Velma had been a messenger, carrying information on her bicycle between towns, farms, and coffee plantations. Whether she was in love with a fellow counterrevolutionary or had brothers or sisters who worked on behalf of the movement, I'm not sure. I know that one day as she was pedaling down the dirt road, unknown drivers, clearly friends of the Sandinista government, struck Velma while she was riding her bicycle and dragged her along the dirt and gravel, shredding the skin and muscle of her right arm.

Realizing she was known now by her enemies, Velma sought the resources of friends who helped her cross into the States. She had relatives in Washington, D.C., congregants of the Seventh Day Adventist Church. So she settled quietly, anonymously into a brand-new version of herself, adopting all that was true and beautiful—as she saw it—in her new religion.

One day I took a photograph of Velma and Robbie in the living room surrounded by toys, Velma's head thrust back in broad laughter as Robbie, wearing a miniature sombrero, grins manically ahead. I bought a special frame for that photograph and put it on our mantelpiece, next to the wedding photos and the one of me in profile, belly ballooning in my ninth month. Aware that this was a typical gesture in the way so many rituals are around a baby, I still hoped Velma would feel a part of our family. I wanted her to know how much I appreciated the animation she brought to my son, and to me. In writing this essay, I cast around for a very long time, searching for metaphors; how to portray Velma, whom I have always seen as unbelievably kind, in phrases that were neither sentimental nor trite. I might capture her in dialogue, which is always best, but there would be a time when an image was called for, yet all I can think about, because it's true, is the sun.

WHAT NEED IS SATISFIED when a narrative gets written? When you sift out fact and circumstance, what gems catch your eye among the detritus in the pan? I did not share Velma's religious belief in personal salvation. Yet I find myself unable to shake the superstitions of my childhood—that evil circumstances are caused, on some level, by witches and monsters, and good outcomes by uncanny magic.

"If you're asking me to look into my crystal ball," our neurologist said during one appointment when I pressed him, "I really can't."

What would I want to know?

Will he use his right hand?

Will he go to a normal school?

Will he use words well, read, learn to drive a car? Will his emotional responses to other people be sensitive, appropriate, intact? Is there any way to reverse *all of this*?

Robbie thrived; he surprised the doctors. The word "remarkable" appears in many medical reports, as well as notice that Velma was always by my side: "The baby was accompanied by his cheerful mother and childcare provider." Or "As always, his mother and nanny attended the session together." In March, six months after Velma had come to work for us, the pulmonary nurse told us that Robbie's apnea monitor tape was clean. There had been no evidence of an event for the past four weeks. It was time to wean him off the machine. She used the word "wean," which—when you think about it—makes no sense at all. In Robbie's case, one simply

unhitched his belt and peeled off the electrodes. I was the one to experience withdrawal. As much as I loathed that millstone encum-
brance, I slept at the edge of my bed, Robbie in the bassinet beside
me, monitor on the floor, and watched periodically throughout the
night the blinking green lights, one for heartbeat, one for each breath,
that assured me he was breathing normally.

The first step was to move him down the hall to the nursery my
husband and I had painted and wallpapered, filled with stuffed animals, then abandoned once Robbie was born. Velma and I spent
time with Robbie in the "new" room, playing with board books and
toys, having him nap in what seemed to me the enormous expanse
of his crib. The carpet, the folded blankets, and larger sized baby
clothes all felt and smelled new. How would we possibly ever use so
many things?

Everything seemed . . . almost normal. This was the transition
we'd waited for since he was born. By now Robbie could crawl and
stand up, holding on to furniture. ("Keep him on his hands and
knees for as long as possible," Gwen advised. "The more weight-
bearing, the denser those right arm bones will grow to be.") One
day, around the time Robbie began sleeping alone in his room,
Velma handed me an unwrapped gift of a leather bible, embossed
with my name. She rarely spoke about her religion, and indeed, I
couldn't count the number of times I'd inquired. The gift was beautiful, I thought, if a little sentimental. I thanked her but had to say,
looking at the gold letters of my name, "I'm not exactly a believer,
you know."

"That's okay!" her shoulders rose in exaggerated nonchalance.
We'd never had this sort of conversation. "Just read it a little—you'll
see. I pray for your family all the time with my church."

I imagined a room filled with Velma's friends, eyes closed in concentration for our well-being. She wasn't the sort of person who invited physical contact from me. I might have asked her many

questions, but instead I held the bible close to my chest, in a gesture that was insincere but grateful.

Earlier that winter, Velma had fallen in love with a man from her congregation and, in a gesture perfect for a film or story, was married in City Hall on St. Valentine's Day. I lent her a white ruffled blouse to wear with her red suit, bought her a silver and garnet pin for the lapel. What fun to exploit one of the most American clichés, I thought. How renegade to marry in a civil service—though, in fact, Velma took this day to heart. Her new husband, Bayardo, was handsome and fine-boned, with sharp dark eyes, and excruciatingly shy. He'd pick her up from work each evening at five on the dime, pull up alongside our house, idling. "He's a good man," she told me, as though I needed convincing. "We don't have money, but we're starting fresh, with God's help."

Velma's ecstasy: She'd skip out the front door in the fun faux-fur coat he bought her, half dancing up to Bayardo's car. Robbie stood at the edge of the coffee table and bounced up and down.

THIS IS AN ESSAY with a happy end, despite moments of despair. Robbie is nine years old now, a special child who loves science experiments and anatomy, and listens to books on tape. A few weeks after their marriage, Velma's husband accepted a good-paying job with a construction company in North Carolina. They left D.C. when Robbie was almost a year old.

In time, I returned to work; I had a daughter and another little boy. My subsequent relationships with babysitters have been more or less successful, though I've felt the typical tugs of war—vying for domestic territory and routine, irritation over tasks not accomplished in the ways I wanted, overindulgence or impatience with the children. No doubt I've idealized Velma. I remind myself that she couldn't be bothered to put a dirty cup in the dishwasher, that she really could *not* cook, even an egg. That she left us with less than two weeks' notice and no forwarding address.

What I cannot manage to feel is the least bit of anger. Only surprise.

Even here in the U.S., hundreds of miles from episodes she would not talk about, a woman with simple work, a church, friends, a quiet husband who was steady and devoted—even so, this need for secrecy? Was her name even Velma? Of course not; that's the name I've given her here. Yet she created the better fiction. I never heard from her again.

To question the depth of Velma's affection for my family is to question ultimately something in myself—my need for reassurance, for example, or an assumption of superiority. Velma's actions had their own integrity. She was a person of her word. Yet when she disappeared, I realized that you should never assume to know a person. This is something to respect.

So I narrate this story here, in lined-up sentences: what was and is, the sadness of what can never be. And my love for Velma, wherever she is now, the way her kindness saved me at that hardest time.

MAMMY POPPINS

Kymberly N. Pinder

*E*very expectant mother imagines her child's face. Whose nose will he have? What kind of chin or color eyes will she get? The long squinting sessions with those tiny ultrasound pictures attest to the way the curiosity eats at you. The face of the child becomes, quite literally, a preconception. Even after the child is born, the guessing continues as the squished features take shape. Little did I know that similar preconceptions apply to nannies, too. Anyone who has hired a caregiver entered the selection process with fixed ideas about what a nanny looks like and how she acts. I could not believe it either but yes, as a black woman, my ideal was "Mammy," like those played by Hattie McDaniel, Louise Beaver, and Ethel Waters.

Right after college, I lived on the Upper West Side of Manhattan. Each morning I'd pass dozens of black and Hispanic women pushing strollers. I'd peek inside, expecting to see a small brown face. But invariably, I'd find instead a child with skin so fair it seemed luminous. While this arrangement wasn't unusual, there was something uncanny about it: these women looking like mothers whose children had been spirited away, changelings left in their stead. But soon even I grew accustomed to the sight. The nouveaux mammies solidified my own idea of what a nanny was. I internalized it to such a degree that years later I could not even see white nannies and would often assume Irish and Eastern European sitters were the mothers of their charges. I know, I know, the mammy is a fiction created by white culture to desexualize black female servants, making them safe to have in the house with white men . . . blah, blah, blah. The truth is, we're not always entirely rational when it comes to our children. Add race to any mix and things become even more complex.

As an art historian I have written, lectured, taught courses, and curated exhibitions about such black stereotypes. Once I asserted that Oprah was our nation's current mega-mammy; she was huggable, nonthreatening, and quick to hush-hush our woes with straight talk and canned therapy. So, who would have guessed that a figure that I considered so steeped in racist traditions would be what I went looking for when I wanted my own nanny?

Here's something you should know: My husband is white. The circles we move in are largely white. And our Chicago neighborhood is predominantly white. The way I saw it, most of my infant son Cyrus's life was going to be inflected with whiteness. But at least I could find him a nanny of color—a mammy, if you will. Since I was teaching only two days a week, I wanted to share a full-time nanny with another mother, and I had the perfect candidate. Helena was a wealthy stay-at-home mom who I met in birthing class. Like me, she was a nonwhite woman (she's Chinese) with a white husband. She was well educated and an artist. Surely we'd be able to find someone to our mutual liking.

Then the applicants arrived. When we interviewed nannies at Helena's condo some would be visibly taken aback when they met us. One Russian college student with flaming orange hair was so surprised when I answered the door that she had to take some time to collect herself. She was hesitant to even come in. Why did they expect only white employers? Do only white people live in luxury condos? Aren't black women working mothers or do they only take care of other people's children?

I was heartened by a Filipino nurse who arrived during the second day of interviews. She made it to our final two candidates. I really wanted her, not so much because she was a nurse but because she was brown. Then we called her references and her former employers were clearly lukewarm about her, confirming the trace of coldness both of us had sensed. Where were all the black nannies I had seen in Manhattan? I was counting on this stereotype as if my life depended on it. I had felt better about having a domestic when I thought I would be bringing another caring black face into my son's life. This other brown-skinned mother was a surrogate for me that I could justify; she would make me feel less guilty about leaving Cyrus and being so far from my own family, whom I worried he would never really know. How strange it was for me to be disappointed to discover that, in Chicago, a large, white underclass of Eastern European immigrants had taken over roles traditionally held by blacks.

During that week of interviews, I asked myself how I envisioned life with my nouveaux mammy. Would it be so idyllic? I thought of scenarios involving an African American woman who would have nothing but thinly veiled disdain for my interracial marriage. I imagined the damaging things she might say to my son: quips about his color, hair, and half-breed status. And what did I know about Afro-Caribbeans, Africans, or Latin Americans anyway? I had many assumptions, some based on experience but many more on nothing.

Helena and I ended up choosing a petite, soft-spoken woman with large gray eyes, ivory skin, and jet black hair. Teo was from Georgia—the former Soviet republic, not the former Confederate state. As soon as Teo entered the room, she was all over the babies. She even struggled to balance both infants simultaneously on her slender frame; she looked as if she barely outweighed the bundles she was holding. Helena and I instantly loved her. Our only hesitation was that we knew she had a lot of emotional baggage. Teo played with the children as if she were starved for their company because she had left her own baby in Georgia three months earlier. Our children became substitutes for her son, who was only fifteen months old and still nursing on the day she left him for the United States.

So she was not the dusky mammy of my dreams and, when all was said and done, I am glad for that. Despite the fact that even after a year, I could not spell her long last name correctly without looking it up, we became very close friends. For Teo, race seemed to be a moot point. I had worried about the cultural and language gulf between us but I had more enlightening and real conversations about racism and intolerance with her than with most people I know. Her own experiences growing up in a region torn by ethnic strife and corruption made her an extremely wise woman at age twenty-three.

Teo spoke often of how beautiful Georgia was and how she missed it, though her life there was not easy. The little I knew about Georgia came from television commercials from the 1970s featuring hundred-year-old Georgian men wearing Astrakhan hats and eating Dannon yogurt. So they're long-lived and have a fondness for dairy products, I thought. Nothing wrong with that. Shortly after she started caring for Cyrus, Teo and I were walking down the street when she noticed some red, white, and blue bunting. She asked me what it was for. Oh, I replied, that's a decoration for the Fourth of July. Her puzzled look told me I needed to elaborate: It's the day we celebrate our independence from Great Britain. She nodded pensively. We have a day like that in Georgia, too. "On our day, people protest in the streets. And Russian soldiers come and kill them. I saw a man stabbed with a . . . the tool you use in garden to dig."

"A spade?" I offered incredulously.

"Yes, a spade. The soldiers stabbed him in the street. It was terrible."

From what I gathered, the Georgians celebrated an event that was more like our Boston Massacre than the signing of the Declaration of Independence. One big difference: Theirs occurred in 1989—and Teo had witnessed it. As a teenager she had been a newscaster for a youth television station during the darkest years of the revolution. She and her friends had taken to the streets with cameras and microphones. Her wonderfully outgoing personality had put her on the front lines of her nation's unfolding history.

When she went to college her parents moved to Greece to work, as the violence increased and they grew tired of living without electricity or running water for weeks at a time. She told me about college professors she knew who actually starved to death! The $1,000 a week she and her husband, a chauffeur, earned in the United States enabled his family to buy two buildings and jump up an entire social class amid the growing poverty in Georgia. Leaving their son changed their families forever.

Teo often compared her son George to my Cy. Yes, his name is George; to express their national pride in their newly independent nation most parents of Teo's generation named their first sons George. One week Teo was very sad and barely spoke, so I asked her what was wrong. She shrugged and replied, "Cyrus turned fifteen months yesterday and that was how old George was when I left him. Now I will not know anything about his growing—I will know nothing." Up until then, watching Cyrus grow was like reliving her time with her own baby. From then on, she would know what she had missed by leaving. Now a void would stretch before her. I remember crying with her when she told me of one bad phone call home. Her hands were shaking and her voice became very high and thin, as it often did when she spoke English. "George refused to talk to me on the phone today. My mother-in-law kept calling to him but she said he would not come. She also told me that he asked for all of the pictures of me to be taken away." My stomach turned.

"Why would your mother-in-law tell you that? Isn't it hard enough that you are away?" I exclaimed and then felt awful. They were all doing the best they could in a horrible situation. My husband would often say, "I would dig ditches rather than leave my kid." But what if you could not get paid to do even that? Teo's strength and resolve frequently made me question mine. I had to admit that I didn't know what I would do in her situation. She had left her child to have what I have. Was I just another spoiled and cynical American who considered the American Dream a myth?

As I write this I am looking at a photograph resting on a nearby bookshelf. It features Cyrus, only four months old, lying in a cardboard box awash with styrofoam packing peanuts, looking like he'd just been delivered, not by a doctor or a stork, but by UPS. He is smiling, the collar of his blue onesie is dark with teething drool, and his plump legs are drawn up to his chest. He is happy. I was the one who took the picture, but it was Teo who posed him that way in the box. Every time I look at it, I wonder if she was living out a little fantasy of her own that day: a secret wish that children could be delivered to us so easily, traveling across oceans and borders without all the trouble of visas and laws, and none the worse for wear.

We decided to stay in Chicago for Cyrus's first Thanksgiving. We invited our friends to dinner so we could commiserate in our exile, admittedly self-imposed, from our families. I also invited Teo, her husband, and their female roommate. While I imagined that Georgia must have a holiday similar to the American Thanksgiving, I was reluctant to ask Teo about it, fearing it might involve someone being stabbed with hedge clippers. Teo and her party arrived bearing two bottles of Georgian wine, four bottles of Georgian water, and a large, vaguely circular loaf of Georgian bread. It was all quite biblical. The wine—let's just say that Georgia poses little threat to any established wine industry. But the bread—it was manna and we still reminisce about it. Teo had brought us that bread once before when Cyrus first began eating such foods. She had come in smiling with what looked like a gigantic wheel wrapped in paper. She told me with great pride that this was the first and only bread her son George had eaten. Discovering a Georgian bakery in Chicago and giving the bread to Cy really made her day. She was making him a little Georgian and a little more like her George.

Sharing Teo with another family was a bit odd since we both ended up knowing personal things about each other. My competitiveness made me want Teo to like us more. She often told me she thought of me as her friend and during the year and a half that she cared for Cyrus, I considered her a friend, too. Being a professor has meant that my time is extremely flexible and I often work at home, so I spent a lot of time with Teo. Some days I felt as if we were coparenting. I rarely dressed up for work so it was common for me to be feeding or holding Cyrus up until the minute I walked out the door. My lifestyle is a blessing but it has been difficult sometimes for my children (and me) to adjust to its irregularity. I like to set up my teaching schedule so I am a mom for half the week and a professor for the other—at home for days, then gone for twelve hours straight. Cy soon learned that when I picked up my work satchel instead of the diaper bag, I was about to leave him and the tears would start.

Teo would stay and chat with me for an hour or more after I got home and sometimes help me make dinner. I paid her for that hour mainly because I wanted to help her out, not because I felt she was still working. It was awkward. One Saturday afternoon we spent a couple hours in my office typing up a résumé for her to get another part-time job. I knew that helping her make more money would allow her to reach her financial goals and leave us sooner. Helena had tried to help Teo and her husband in even bigger ways such as paying for an immigration lawyer to discuss getting her son over here.

We both had fantasies about Teo relocating here permanently and our children growing up together. I had always considered nannies to be long-term. The mammy in films and literature remained devoted to her children, her own and her employers', until she died.

Helena also offered Teo and her husband extra work cleaning and making repairs in the various apartments and condos Helena owned. Teo was a bit insulted by the offer. Helena often mentioned to me that all of her friends' nannies cleaned their homes when the children napped and she wanted Teo to do the same. Of course, I wanted her to clean too. Who wouldn't? But I felt too uncomfortable with the whole employer role to ever ask. I also had a lot of class anxiety around Helena because, whether or not she and her husband actually were, I still considered them to be rich. They were landlords who owned identical silver BMW SUVs and shopped exclusively at Whole Foods and the toniest boutiques in the city. Helena was thin, tall, and stunning on top of it all.

As she told me how her daughter was applying to the École Français and how excited she was about socializing with the international set who went there, I knew I would never hear from her once Teo went to Georgia. I wanted to scoff at her social climbing, but she was so charming, so funny, and so beautiful, I still wished she liked me. Of course, I had secretly hoped she would invite me to some of their fancy dinner parties, the ones that Teo told me about. There I was—a grownup, a professional, a mother, and I felt like I was in high school. On the other hand, Teo's complaints about Helena proved some fictional class alliances I thought I had with Teo against her wealthy boss. I convinced myself that my relationship with Teo was fundamentally different and better (that is, less capitalist). Helena was paying a nanny but I was helping out a dear friend. Oh, the things we tell ourselves!

So my son grew to love his white nanny. Teo was always so proud of him, as if he were hers. She often said, "I grow him, too" when he reached another milestone. In turn, Cy was often drawn to women who looked like her. During his first Christmas at my in-laws, he would not stay away from a young cousin because her large, blue eyes and slender frame reminded him so much of Teo. Later that year, while in a gym class at the neighborhood park, my son kept staring at a woman with Teo's eyes and long black hair. He eventually went up to her and grabbed her hand. I smiled at her and said, "He likes you because you look like our nanny." Her face fell almost into the trike she was holding for her young daughter. *How the hell could I look like that woman's nanny?* her expression seemed to say. She was so shocked that she actually said nothing, just forced a crooked smile onto her face and walked off. She moved away from me and furrowed her brow for the rest of the class. I later imagined that she told her husband or sister or mother about the incident and how that conversation may have transformed someone's ideas about race in some way. Maybe it just made them complain about uppity, middle-class blacks but at least it made them acknowledge there were some. Maybe it made someone go on a tirade about immigration and the workforce. Maybe it made someone ask herself why it bothered her enough to bring it up. I also hoped that she had different thoughts now about the many white immigrant nannies whose guttural chatter she heard at the park or when she saw the few black nannies that sometimes appeared in our neighborhood. My little brown cherub had called out her whiteness with the innocent gesture of taking her hand and it shook her world. Was a black woman having a white nanny still so earth-shattering in 2001? (I used to mess with old white women on elevators or at bus stops in New York City by moving my purse away from them or hugging it tighter when I got near them. It caused the same shocked face I saw on that mom. These were just little political interventions I "performed" while a graduate student. Okay, I still do it sometimes.)

My husband and I have always been aware of the tangle of history that surrounds our interracial relationship. A walk down the street holding hands can prove it. Our existence and that of our offspring has a political dimension that we unconsciously assert each moment of our mundane lives—we go out to dinner with a set of grandparents and it's perceived as a rainbow-coalition event by on-lookers. When you are in a nontraditional family, your boring life constantly has onlookers. So when the specter of "mammy" appeared on the scene I had to wonder if I was trying to both rewrite and relive some racial past. Was I now taking on the traditional role of the white mistress and therefore wanting no competition for the white man in my home? And why was I not threatened at all by my very young, very attractive white nanny who often wore skintight jeans and T-shirts? Wouldn't any other woman be?

We had Teo for a little over a year because my husband quit his full-time job to stay home. Teo was planning to stay only a few more months anyway before returning to Georgia. Her goal was to be home for her son's third birthday in mid-December. We loved Teo and still do. She calls each Christmas or Thanksgiving and we receive sporadic e-mails each year. Her roommate, who stayed on another year, also kept us abreast of news from Teo. Teo gave birth to a girl less than a year after she left the country. We were so thrilled for her; having more babies was one of her favorite topics of conversation. I remember how she jumped up and down and kissed me when I told her that I was pregnant just a couple of months before she left. The news was an odd going-away gift since she would never meet the brother of the boy she called her second son. Although he does not remember it, Teo's departure remains the first great loss of Cyrus's life. That he does not remember it only makes this fact sadder.

Teo was our only nanny. After she left, we barely used babysit-ters though, ironically, the handful we have used look a lot like Teo. I did not realize this dubious coincidence until my neighbor began her search for a nanny last year. All three candidates I recommended were practically Teo clones! One was her Georgian roommate and the other two were American graduate students of mine. My neigh-bor ended up hiring an older woman from an agency. Gloria was from Zambia. She was about fifty, dark, stout with shining eyes and a musical accent. Through the windows, I would see Gloria many times a day walking the baby slung over her shoulder or cradled in her arms. She had a large frame with an ample bosom and loved to hold my neighbor's infant son close. She *was* the mammy, made of fact and fiction, that I had so desired five years earlier. I found my-self hanging out with Gloria whenever I had to stop by for some-thing. It was as if I were trying to see how it would have been with my ideal nanny.

But, of course, she wasn't ideal. She wore strange wigs and seemed a bit too conservative. She also quizzed me often about when I was baptizing my newborn daughter and if I had seen the mineral deposit that looked like the Virgin Mary recently discov-ered off the highway. As my mammy fictions crumbled, my neigh-bors put their son in daycare and Gloria left. I could not insinuate myself into her life any further. I still ask about her and get a small thrill when I see her car in their driveway when she babysits occa-sionally, but now I don't go over.

MY NANNY, MY SELF

Jane Meredith Adams

When I was a kid, my mother smoked, drank, and refused to engage in anything that might be construed
as child's play. She had her talents, but raising children was not one of them. While my father worked, my mother
took care of my four sisters and me, and I understood *mother* to mean
a weary figure who lay on the couch critiquing the accomplishments
of her children. Show her your story in the school newspaper and
she'd sniff, "Well, it's not the *New York Times*." Bring home a tro-
phy from a tennis tournament and she'd question, "Exactly how
many people were in this tournament?"

In deciding to become a mother myself, the last thing I wanted
was to bear sole responsibility for the mental health of my offspring.
Mercifully, our San Francisco family would have two moms, my
girlfriend, Crystal, and me, and two dads, John, the biological father, and his partner, Eric. And of course, since I planned to work
part-time at home, we'd have a nanny.

It was upon the nanny that I laid my hopes. In searching for
someone to teach me how to take care of a baby—to teach me, ac-

tually, how to be a mother—I thought it wise to reach beyond my relatives and seek the services of a paid professional. My mom was dead and unable to criticize the next generation, my dad was busy, and two of my sisters in Massachusetts greeted the news of my pregnancy with the kind of horror usually reserved for the coming of the antichrist. Fearful of crossing the antichrist contingent, my other two sisters (also in Massachusetts) weren't rushing to lend a hand with the diaper changing, either. On Crystal's side, her parents were dead, her sister lived in Texas, and her Christian fundamentalist brother refused to speak to her once he got wind of the fact that, like him, we'd felt entitled to reproduce.

As for our own family structure, four parents sounded like a lot, but after I'd been vomiting for six months, it occurred to me that as the biological mother I was hoisting way more than my quarter of the load. While it was terrific that John and Eric lived only five blocks away in our Noe Valley neighborhood, they would be safely out of earshot of a wailing infant. Their plan was to show up three evenings a week for some quality face-time; the rest was up to us. Crystal worked full-time as a construction superintendent and needed her sleep; the lion's share of the burdens rested with me. Even more worrisome was the fact that I was carrying twins, a situation that caused friends and strangers alike to recoil in alarm.

Vastly pregnant, I drove to a meeting of the San Francisco Mothers of Twins Club to decode the mystery of how to obtain the perfect nanny or, barring that, an affordable nanny who wouldn't carve Satanic symbols onto the babies' foreheads. Pregnancy had put me in a mood of doom—feeling obese, nauseated, and terrified can do that to a person—yet I had no choice but to curb my personal litany of complaints when I entered a room clogged with double strollers. Here were my people: seven hormonally crippled women who had slogged through miserable pregnancies only to be faced with labor, delivery, and the gymnastic challenge of breast-feeding two babies at once. Inside a conference room at Children's Hospital, many of the women were, as I was, close to or slightly beyond age forty, the reproductive no-fly zone that leads to fertility treatments and hence two babies or perhaps, heaven help you, more. To be frank, a few of the moms were obvious wrecks, with puffy eyes and wrinkled clothes that looked slept in. I lowered myself into a chair next to the group leader, a graying brunette who introduced herself as Linda. "I left my twins at home with their nanny," she explained. "It's easier that way." I didn't doubt it.

In the back of the room, pacing the perimeter with swaddled babies in their arms, were two actual nannies, one a Swedish teenager and the other a fiftyish Mexican matron in a tight white nurse's uniform. Their presence at the meeting seemed strange, but I soon saw the brilliance of traveling with a trained assistant. Why be alone with two crying babies, even if you're at a meeting to talk about what it's like to be alone with two crying babies? The young Swede laid two preemies side by side on a blanket and expertly changed their cocktail napkin–sized diapers, while the Mexican matron confidently rocked a bald infant in one arm and soothed another baldy on her shoulder. Looking at the two helpers, I knew instantly that I'd never hire a nanny who was younger than I was. I didn't want anyone like the young Swede asking me for advice about dating or finding an apartment, or asking me anything at all. The Mexican matron's white uniform was too over-the-top authoritarian for my taste, but with her neat dark hair and quick smile she seemed kind and maternal. As she cooed at the baby on her shoulder, I imagined her at home with me. I'd be resting in the gliding rocker while she bustled around changing diapers, holding fussy babies, and, if need be, performing the Heimlich maneuver on the twins. As soon as she got the babies settled, she'd return to her most important task. "I think it's time you took a nap," she'd say, rubbing my shoulders. "Here's a nice tall glass of seltzer water with lime and crushed ice, just the way you like it. But before you go, would you be so kind as to recount, once again, how wretched being pregnant was?"

I raised my hand and inquired as to how I would find one of these incredibly useful nanny persons for myself.

The answer was not clear. Two moms had gone the nanny agency route, replete with visas and expensive fees. Another was using a friend's former nanny and, from the sound of it, she'd timed her pregnancy to coincide with the month the nanny would be available. Someone else had found a nanny through an advertisement in *The Diaper Rag*, the newsletter of the Mothers of Twins Club. "I don't have a nanny," said a youngish woman with a ponytail. We regarded her with concern.

A tired-looking brunette in jeans and a polo shirt spoke from the floor, where she was attempting to change the soggy diaper of a bleating six-week-old. Her voice rose like that of an oracle. "Get as much help as you can," she intoned. "Borrow money. Refinance the mortgage. Do whatever you have to do. Get help."

Apparently, what would be required was a far-reaching nanny search. Three days later I was diagnosed with preterm labor and confined to bed for the remainder of my pregnancy, bringing a halt to that idea. While I lay around reading *Leftsider*, a magazine devoted to frightening pregnant women with the information that if we don't lie on our left sides, we can cut off the babies' blood supply, Crystal ran into a friend at the supermarket who had a word of advice in the nanny department: "Latins," she said.

I envisioned a three-person Latin staff: nanny, housekeeper, and cook. Having non-English speakers around the house would be just the ticket. They wouldn't make me nervous with personal chitchat and at the same time, they'd introduce the babies to the fundamentals of Spanish. Although Crystal and I couldn't properly pronounce burrito, I thought that with a little effort, a few Spanish tapes in the car, and the staff chirping *en Español*, we'd be a bilingual family. When Crystal pointed out that the staff would have to be paid, we pared down our plans and considered the part-time services of a wizened Guatemalan named Esmerelda.

For three years Esmerelda had taken care of the boy across the street. I'd often seen her and wondered, *Who is this mysterious, ancient woman?* With her stocky build and somber expression, Esmerelda seemed to have wandered out of a remote mountain village, vowing never to laugh again. Our street ran up a steep hillside which she climbed with slow, sherpa-like determination, pausing to make base camp in stairwells. Her age was difficult to pin down; the wrinkled face and gray-haired bun indicated that she was well past sixty, but the idea that she was working past seventy was too grim to consider. Since she was our only candidate for the job of nanny, we concentrated on her strengths: The boy across the street adored her and his mother reported that Esmerelda had a habit of sponging down the kitchen appliances. After the birth of our twins—eight weeks early, with loose-skinned, four-pound bodies—I telephoned Esmerelda's daughter, Anna, who spoke English, and arranged for an interview with Crystal and me.

Anna, who was stout, middle-aged, and occasionally willing to smile, had followed her mother into nannyhood and worked for a family across town. Heaving herself into a rocking chair in the living room, she launched into a litany of complaints about her mother's previous employer, the Treadways across the street. "Mrs. Treadway didn't know how to make her baby stop crying, ever," she said gravely, leaning perilously back in the rocker. "All Webster has in this world is my mother."

"*Ay, Webster, ay, mi bebé,*" Esmerelda murmured, sitting in a matching rocker with her eyes half closed.

"My mother and his cat," Anna continued. "If it weren't for my mother . . ." She shook her head and made clucking noises.

Crystal and I didn't know the Treadways very well but I was fairly sure it wasn't a good idea to gripe about your last employer before you've been hired by your next. While I admired Esmerelda's devotion to her young charge, I sensed she saw herself less as a babysitter and more as a missionary wandering the hills of Noe Valley bringing love and joy to neglected infants. It was an interesting stance for a morose woman with a morose daughter. Crystal steered the conversation to what we had in mind for hours and pay and Anna translated. Since I was nursing the twins with a frequency that had moved me into bra sizes I'd never known existed, I explained to Anna that I would be on the premises and would take care of the babies alongside Esmerelda, at least in the beginning. "We'll be a team!" I said cheerily. Ignoring my words, Esmerelda rose, silently removed Claire from my arms and Andrew from Crystal's, and sat down again. Leaning her face next to theirs, she whispered feverishly in Spanish, probably along the lines of, *Don't worry children, I will save you. No one will ever love you as I do, not even your mother and that other woman, whoever she is.* We hired her.

Maybe if I'd spoken her language I would have taken a stab at explaining to Esmerelda the reproductive details of lesbian motherhood. As it was, I saw no need to trouble her with the news that she was employed by homosexuals. I'm not sure she understood our arrangement, but she never indicated she saw anything unusual about two women raising babies. From what I could tell, she traveled in a manless world herself, never mentioning who'd fathered Anna, just as Anna never mentioned who'd fathered her two children. Our family actually had more men in evidence than their household. Later, when John dropped by the house, I introduced him as the babies' papa. Esmerelda gave him a withering look, perhaps surmising that he'd run out on me. "My name is Juan," he said earnestly, but her nod was curt. "She doesn't like men," John said after he'd received the withering look a half a dozen times. "She likes Andrew," I replied. "Okay," he said, "she likes baby men."

On the first day of work Esmerelda arrived at 8:40 A.M., twenty minutes ahead of schedule. From the window in the living room, I watched as she doggedly climbed the sixty-six steps up our walkway. She looked up at me, nodded her head, and proceeded to the summit. Upon reaching our enclosed porch, she sat down on the floor. Did she want a little private time before reporting for duty? Was sitting on the floor some kind of pre-work ritual? Not wanting to compel her to work before her official starting time, I turned away from the door, pretending it was no big deal to be walking around with two five-pound babies strapped to my body, Andrew in a BabyBjörn frontpack and Claire in a sling resting on top of him. Sure, fine, a little break before you begin your day, fine. Five minutes later, I passed through the living room only to see Esmerelda's face at the front door, her lips pressed into a tight, irritated line. I uttered the first of many apologies. "Sorry, sorry, hello, come in," I said, opening the door and handing her one of the babies.

Soon after her employment began, Esmerelda and I brought the babies to the doctor for their first vaccinations. As the two of us wrangled the twins into matching striped cotton outfits, carried them down sixty-six steps, and wandered the street until I remembered where I'd parked the car, I thanked God and the lax enforcement policies of the Immigration and Naturalization Service that I didn't have to do this alone. At the doctor's office, I kissed my clueless, peaceful offspring on their cheeks and held them out one at a time to the doctor, a white-coated stranger who would stab their thighs with needles. Claire went first. Because her underdeveloped lungs weren't yet able to produce a real bloodcurdler, her screams were more like those of a kitten getting its leg amputated, a raw mewling with bitter undertones of fury and injustice. When it was his turn, Andrew demonstrated a scream that was bold yet weak, insistent yet unsure, increasing in rage as the doctor progressed with each of the five shots. Thrashing in my arms, Andrew seemed to want nothing more than the ability to crawl, run, or levitate himself away from me, a person he'd once considered his best friend in the world. Yes, polio would be a drag, but it was a distant, far-off drag compared to the immediate torture unfolding before me. Why in God's name hadn't a doctor put her mind to it and concocted a cherry-flavored vaccine brew for a baby to inbibe? Sympathetic milk leaked from my oversized breasts, creating two wet bull's-eyes on my T-shirt. After the last needle was withdrawn, I clutched Andrew while Esmerelda held Claire, and we emerged, stunned, into the waiting room. "Should I nurse them?" I asked, nearly in tears myself. Esmerelda looked at me blankly. I motioned to my breasts. "No," she said, pressing Claire tight in her arms and leading us out. Something told me I hadn't so much hired Esmerelda as surrendered to her.

Every day she arrived early, slogging up the hill with her swollen feet stuffed into flat blue shoes. I counted the minutes until she appeared in the morning and I dreaded her exit in the afternoon, two or three hours before Crystal's return from work. She never called in sick, never asked for time off, and always said yes if I asked her to stay an extra hour. I felt unbelievably lucky.

Our strategy boiled down to zone or one-on-one. If I was in the kitchen doing the dishes, Esmerelda worked zone, holding the crying baby while cooing at the happy baby. If I was available, we worked one-on-one, each taking a baby and pacing around our cottage. Communication was by hand signal. Holding her fingers open in the shape of the letter C, Esmerelda brought her fingers together like eyelids to signal that a baby had fallen asleep. Heading for the changing table, she flashed me the international symbol for poop: a fist clenched and then violently opened. Any thought that our children would be free to form their own opinions of gender roles vanished as Esmerelda smothered Claire with cries of "*la princesa.*" Dropping her voice to a bass and raising Andrew's scrawny arm into the air, she declared him a man with a cry of "*hombre!*"

Before long, Esmerelda communicated by strapping on a Baby-Björn, loading Andrew in, and pointing out the window. A walk. Terrific idea. She was halfway down the steps by the time I had my Björn on with Claire packed inside. Sprinting, I caught up to her on the street. As a bus roared by, I saw our stroll as an opportunity to show Esmerelda that not only did I respect her as a person, I valued her culture and her language. Pointing to the belching vehicle, I asked, "Co-moe-say-dee-say bus?"

"Boos," she replied indifferently. For a slow walker, she seemed to have found her stride.

Tree? Bird? Leaf? For two blocks, each query of mine was answered in unintelligible Spanish, which I mangled and repeated. At the next corner, Esmerelda jerked her head to indicate she'd be turning. Pointing an index finger at me, she signaled that I was to go back to the house without her. I slogged back up the hill with Claire strapped to my chest and repeated boos, boos, boos, trying to get the Spanish accent just right.

Even with two of us on duty, life with twins was chaotic. I'd assumed Esmerelda would be one of those baby whisperers who knew how to lull to sleep the screaming, colicky baby that was Claire. Instead, as Claire cried inconsolably for hours, Esmerelda glumly paced and chanted, "*Jésus, José, Maria.*" Once, exhausted by Claire's crying, Esmerelda went so far as to emit an English word: "Tylenol." We dosed Claire without much effect.

Meanwhile, my pals in the Mothers of Twins Club seemed to be pulling themselves together. I'd return from a club meeting full of resolve to make the babies' routines, such as they were, more orderly. Linda, the group leader, had her twins on a schedule. In a move that seemed to me a mark of insanity, she deliberately disturbed her two sleeping babies, waking them at 7 A.M. sharp so their daily naps and nursing shifts would proceed in an orderly fashion. As I recall, her twins napped from 9:03 A.M. to 10:17 A.M. and again from 1:13 P.M. to 3:34 P.M., and were nursed at three-hour intervals until midnight, at which point they were cut off with a little pat on the back and instructions to "quit crying and grow up." Getting them on a schedule involved letting them scream until they passed out. "It's tough at first," said Linda. "But it's definitely worth it."

A schedule, I thought. That's what we need. With a thick paperback Spanish-language dictionary in my hand, I looked up the word for schedule and pointed to it for Esmerelda's edification. "*Ay,*" she said, an all-purpose sound that seemed to mean either *I understand completely* or *I don't know what you're talking about and I don't care.* My Spanish was worse than rudimentary, but I pressed on. Someone in this house would have to become bilingual and it looked like it would have to be me. "*Itinerario necesita nosotros* (Schedule we need)," I said. "*Problema tenemos bebés siesta* (Problem we have babies nap)."

At ten in the morning, I lowered the babies into the crib they shared, and instructed Esmerelda, "Must nap babies. Is time now." While the babies cried their heads off, I stood guard around the corner from the crib, waving my arms to keep Esmerelda at bay. Twice she started for the crib and I fended her off. "Cry sad yes but good. Schedule," I said. Nineteen minutes later, after I'd ducked into the bathroom for some peace, Esmerelda liberated the babies from their crib. "*Ay,*" she whispered into their tear-soaked faces. "*Ay, mis bebés, ay.*" She motioned to me to fetch and open the two single strollers we kept on the porch. After plopping each baby into a canvas seat, she stood in the living room like the axis of our personal solar system, pushing one stroller to the right and one to the left, in and out, until the babies fell asleep.

If not a sleep schedule, then perhaps we could have a nursing schedule. After issuing an edict that nursing would happen every *tres horas* and no sooner, I left the house until the appointed mealtime. That worked okay, for me at least, but the next day I foolishly attempted to work upstairs in my office. After about an hour at my desk, I heard the distant sound of the twins warming up their vocal cords. Flicking on the baby monitor connected to their room downstairs, I listened to what sounded like a difficult session of cattle branding. A few moments later, Esmerelda stood outside my closed office door with two shrieking babies. I couldn't say no. As the days passed, no matter when I left the house, I returned to a similar scene: Claire screaming, refusing to take a bottle, and Andrew screaming because Claire was screaming.

Forget sleeping and feeding schedules, then. At least the twins could attend the same Tuesday-Thursday playgroup as a couple of other sets of twins from the mothers' club. Linda raved about the group, which was held in the basement of a nearby Lutheran church. Songs! Water play! Circle time! Esmerelda would have to go along, as Claire and Andrew were too young to attend without a caretaker. Waving a cheery farewell, I dropped them off on a Tuesday morning. When I picked them up, Esmerelda's face expressed a new level of somberness, something I hadn't thought possible. On Thursday, when I gathered my car keys and asked, "Playgroup now okay?" Esmerelda shook her head and walked into the kitchen. At twins' club meetings, I dodged inquiries about nursing schedules, naptime rituals, and the Lutheran church playgroup. At our house, we seemed to be forging ahead in baby care with a distinct lack of knowledge, insight, or planning. There was something familiar in the hard gaze Esmerelda directed at me. Something that made me remember that the secretary at my sister's office referred to my mother as The General, and left little pink slips of paper with the message, "The General called." And this was just from hearing my mother on the phone.

One day, more than a year after the strollers became part of our living room furniture, Esmerelda's fourteen-year-old granddaughter, Maria, came in to see the babies, as she often did. As we chatted, she mentioned that her grandmother had been a nurse in Honduras. "Well, not a nurse, exactly," she said. "Kind of a healer. A medicine woman."

Really? As it happened, I was in need of medical expertise regarding my itchy and bloodshot eyes, the end product of months of stunning sleep deprivation. Pointing at my eyes to Esmerelda, I held my hands up to indicate bafflement. When she seemed puzzled, I darted to the bathroom and returned with the empty bottle of Visine.

"No, no, no," she said, shaking her head at the foolishness of Western medicine. She moved to the kitchen cabinet and withdrew a canister of salt. Taking a fresh lemon from the bowl on the counter, she mimed slicing, squeezing and mixing the juice with salt and throwing in a little water. "*Bueno*," she said, patting her eyes.

As soon as Esmerelda and her granddaughter left with the kids, I sought solace in her folk remedy. Eagerly I mixed the salty potion, leaned over the kitchen sink, and scooped the liquid into my right eye. It's hard to recall which sensation dominated the experience: the ferocious burning, the torturous stinging, or the realization that I would no longer be troubled by itchy eyes since I'd blinded myself. One thing became clear, though. While it was perhaps true that I knew very little about how to take care of babies, I was an idiot to think that Esmerelda knew a lot more about everything.

Naturally enough, the twins eventually started talking. Obediently, they'd fetch a *pelota* or a *calcetina* at Esmerelda's request, but I never overheard them chatting in Spanish as they rolled along in the double-wide. At every chance, I played Spanish-language tapes in the car, but the only one who learned how to ask for a hotel room with a bathtub was me. As I nursed them on the obscenely large blue nursing pillow, I watched a Spanish TV soap opera and learned how to beg for a divorce from a man whom I thought had died ten years before in a car accident. As the twins reached twenty months old, it was clear that Esmerelda didn't like children who spoke or moved or inched their way toward independence, even if independence meant refusing to take off their soaking wet diapers. As they became toddlers who screamed "No!" and ran down the hill away from her, her face assumed an expression of chronic hurt and disappointment. The turning point came after she took a second part-time job. My guess is that the other family paid her slightly more money to care for one sleepy newborn than we paid for her to chase after two defiant, unscheduled, non–Spanish-speaking toddlers on a hill. Exhausted by two jobs, her temper flared. "*La cochina!*" she yelled at Claire one morning in the bedroom. From my office, I ran in when I heard the tone of her voice. Claire was lying on the floor. There was no evidence of any crime or misbehavior. Esmerelda picked her up and hurried out of the room. A neighbor translated the phrase as "little pig." "It's not necessarily bad," my neighbor added. "But I wouldn't want my daughter called that."

Being unkind to me is one thing, but being mean to my kids is another. I called Anna and told her we'd decided to put the kids in preschool starting in one week. This was a lie. I was going to find a new nanny and in fact, after one day of asking around at the park, I'd met a calm, fortyish El Salvadoran woman I liked. When I told Anna we'd need her mother only for another week, Esmerelda refused to return to the house. Bereft, Claire cried inconsolably. Andrew looked at the front door, waiting for Esmerelda to walk through.

This would not do. I called Esmerelda's other employer and asked if we could come over and say a proper good-bye. Of course we could. When we arrived, Esmerelda wouldn't look at me, but she scooped up the kids in her arms. After a few minutes, there was nothing to do but have the kids say *Adios*, Esmerelda, and leave. So we did. If I'd watched just one more year of Spanish soap operas I'd have fired out a parting shot. "You not mother," I'd have told her. "Babies mine."

FINDING MARY

Joyce Maynard

What I would give now for a day with my children when they were small. Two, four, and eight; three, five, and nine; five, seven, eleven; zero, two, and six. I'd take them at any of the ages they ever were when they still lived under the same roof with me, and I wouldn't care if they spilled their milk or failed to pick up their Legos. That's how much I miss those days.

When I was living them, it was a different story. When they were little, and I was young—trying to take care of them and still hold on to some scrap of the woman I was before they arrived on the scene—I dreamed of reclaiming a portion of what I have now in abundance: time alone. An empty house. An uninterrupted hour in the bathtub. A telephone conversation that could be carried out without hiding in the closet (phone cord stretched to its limits, because these were the days before cordless phones were invented).

Everything I long for now is everything I had too much of then. Today, I want to hold a baby. In 1978, I longed for someone else to take her sometimes. I longed to do my work, but

*though I didn't understand this at the time, there was some-
thing else necessary, before I could even get to that. For me, the
first gift our first babysitter gave me was simply this: the chance
to do nothing at all for a while. To simply sit alone and remember who I was before I was a mother.*

In 1978, when I gave birth to Audrey—baby number one—I had
never known anyone who had a baby. Nobody my age, anyway—
twenty-four. My mother lived far away. Most of the women I'd
known in my days as a young student in the newly co-ed Ivy League
were off pursuing high-powered careers of the sort I'd had, very
briefly, and abandoned for a home birth and a life of gardening and
bread baking on fifty acres with my artist husband. My former class-
mates were in graduate school or working in the city, wearing Diane
von Furstenberg wrap dresses and going out at night. They couldn't
relate to my life with a husband and a baby—couldn't relate to the
levels of love and selflessness my daughter inspired, or to the feeling
that overtook me sometimes, holding my daughter as I unbuttoned
my blouse to begin nursing her: a wave of sadness so vast I couldn't
get my head above its dark and murky waters.

I was lonely and depressed, and something else: I was overtaken
with guilt for feeling that way, at the exact moment in my life when
I knew I should have been ecstatic, because I had this baby girl, and
she was more wonderful than I could have dreamed, and that should
be enough.

Of the few friends I'd made in the small town where my husband and I had come to live, only one had a baby. The one who
did—Betsy was her name—used to stop by for visits with her three-
year-old. "Your breasts will be ruined, of course," she told me, with
an air of something close to satisfaction. "My husband and I used to
have all this great sex," she confided. "That's over now."

"I used to be an artist," she said, hearing of my writing career in
the city. Then she laughed.

Only a year earlier, I'd been a young bride, reciting poems to my handsome husband, lying naked on the grass as he drew my portrait, twirling across the dance floor with him at our wedding. Here I was now, only eleven months later, sitting at my kitchen table while a woman I didn't even particularly like held forth for a solid hour on all the things you could tell about your baby from analyzing the consistency of what you found in her diaper. I listened earnestly, but after she left, I put my head on the table and wept. I loved my daughter more than I had known was possible, but what I hadn't bargained on was how, in the course of becoming her mother, I had somehow lost sight of my own self.

We took a trip to New York City—my husband and I, and our infinitely precious baby girl—when she was three months old, and we ended up at the top of the Empire State Building, on the observation deck. Looking over the edge, with Audrey in my arms, I knew I had to get out of that place. The image of throwing her off the side of the building was filling up my brain.

It was around this time, pushing my grocery cart through the Grand Union with Audrey in her front pack, that a woman happened to stop me in the produce aisle to admire my baby. At the time, she seemed very old, though I realize with a shiver, writing these words, that she was probably around the age that I am now: fifty-two. Her hair was gray, but she was tall and she carried herself like a queen. She introduced herself to me: Mary.

"People are going to tell you that beautiful hair of hers will all fall out," Mary said, inspecting Audrey's head. "But don't believe them. She's a black-haired beauty."

And then she turned her gaze from my daughter to me. "You look like you could use a break," she said. "You better take care of yourself, or you won't be any good for this precious baby of yours."

Five minutes later, I was in the checkout line, paying for my groceries, and saw that one aisle over, so was Mary. She was just picking up her bag to go when I caught up with her.

"I know this sounds crazy," I said. "But would you ever consider just . . . I don't know . . . taking her for a few hours some time?"

At eight the next morning, I was sitting in Mary's apartment, handing over the supplies: two changes of sleeper suit, a few Pampers, Audrey's blanket, and a precious bottle of expressed breast milk, still warm. I had never left my daughter with anyone before. Even my husband took her only occasionally, and never for long. For three months, I had seldom if ever had her out of my sight for more than an hour.

Mary listened patiently enough to my recitation of all the things about Audrey that I thought a person needed to know before taking charge of her for a morning—none of which was all that important. When I'd finished she said, "I know what to do," and it was clear she did. She had raised her own three children mostly by herself, on the small wage she earned cleaning the house of the Catholic priest in town and cooking his dinner now and then. Her wage, from me, I think, was a dollar-fifty an hour.

"You get on home and take care of yourself," she said. "I'll take care of the baby."

The plan was that I'd use the time Mary took care of Audrey to do something constructive—meaning, to earn some money writing articles for magazines. One thing was clear: We needed money. In the months since I'd become a mother, I had been able to think of little besides my daughter, and our finances showed it.

The first morning I left Audrey at Mary's, I drove away crying. When I got back home, I sat down at my typewriter and rolled a piece of paper in the carriage. I stared at that sheet of paper for a long time, typed a few words of one sentence, then a few words of another, before getting up, fixing myself a bowl of cereal, and staring out the window at the mess that was once my flower garden. It was just the season when a person might have planted tomatoes, but the whole process seemed impossibly complicated now. Where was my hoe, my shovel? Should I buy Big Boy or Early Girl? Or try peppers and beans instead? Or maybe sweep the porch and take off the storm windows?

The whole morning went like that. I put on a load of laundry. I started slipping record albums back in their cases. I thought I'd organize Audrey's dresser drawers, but then I noticed a rip in her leggings and thought I'd mend it. I decided to eat a cookie instead, and when it turned out there were no cookies, I thought I'd bake some, only we were out of chocolate chips. Then it occurred to me to wash my hair, but taking a shower required me to look at my naked body in the mirror, and that made me cry. So I did a dozen sit-ups. Then cried some more.

Then it was time to pick Audrey up. Not quite time, actually. I showed up at Mary's a half hour early.

My daughter smelled different, and unfamiliar. Mary had given her a bath, and managed to style her hair, with a single pink barrette. When I got there she was eating baby cereal, and seemed to like it. Audrey was kicking her feet in the infant seat propped on the counter. "She likes peaches stirred in," Mary told me. "Just a teaspoon."

After that, I brought Audrey to Mary's every morning. Then I'd drive home and sit at the kitchen table, trying to think of something to write about. Often, a whole morning would pass in which all I did was sit there. Or I'd walk through our house, tidying up small messes. One day I wrote a letter to my sister. One day I made a pie. One time—guiltily—I took a book down to the waterfall at the end of our road and read on the edge at the place where the water tumbled over the rocks until it was time to pick my daughter up. One day I took a book down to the waterfall, and didn't even open it, just sat there.

Now and then my husband asked how things were going, and I always told him "fine."

"I'm getting a lot done," I said, feeling like a criminal. A dollar-fifty an hour wasn't a lot of money to spend on childcare, but it was a dollar-fifty an hour more than I was earning.

Still, I kept bringing Audrey to Mary's house for those half days. I couldn't give it up. I wasn't writing anything, but a change was taking place. I was thinking about things besides being a mother. I was putting on clothes other than sweatpants. I was doing sit-ups. But probably more significantly, I was doing nothing. Just sitting at the table, thinking. Sometimes about Audrey. Sometimes not.

As much as I loved dropping Audrey off at Mary's, I loved picking her up. I was always happy to see her again—to bend down and take her in my arms, carry her out to the car, buckle her into the car seat, and later—home again—give her my breast. But sometimes, too, I was in no hurry to leave Mary's. We'd sit in her living room and talk about the baby, talk about the news of town, or her own children, and how things were for her, when they were the ages mine was now.

Once, when I was having tea with Mary, before taking Audrey home, Audrey had gotten into a stack of magazines and ripped off the cover of one. "Audrey," Mary told her sternly. "Go to your room now."

Audrey was eleven months old—not yet walking. But she turned around and crawled off to Mary's back bedroom. No tears, and no particular sign of unhappiness either. She was just following the rules, though they were rules that did not exist at our house. And it occurred to me, watching her, that already my daughter had a life apart from me—not just a place to go, but a set of experiences, and a relationship I wasn't fully part of. I didn't know everything about her anymore. In the same way that I'd been living a life separate from her, in those few hours every day that she spent in Mary's care, she'd been living a life separate from me, too.

One time when Audrey was at Mary's, I drove into town to buy groceries, and spotted the two of them, Mary and Audrey, walking down Main Street. Seeing them, I felt as guilty as I would if I'd been headed to meet a lover. I was the mother. What was wrong with me that I liked being away from my baby? And not even because I was working on anything important. Just because I liked it.

When Audrey was eighteen months old—walking now, on her own—I met a famous young woman fiction writer, whose new novel (her second) had just been published to considerable acclaim. I came home and wept to my husband that I would never find the time and concentration to write a novel like that woman did. (She was childless, I knew. She had a flat stomach, without benefit of sit-ups, probably. She was just back from Key West, she told me. There, and Hollywood.)

Hearing me talk about the celebrated young fiction writer, my husband had looked at me sharply. "For Pete's sake quit complaining and just do it if it's that important to you," he said. "Leave Audrey at Mary's a little longer, if that's what it takes."

Up until then, I'd left Audrey with Mary from eight A.M. to noon, but now I asked her whether she could keep my daughter for some afternoons, too. So, I left Audrey for a full eight-hour day at Mary's, and for three days I just sat at the kitchen table, feeling guilty. On the fourth day—maybe because it seemed too awful to leave my baby all this time and not accomplish anything—I decided it was time to type some kind of a sentence, and since I was thinking about my daughter, and being a mother, the words I typed were "Five girls sit on the steps of the Laundromat with their babies." After that, I couldn't stop, and four weeks later I finished a novel I called *Baby Love*, the first novel I ever wrote, and a year after that, it was published.

I didn't abandon my daughter. I didn't even make a habit of leaving her for eight hours a day at Mary's, once the book was done, though when it *was* done, I started thinking about another one. But when I look back on my life as a new mother—more than a quarter of a century later—it occurs to me that this was the moment when I first felt how it was possible to be a mother without ceasing to be my own self. In the space of those four-hour interludes when I was home at my desk, and she wasn't, I had carved out for myself a life that didn't fully include Audrey, but that was alright, because she had a life going on, too, that didn't fully include me—with her own small secrets. (Gerber peaches and trips to the Catholic church rectory. "Go to your room" and a brand of shampoo I didn't recognize, that smelled like strawberries. Mary's granddaughter, Melissa, and a cat, and a nursery rhyme I didn't know, that Mary'd learned from her own long-ago childhood in England.)

That was the first of a long series of small steps we have taken, she and I, to make our own way in the world, over the course of the twenty-eight years since that day. And though we always come back to each other, I know (as I began to realize, even then) that she is not all mine, any more than I am hers. Another woman sometimes washed her hair and changed her diapers, comforted her when she cried and made her laugh. She had her life with Mary. Same as I had mine, with my work. Neither one of them meant that we loved each other any less, at the end of the day, or that I had less to offer her. More, sometimes, because I had more to give. There is no way of offering a sip of water to a child, when your own well's gone dry, as mine did for a while there, before Mary helped me find the way to fill it.

Part Two

SISTER SUFFRAGETTE: IN IT TOGETHER

THE NANNY CONUNDRUM:
What I Didn't Understand About the Women Who Took Care of My Children, and How I Found Out

Susan Cheever

*I*f there's a good woman behind every great man, behind every great woman there's a good nanny. As the family has been restructured and most mothers of children have continued working, babysitters, nannies, and daycare have become our necessities. This demand for childcare has been met by a patchwork of agencies, a few experienced nannies, and thousands of immigrant women looking for jobs that require no training, no degrees, and usually no papers. Often these women leave their own children at home in order to support them with money they make looking after other women's children. A babysitter's salary in New York or Los Angeles is the equivalent of a doctor's salary in Sri Lanka or the Philippines. This collision of the needs of two kinds of very different women is difficult for working mothers who have to find reliable childcare in an unreliable market, and it's difficult for the women who work for them with no protection and no guarantees.

THE MOMENT I HELD my baby Sarah in my arms, my life changed. The love I felt knocked me off my feet. For the first time, feelings for another person cut through the elaborate web of defenses I had constructed. I could feel my new self floating away from the old, and I was frightened as well as exhilarated. My little girl instantly became the center of my world. How could I learn to care for this exquisite creature? In understanding selflessness, in actually feeling that I would rather be hurt than have her hurt, I also understood that I was vulnerable in a new and terrifying way.

Before being a mother I was careless. Few things frightened me. Now everything—New York City traffic, germs on doorknobs, chemicals in baby formula—frightened me. I needed help. I hired a woman named Ferdi from El Salvador who had worked for a friend of mine as a cleaning lady. My friend said Ferdi was quiet and reliable, and I knew she had a son of her own.

At first Ferdi and I worked well together. I sponsored her for her green card, filling out and copying many forms. I helped her go back to her country in order to make a legal entry into the United States where she had been living for a decade. Thanks to me she was no longer an illegal alien. I started paying her Social Security. I didn't mind. She was as much my daughter's parent as I was, it sometimes seemed.

I loved the sound of Ferdi's key in our lock each morning because it meant I would have time off from being a mother, time to take a shower or read a book. It meant I would have time to work. I loved listening to her play with my daughter in the next room as I wrote, or as I did business on the phone, or just drifted into the doze of the perpetually sleep-deprived. I loved hearing the sweet song Ferdi sang in Spanish about a little white horse that was homesick. I adored my daughter, but I needed help taking care of her, although it was sometimes painful to admit that.

It wasn't just the physical help; the dressing and undressing required by a three-year-old, the cleaning up which followed every sloppy meal, the endless hours of playing on the floor with small pink plastic horses that had to be put back in their stalls after each canter around the rug. Ferdi was my only company in that intense place that was the texture of my daughter's life. My husband sometimes gave a hand, of course he did, but when it came to the tough stuff, the laundry, the tantrums, the applesauce, the comforting, the coaxing into sleep, it was Ferdi who understood what was needed and Ferdi who knew what I was doing even when she wasn't there.

Then after three years, Ferdi announced one evening that she wanted to take the summer off. It was already May and she wanted to leave in June. Could I have heard correctly? My daughter started at the strange sound of my voice speaking angrily to her beloved Ferdi. I was horrified. Without Ferdi's help, even for a week, caring for my three-year-old girl would have left me exhausted and strung out. I was in a bind. I was trapped and that made me desperate. Ferdi was the answer. I couldn't even imagine three months without her help. It was too little time to hire a replacement and way too much time to go without a babysitter. A whole summer was out of the question. I said no.

Ferdi and I began to argue. She used the telephone too much. She fed my daughter unauthorized cookies. I hectored her about my needs and my work. As she was cleaning the kitchen counter one morning while my daughter napped, I told her that I thought we should have a serious talk. She nodded. I reminded her how generous I had been. I was on a book deadline, and I tried to explain what that meant. The narrow room smelled of Clorox and fried eggs; sun poured in through the sooty window, the coffee pot was half full. Ferdi wouldn't answer me; she just kept sponging the counter.

After that morning, she got quieter and quieter. Once, when I heard her singing about the little white horse to my daughter, I went to stand in the doorway. When Ferdi saw me, she stopped singing. The next day she called me to say she couldn't come in because she was sick. A week later she brought a note from her doctor saying she needed the summer off. I joked sarcastically that I would love to have a doctor who said I needed the summer off. I wanted Ferdi to see my doctor. I made an appointment for her; she said she couldn't find his office. Then one day she was gone. She left a note saying she was sorry. A few months later I found out that Ferdi had gone to work for a friend of mine.

Later, sifting through the wreckage of my connection to her, I realized that I had never known Ferdi well. She had intimate knowledge of the details of my life. She washed my lingerie, and she heard me fight with my husband. Yet I had barely met her children or her family and I had never been to her home. The story of our breakup, if I had been in a position to understand it, might have shown me the inherent difficulties in the situation between mothers and babysitters in our society in the twentieth and twenty-first centuries. At the time, I couldn't acknowledge that I wanted the impossible: a babysitter who would love my daughter as if she were her own, admire me, work for minimum wage, and make sure that my daughter didn't love her more than she loved me. Instead of learning from this experience, I hired another woman I didn't know. This time, I was lucky.

Our second babysitter, Leona, was a warm, smart woman with six children of her own left behind on the other side of the Pacific. There must be a special god who looks out for clueless mothers, because although I hired blindly, I could not have found a better nanny. Again, I wanted the impossible; what I got was something even better, a woman who gently parented me into being a mother as she helped me mother my beloved children. In the Philippines she had been a teacher. She had come to New York with a specific goal—to educate her children and bring them to the United States. After she had worked for me for a while, we talked frankly about that goal. I wanted to help her, and as a result she wanted to help me. When my daughter was seven, I had a son who was equally precious to me. Leona seemed to adore my children and took care of them with good humor and affection.

Still, leaving my kids, even for a few hours, was often tough. No matter how many times I reminded myself that I had to work, no matter how many times I told myself that I was being a model for my daughter, no matter how often I assured myself that an unhappy mother was bad for her kids, walking away could be agonizing. I often exited the apartment and stood leaning against the outside of the closed door breathing in the air of my children's lives until I felt strong enough to leave. It was impossible to avoid the parallel between my life and Leona's. In those moments my heart went out to her. I couldn't imagine how she found the strength to bear it.

Leona was expensive. She was struggling to send enough money home to pay for her children's housing and education. She asked me to pay her in hundred-dollar bills because they were worth more in the Philippines. Each Friday I went to the bank, withdrew a stack of money and counted it out. My friends told me she was taking financial advantage of me. Thank God I didn't listen to them. Every time I thought about firing her to save money, a quick flash of imagining what our lives would be like without her brought me to my senses. Still, when Leona was offered a good teaching job I was happy for her, although I was sad for my family. She gave me plenty of notice and she was obviously thrilled to be teaching again.

Working with Leona I began to see that the babysitter or nanny was not an ordinary employee but the most important person in my life. The woman (and it was always a woman) who stood shoulder to shoulder with me through the joys and nightmares of raising my children was at the center of each day, more important than my friends, more supportive than my family, and more relied on than my husband. It took me a long time to realize this.

Later I learned that the relationship between a mother and the other woman who cares for her child or children is as volatile, passionate, and complicated as many marriages. It must often transcend a difference in cultures and languages. It's a difficult relationship for the mother—whose anguish at leaving her child with another woman may carry over into it. It's also difficult for the babysitter who must lavish love and care on children she may never see again. To soften the reality of the situation, we create a kind of mythology of friendship. We imagine that our babysitters are not just working for money. They must also love our children—how could they *not* love our wonderful children?—although they have no real power and no real stake in our children's lives. It's a tall order for women who usually get paid less than the plumber or the veterinarian.

It wasn't until my daughter was twelve and I wrote a magazine piece about Dominique, our third nanny, that I bothered to find out more about the elegant woman from Trinidad who was taking care of my children. As a journalist I was curious and interested. As a mother I had been strangely clueless. I took the time to do the research that I had never done before. I went to Dominique's apartment in Brooklyn. I saw that although she didn't have much furniture she had a flair for modernism and she owned a few nice pieces. I saw the Bible she kept under her pillow and the Snapple in her fridge. I met her friends. I heard her life story and saw photographs of her daughter.

Some mornings I commuted with her to my place, a commute involving two long subway rides, and I stopped with her to say a prayer at a local church. I got to know her as a friend. I heard her stories and her friends' stories about bad employers. Some mothers treated the babysitters like servants; some fathers treated them like whores. It was a shock to hear about parents from the nanny's point of view, especially when the parents did things that I had done: refusing to give paid vacations, asking them to walk and feed the dog, expecting them to iron and sew and cook when I needed help with those things. Dominique completed my education. Just as I no longer needed help with my children I began to be qualified to employ help.

Our generation has made a religion of parenting. Our mothers had Dr. Spock; we have a library of books telling us what to do and how to feel. They had a family doctor; we have pediatric dermatologists who scrutinize every passing rash. In many families the babysitter becomes the true second parent, the one who works with the mother to create ways for the children to thrive. Honesty and professionalism can go a long way toward defusing this fraught situation. If I had made an agreement with Ferdi when I sponsored her for her green card, we wouldn't have been so surprised and infuriated by each other's needs. At the same time the situation has many more intractable problems.

We've decided to let other women help raise our children so that our children can have better lives; at least that's what we hope for. It's an excruciating situation, as the nannies know better than anyone since many of them have made exactly the same decision on a larger scale. We are more like our nannies than we realize. We're all strung out between the old ways and the new, torn between the demands of money and the demands of love. They have chosen to give their children less mothering and so have we. There are bad nannies and good nannies just as there are bad mothers and good mothers, but it's our similarities rather than our differences that make the situation so painful.

THE UNFLAPPABLE LINA G.

Karen Shepard

O ur oldest boy was five; our new baby son was four months. I was in that manic new-mother stage of making lists and trying to cross things off. I am, my loved ones would report with some kindness, always in that stage. But at that time I was even more so because I was going back to teaching, and with a new baby, teaching had less than the necessary appeal. Whatever part of teaching is about fulfilling some maternal need had been temporarily eradicated. That fall, I stared out at my students thinking, *You are not my baby. Why, exactly, should I care about you?*

And yet here I was getting ready to entrust the care of my baby to someone who could look at him and think exactly that: *You are not my baby.*

So perhaps it was the perfect timing for someone like Lina. She was a senior at Williams College, where both my husband and I teach English and creative writing. I was reassured by her unflappable nature, by her matter-of-fact way of going through the world. I, usually unflappable myself, had been flapping away like a penguin trying to take flight since the birth of my son. We moved houses when he was two months old. Our books were still in boxes. There were shelves to be built. Things were not in order, and I seemed to have been rendered constitutionally unable to fix things in my usual way. Enter Lina.

She'd been a friend's sitter. I'd heard rave after rave about her way with children, her level of responsibility, her experience with infants. (To this day, that friend insists I stole Lina away from her. I lost not a moment of sleep about the truth of that statement. *That's* how needy I was. Actually, I was so needy that I tracked down Lina's home number in Peoria, Illinois, and called her over the summer. If I had stolen her away, couldn't somebody else have done the same? I wanted to lock her in before anyone else got to her. Lina gave me grief about that phone call for months.)

In September, she came to the house for an interview. She had thick black hair that she wore pulled back in a sensible oversized barrette. Her nose was prominent. Her eyes an alert brown. Her hips wide. She had a way of walking that was both casual and no-nonsense, as if she were wearing house slippers outside. She had three brothers and was the only daughter of an ardently Catholic Columbian mother and a recessive Midwestern father.

During that interview, I learned some things about her that I still find myself telling people. As a child, she'd decided that she was going to have a baby, man or no man, by the time she was twenty-nine. To that end, she'd opened a savings account and had been making regular contributions to it for years. Since elementary school, she'd been carrying a list of possible baby names on a small piece of paper in her wallet. She announced this sort of stuff as if supplying references. I stared at her, speechless.

She was the student liaison for the women's studies program. She did internships at family centers in the bleak former mill town that neighbored our elite college town. She worked in a restaurant, where she routinely spun around to put a finger in the faces of her male coworkers whom she was sure were looking up her skirt, saying, "*You*. Can you say, *sexual harassment*?"

All sounded good. All sounded familiar to us, teachers of the overachieving types this elite liberal arts college routinely attracted. Just the kind of person we'd imagined for our child. Just the kind of resource we could have in our lives while genuinely sympathizing with the plight of our friends who lived in towns without college students like ours.

She worked for us during her senior year, at least twenty-five hours a week. When we expressed concern about her classes, she reassured us. The reading wasn't absolutely necessary in many of her courses.

She was, it turned out, the most cheerfully anti-intellectual student my husband and I had come across in our combined thirty-five years of teaching.

Coming over to our place after a meeting of her modern European history class, she announced, throwing her bag down, slipping off her shoes, heaving our son onto her hip, "God. So I was reading about World War II? And was Eastern Europe a grim place, or what? I am *so* glad I didn't live there then." She swung the baby to the other hip.

One day my husband told her he was showing a film to his class that he thought she'd like. She slid her eyes over to take him in. "Is it in black and white?" she asked, fatigued.

We laughed and teased her about this. We told these stories to people who knew her and people who didn't. Had I imagined entrusting my children to someone who told me that she'd been signed up for my English class her freshman year, but when, on the first day, it had become clear how much work there'd be—no more than the average Williams class—she'd dropped the course?

No. But what I had thought was going to matter most had turned out not to matter almost at all. And isn't that always the way when parenting is the issue?

What turned out to be more important was the unobtrusively democratic way of looking at the world that Lina modeled for my children. The easy way with which she took them to the kinds of places that I, born and raised in the upper class of New York City, would've found a little cheesy, and by implication, a little beneath me. She took them apple and pumpkin picking at the kind of farms where they could have their pictures taken in those big wooden cutouts, her own face inserted in the holes next to theirs. She took them to the kind of small-town attractions—Memorial Day parades, sheep-shearing festivals—that my husband and I tend to avoid.

Why not? her position seemed to be. Why not do X or Y? Whereas I had spent my life controlling myself, asking, always, Why?

Which brings me to my mother. Because, of course, any essay about a nanny has inextricable ties to one's own mother. Where else does one get one's definitions of caretaking, good and bad? How often do young parents take comfort in the thought, *Well, at least I'm not going to fail at this whole thing as miserably as my own parents did.*

My own mother—a relatively young grandmother (fifty-seven when our second child was born), divorced from my father, living on her own in New York City, teaching Special Ed and traveling to her native country of China once a year—had often pointed out that she had devoted herself to me, her only child, from my birth to age three, when I had started nursery school. After that, there had been one part-time sitter, but only after my independence had been established. One doesn't have to be an expert in psychology to find the holes in the logic of that sentence.

Her implication was always that as a teacher and writer, I was giving my children the short end of the stick, not living up to my role as a mother, which might've made me feel guiltier if she hadn't spent my childhood training me to be able to do without her. I took the city bus to school when I was five. I had a key to the apartment at the same age. I had my own checking account at twelve, out of which I paid for my phone bill and my share of the cable bill.

She was successful at her project. I am, for the most part, able to do without her, logistically and emotionally. But then I had children. And what I needed and wanted from my own mother changed. Things I'd put up with for years, things I'd used as fodder for comic anecdotes, turned out not to be that funny.

I have three children now, fourteen, eight, and three. My mother has seen the three-year-old twice. The first time when my daughter was two months old. When my daughter passes the wall of photos on our stairs, she sometimes points out my mother's and says, "Who's that?" When I answer, she says again, "Who's that?"

How much does this bother me? So much that, for all intents and purposes (one of my mother's phrases), I keep my distance from my mother. We can go months without any contact. An exchange of two e-mails can keep us going for almost a year. I don't call her when we go to New York. I've stopped inviting her for holidays. I've stopped sending birthday presents. I routinely worry about how I'll respond to real need on her part. Will I be able to offer the kind of caretaking she might need when she gets older? Even if I'm able, will I be willing?

Am I proud of this? Not especially. But I don't see any other way. My mother says I want her to be someone that she's not. She says I need to accept her for the kind of mother she is, and not try to mold her into some kind of idealized version of what a mother should be.

Sounds reasonable. Who wouldn't agree that our interest in others should be based in desire and not only obligation? But I keep thinking that if she got to know my children, she might actually *want* to spend time with them, not because grandparents are supposed to be interested in grandchildren, but because these are interesting children.

Which brings me back to Lina, who had her own mother issues.

Her mother was the volatile ardent Catholic Columbian. We heard about her mother a lot.

Her mother's routine punishment was to ostracize her. No place set for her at the family table. No riding in the family car. Brothers and father forbidden to speak to her. This treatment was usually tied to revelations about Lina's sexuality. As in, her having one. The first occasion of ostracism followed her mother's asking whether Lina was sleeping with her freshman-year boyfriend. That banishment had lasted six weeks. Lina had been welcomed back into the fold only when she'd agreed to see their priest for a "revirginification" process. (Surprisingly, I've never had the desire to pursue the details of that process.)

Her mother had asked the same question about Lina's senior-year boyfriend. This time, Lina had said, "Are you sure you want to know the answer?" and had reminded her mother what had happened the last time.

Which, as far as Lina's mother was concerned, *was* an answer. This time Lina was out of the family for four months.

This Draconian level of abandonment went back even further in her childhood. When one of our mutual friends left his infant, by accident, in the college gym, Lina said to him, waving her hand, "Oh, that's nothing. Our mother used to do that to us all the time. I can't tell you the number of street corners we've stood on, waiting for her to show up." I never found out how young she'd been or how long she'd waited.

My own mother used to wait until I was asleep and then go out to—I don't know—visit friends? Have a date? Who cares, really. I would call my father, and weep into the phone, making myself sound worse off than I was, knowing that he'd get in a cab, race across town, put me back to bed, so I could wait up until Mom got home and I could listen to him let her have it. Of course, all I wanted was for someone or something to force her back to me. It was clear that that would have to be someone or something other than me.

(This was probably why, when listening to Lina's stories, I was more appalled by her father's reactions than her mother's. It was one thing, I thought, for her father to be told to stop speaking to his own daughter. It was another for him to *follow* those instructions.)

What *were* her reactions to all this aggression? Well, she never shut her mother out. She let her do her insane and deeply hurtful things, and then went on, loving and hating her in that delicate way that mothers and children do.

She did, in other words, what I, with all my years of wisdom, have not been able to do.

I would never, I knew, be guilty of the kind of things Lina's mother was guilty of. But what *would* I be guilty of? What *was* I guilty of? Once, a year or so ago, my husband and some friends and I were talking about my mother. Our oldest had been listening in that thirteen-year-old's way, and he said, "Where is she stationed, anyway?"

We all laughed. I laughed the hardest, at the idea of my mother as a transient member of some odd and obscure branch of the armed services. But whose fault *was* it that that's how my thirteen-year-old thought of one of his grandparents? What I was teaching my children was that disengagement, withdrawal, self-protection was the way to go when someone you loved did something you found unforgivable. In the lives ahead of them, would I do something they thought unforgivable? Absolutely. Would I want them to react the way I had reacted? It would be my worst nightmare.

Thank goodness, then, that they had someone like Lina in their young lives. Someone who, when ostracized, got over it. Someone who waited a prudent amount of time, and then came back. Someone who, when called names, gave her mother the benefit of the doubt and tried to figure out what her mother was trying to say in her own inarticulate way.

But I don't mean to make Lina sound *only* like a poster child for mental health. As a corrective, two stories. The first has to do with her then boyfriend, now husband. He was, according to reports from her during their first spring together, her soulmate. However, if he ended up finding a job more than two plane changes away, she added, the relationship was over.

The second has to do with her own daughter, a girl born around the same time as our third. Lina and her daughter came to visit us. We played in the room that Lina and my son had crawled around in together. My son, delighted with the baby, put on a scary rubber mask and stood, undetected, behind her. Lina got her daughter's attention, pointed, and said, "Look." Her trusting daughter turned around, saw, and burst into tears and screams. Lina laughed and laughed, expanding for me, once again, my definition of what a mother could be.

Sisters

Marina Budhos

Sheila came to me by word of mouth. Another mother in my Upper West Side building had a daughter who would be starting school full-time, would need her for only a few hours in the late afternoon. My son had been born in the summer, and I was looking for a nanny to begin part-time at first. My sense of the job, of how many hours, of even what I expected a nanny to do, was completely vague.

Our first meeting was hardly an "interview." We both were too embarrassed. We sat on the couch in my apartment, my arm draped across the back, she with her shoes off, and chatted about giving birth, babies, our families. There was nothing unusual about our impending arrangement; all over my neighborhood mothers like me, in their thirties and forties, were hiring mothers like Sheila—immigrants, mothers themselves—to look after their children.

Sheila is from Guyana. Her mother was Portuguese, her father Indian, and she lived with her family and her daughter in Queens, not far from where I had grown up. She had dark brown hair, tinged red from henna, and her skin was tawny brown.

She looked like my sister. In fact, Sheila could be my sister.

∞

MY HOME WAS THE CONFLUENCE of two immigrations: my father, like Sheila, was of Indian descent and grew up in a tiny village in Guyana. On my mother's side, my Jewish grandparents fled the pogroms of Russia, and my mother grew up speaking no English until she was six years old.

Growing up, I was surrounded mostly by foreigners and immigrants, as we often played host to newcomers, and we also lived in a garden apartment complex built for UN employees and other overseas families. My eye was on two worlds: the mostly assimilated American world of my school friends, and that of my foreign-born neighbors, whose servants literally slept in the closet.

In our home, it was always pointed out to me that American kids were "bratty," with no discipline or sense of history. I was to be American, yes, but not too American. *Oh you see how they dress their daughter, in those store-bought clothes*, my mother would remark. (I had handmade dresses and crocheted and knitted sweaters). *They never sit together and eat as a family and they only eat frozen foods.* (We always had full meals, often Indian, and always with a pot of rice for my father.)

So I became quiet, withdrawn, and dutiful, as my mother was to her immigrant mother; I was the pleasing daughter to my slightly befuddled, slightly alienated father. While on the outside I was like any other kid in my school, watching the same TV shows, riding a banana-seat bicycle, inside there was a veil of distance; I could hear that warning bell of my parents, not to go too far into America.

By the time I was a teenager, though, my mother had gone back to school to find herself and I was often left alone, feeling confused, angry, and neglected, coming home to a darkened apartment with pork chops sitting cold in a skillet. One of the ways I assuaged my own loneliness was to take care of the neighborhood children. I soon had a flourishing business; my fluidness at being at home in American and foreign homes meant that everyone would call me up.

Sometimes I would spend time in the apartment of our Egyptian friends, the Zehdis; they had a servant, Fatima, who slept under the dining room table, and taught herself to speak by watching TV. Soon Fatima began to confide in me: She told me that the Zehdis were going to send her back to Egypt, where she would be beaten by her stepmother and married off to a man who would also hurt her.

In surprisingly clear English, Fatima would beg me to help her stay. I was stunned; I was twelve years old. What could I do? But I was also fascinated by her story. Here, under the domestic surface, doors opened and opened and I was suddenly in Egypt, not just the upper-class Alexandria, but learning about lives in the twisting by-lanes of poor Cairo.

I was a weird combination: a dreamy, yet intensely disciplined kid. I saved up hundreds and hundreds of dollars from my babysitting jobs, but I wanted to spend it all on a trip to Los Angeles, where I hoped some movie director would discover me. I wanted to be part of America, to appear on a TV show with white skin and freckles, but strangely enough, I identified with those flitting servants I saw unrolling their beds under the dining table. I wanted to be in both places at once, on the shadowy margins of the servants, and boldly in the center, like a real American.

∽

LIKE MOST OF MY FRIENDS, I became pregnant in my late thirties—nearly a decade older than my mother was when she had me, her second child. I never doubted for a moment that I would have help, as my own mother did not doubt that she would stay at home. Even though my mother was a serious student and yearned to do more with her life, she was a mother first, and those ambitions took second place. She loved babies, certainly, but I also remember best the frustration lining her face; how she grew impatient if we spent too many hours together and expected me to converse with her as an adult, to be her company. I lived in fear of becoming the madwoman in the attic, with unrealized dreams and baby toys strewn around me. Or worse, I worried that I would be a "bad" mother because I would always be distracted by my own frustrated yearnings.

However, since I was a freelance writer and teaching part-time, money was tight and it wasn't quite as easy to justify getting a nanny. Couldn't I stay at home, tapping at the computer, while the baby napped? Yet I knew, deep down, that this was impossible. My habits were too well formed, routines that I had established through my twenties: to wake, drink coffee, and sit at the desk and write in hushed silence. A nanny, a woman there exclusively for me and my son, seemed the only way to preserve that sanctuary. I lived in fear that if I didn't set this up, everything I had accomplished would be struck down and buried in a storm of tantrums and diapers. I wasn't that different from most of my friends: stubborn about my career, while also afraid that it was all too fragile, and could easily be swept away.

At the same time, I was divided: I didn't want to be seen as one of those demanding, self-absorbed "American" women—everything my family had warned me against. In my family, to hire a nanny was completely new—it signaled that I had moved up in class, something that they watched with suspicion. My brother had married a woman who immediately gave up her job and stayed home with the children, taking pride in the fact that they never used babysitters. But I knew it could be no other way; it was no coincidence that I had married a man whose own foreign-born mother had herself been reared with servants, and who always had nannies and au pairs to help rear her son while she worked as a professional set designer with her husband. From an early age, I wanted to move up in class and culture, to be like the Zehdis and the other glamorous families I had watched in my community.

Yet I was still the good, local girl taking care of all the children and listening to servants as if they were my best friends. I listened to my friends talk about hiring help, and cringed. To them, a nanny was still a woman from another world, a foreigner; to me, I wasn't so sure. That first day, as Sheila and I talked, I was still that in-between person, alert to her story, more afraid of being sized up wrongly, and I kept reassuring her that I was easy and relaxed—I wasn't one of those "usual" employers.

I remember, during that first conversation, for most of the time, Sheila was very quiet, her eyes a little murky, which bothered me a little. Our interview eventually ended, though it was more like the natural slowing of a conversation between friends. Before she left, though, I asked her about her own family.

"I have a daughter, two years old," she explained.

For some reason, this surprised me. And God help me—the thought popped into my head, *Her daughter doesn't matter that much to her.*

An instant later, Sheila turned to me. There was a shift in her otherwise impassive face. She explained she had been married a long time and she had her daughter only two years earlier. She blurted out, "I didn't even think I could have a child. I'd had abortions." The sudden intimacy surprised me.

"What's her name?" I asked.

"Jennifer," she replied, and crept out the door, quiet as a cat.

✌

SHEILA MOVED INTO OUR LIVES, as easily as she slipped out that day. She always took her shoes off in the foyer, Indian style, and joined me in the bedroom where my son Sasha lay squirming on the bed, ready to be dressed. I would then pump breast milk for his noon bottle and she would wheel him out in the stroller and walk around the neighborhood. After they left, I shut the door and wrote in my little study, rigged up in one half of the room I shared with my son.

From the start, Sheila was like a member of the family. The two of us would fuss over Sasha as if he was our shared child, swapping stories about his latest amazing feat. I could see she loved his black eyes and long physique and liveliness, and enjoyed showing him off to the other nannies and doormen. As he grew older she would arrive as I was preparing his lunch. This was my prideful ritual. I wanted Sheila to peel off the plastic lid, so the other Caribbean nannies could see I fed my child rice and meat and vegetables—grown-up food, the way I was raised, the way children are raised elsewhere.

Because my husband traveled weekly to Chicago for his job, Sheila made it possible to keep a calm balance in our home. She had infinite patience. Children were never yelled at. Never. She always folded Sasha's cotton socks down, just so. She tied his shoes carefully and buttoned up his shirts all the way, so he looked like a boy ready for Catholic school. She also began to run small errands for me—taking in the dry cleaning, buying milk, diapers, baby food. Her steady, methodical way became a ballast for my life. While I usually raced through the day, juggling too many projects, Sheila made an art of the minute; she was able to be in the present, far better than me. I was always tripping ahead to the next anxiety, the next goal or ambition.

And to my surprise, despite my fears that motherhood would efface my hard-earned sense of self, I felt quite the opposite: It's as if I had stretched and grown larger, more capacious. I grew more driven with more work, more desirous of succeeding, for his sake.

Over time, we began to look and behave like sisters: Some days we dressed almost the same, in black pants, a ribbed top, a similar leather jacket. My first splurge as a new mother was a pair of shiny red loafers; a few weeks later Sheila bought the same in a knock-off version. We chatted about the other nannies and children; she'd give me the latest gossip or cluck her tongue over a lazy nanny who cared only about shopping.

In fact, Sheila was one of the younger sisters of a huge family that lived in the same house or nearby. I envied her for always being surrounded by her family—there were ten brothers and sisters, and someone was always showing up at their house. At the end of every week, when I asked her what she would be doing that weekend, it was as if she had to make no decisions; she would just flow into whatever others were doing that day. My father had come from such a large family, but he always kept a safe distance between him and most of his siblings, who stayed behind in Guyana. I was raised to think of them as the "backward" relatives, always pressing my father for money, never moving on, into the future.

I began to feel a sharp undercurrent of guilt about her daughter. More and more, she talked about Jennifer—how proud she was that she knew her ABCs; how she wanted to teach her to speak up, and not be held back as a girl. She worried because while she worked, her daughter was stuck in the house all day with her mother, with no stimulation, except for her cousin, who was about the same age. She worried, too, about her daughter's weight problems, since she was always being fed traditional *roti* and meat dishes.

So I began to act like an older sister: In much the same way as my mother and father were always proffering advice to newcomers, I too took on this role for Sheila. I gave her books for Jennifer, encouraged her to look into some preschool programs, told her to bring Jennifer with her to our house. I kept pushing her to start taking GED classes or think about eventually working as a teacher's aide, since she was so good with children. I bought her eyeglasses, as her eyes were starting to be strained, but she never picked them up.

Sheila was alert and observant; she saw the possibilities of other lives outside of her world, but just didn't know how to get there. She had dropped out of high school to get married, and had never gotten her degree. Later she attended a GED class and had done very well, but didn't manage to take the final test. In the meantime her life had gone up and down. She had lived for years with her family in the United States, then her husband wanted to make a go of it back in Guyana, and restart the family's rice farm. In time, she joined him, but the farm went bust. By that time, she was pregnant with Jennifer.

There was in Sheila a passivity, especially about her own destiny. The very quality of patience that I benefited from also seemed to be her undoing. We talked endlessly about her getting her GED, Saturday courses, looking into teaching, but even as she wanted more for herself and her daughter, she had a hard time organizing herself, or seeing ahead to some better picture of the future. I realized that underneath Sheila's calm lay a reservoir of deep shyness, a lack of will. This was a woman who also stayed with a man who beat her for years; who followed him back to Guyana for some crazy scheme about making it rich in rice. Every time I tried to push her to do more for herself, a murky passivity would come over her, the same quality I noticed in our first chat. There was some gap, some lack of belief that she could actually change her circumstances.

The only area I couldn't help Sheila with was health benefits. We could not afford them. Yet this troubled me. There was the cyst that had to be removed, her eyesight, her headaches, and her daughter's usual routine of doctor visits. Finally her husband got a job working in a shipping department. A real job, not some off-the-books gig, and I felt relieved, for her sake.

When do you get on his coverage? I kept asking.

Not yet, she would reply. He's finding out.

Otherwise the balance we created was perfect—her patience, my constant drive and organization. We cooked together—she taught me how to properly make *roti* and I gave her other recipes. Half the time when she rolled the Maclaren stroller with my son, she was mistaken for being his mother. Half the time I was mistaken for the nanny. We both enjoyed the mix-ups. There was no difference between us, we felt. We were family.

That is, until the tugs came from our real families.

∽

JUST BEFORE CHRISTMAS, my mother-in-law had trouble breathing and was checked into the hospital and put on oxygen therapy. My life suddenly accelerated, between my end-of-semester duties, monitoring her progress at a rehabilitation center, finding her in-house help, and taking care of my son. My need for Sheila became ever more urgent. But she had grown strangely withdrawn, even spacey. I would ask her to come back early with Sasha to help, and she'd forget.

One Friday, I was frantic to pack our suitcase, so we could stay at my mother-in-law's and help her return from the hospital and set up home care. I wanted Sheila around, mostly to feel her patience, her steadiness, to make sure I packed everything right before leaving.

But I couldn't find her. I knew she sometimes went up to my friend Kathleen's apartment, as she still took care of their child in the late afternoons. Or she went to another friend's around the corner, who had a baby the same age. But she wasn't anywhere. I paced and cursed. When she came back, I lost my temper with her for the first time. I told her how upset I was, that this was a stressful time and I needed her help. Her eyes went blank. She retreated to some place I could not reach.

Months later, after my mother-in-law was healthy and life went back to normal, I asked casually whether her husband was getting medical coverage.

She began to cry.

"My husband and I, we're not together anymore," she said. "I asked him to leave."

And then out poured a story I had only half glimpsed: how her husband's drinking habit had grown worse. He used to beat her so badly, he once cracked her rib. One time, when she went to rejoin him in Guyana, she found the house in disrepair and him roaring drunk. She fled in the middle of the night, terrified. I remembered, suddenly, sitting and listening to Fatima's tale—there it was again, these shadowy worlds of other women's lives, where they had no control.

"When did this happen?" I asked.

"Around Christmastime."

Those days when she withdrew from me, she had gone to sit quietly in a park, the library, a bookstore, or Kathleen's apartment. I pictured her in those dark, empty rooms, just trying to gather herself together, build up the courage to kick him out. She was not only standing up to him, after years and years, but to her family as well, for whom a divorce was the worst thing possible—worse, it seems, than her daughter's broken ribs. "You have no idea how much I stuck it out," she kept saying, almost to reassure herself that she was allowed to finally cut him loose.

"I would sit in the park, feeling so terrible," she continued. "It was Sasha who made me feel better."

I was amazed that it was my child that nurtured her, provided her with solace.

"Why didn't you tell me?"

"I was going to. I just didn't think it was the right time, with so much going on. It was a bad time."

She was right. It was a bad time, what with me racing between our apartment and my mother-in-law's house, dealing with the home aid agency. But I wasn't coping with a husband who drank himself senseless.

"What made you able to do it?" I asked.

"It's one thing for me to put up with him," she said, her voice cracking. "But not Jennifer. I did it for her."

And it was then that I saw open up the real difference between us: how much I felt I had control over my own destiny. Despite my parents' exhortations to be the good daughter of immigrants, the one thing they had instilled in me was a very American sense of will, of individuality. Even my getting a nanny, though it strained us financially, was unquestioned.

I had tried to give Sheila a sense of ambition, of a different future. But I could not. The only person who moved her to change was her daughter. Each time Sheila mentioned Jennifer's name, her voice cracked. It's different now, she kept saying. I have to do things for her. I remembered the awful thought I'd had about her daughter not mattering to her. A selfish convenience on my part, ensuring that my child would be the star, the one that mattered. What I hadn't taken in was Sheila the mother, the protector who would do anything for her flesh and blood, even forsake her husband of twenty years. Same as I would do for my own son, if pressed. This I understood, above all else.

It was as if I hadn't seen her for who she really was. Not a sister, but a mother, like me.

SOMETHING TO TELL YOU

Elizabeth Graver

*I*lse knocks on my study door and comes in, pushing a long curl off her face. I am sitting in my armchair, student papers all around. I should be grading but I've been lost in my thoughts, someplace far away. When she looks up, her eyes are panicked, pink-rimmed, and as my mind lurches back into the here and now, my first thought—always my first thought—is the girls: Something has happened, why aren't they at her side? Then I remember: They are napping. It is two-thirty. She almost always gets them down beautifully, in concert, then folds the laundry in smooth packages, picks up toys, makes a cup of tea, and begins her homework. They're napping, but then what feels so *wrong*?

"What?" I ask. "Is everything okay?"

"I have something to tell you," Ilse says.

WHEN WE'D HIRED HER, some three months earlier, she had seemed—I remember saying this to my husband, Jim—too good to be true. Our previous nanny, Edith, who'd been with us for a mere four months, had fallen into a deep depression during her winter vacation and had never returned. For three weeks in January, we'd been searching for a replacement, women filing in and out of the house. We found candidates on Craig's List and Sittercity.com; we found them through a fancy service with a horrifying placement fee. I put up notices in the library. Jim put an ad in the paper. The phone rang; e-mails came pouring in. My stomach—always a relentless barometer of my state of mind—seized, bucked, and refused food. "Why is another babysitter coming over?" our older daughter, Chloe, then three and a half, kept asking. "And why can't she just play with me?" "We need to talk to her," we said, "to see if she's the nicest babysitter for you."

Who were they all, this stream of people, the ones we did not welcome into our lives? We will never know. One woman, who had sounded wonderful on paper, came across as tight-lipped and rigid in person. "I believe in boundaries and will not fold the parents' underwear," she said, and though it was a perfectly reasonable sentiment, I knew she was not for us. Another woman's shoes were tied with red yarn, and she played clapping games with the girls in a manner so animated that it seemed to straddle the border between sweet and psychotic. I called her references. Keep looking, the father said.

Ilse's voice, when she called the first time, was kind, calm, and accented. She had grown up in East Germany, she told me. She had lived in the United States for three years, was getting her Masters in Social Work, and had been a full-time nanny the whole time. She had seen our listing on Sittercity.com. She loved reading, she said. She loved music and art, nature, imaginary games, all things I'd mentioned in my ad. She had grown up in a small village. In Germany, she had earned Masters degrees in art history and political science. She was twenty-nine years old. I told her about us; she asked thoughtful questions. We spoke for a good forty-five minutes on the phone, and as we talked, a hunch began to form: This one. Could. She. Be. It? The semester was about to start; I had a full-time college teaching job and a book tour coming up. Jim worked long days in the city. We had to move carefully but quickly. Before the depressed nanny, we'd had Kiki. We all adored her, and she was with us for three and a half years. Yes, Kiki had a boyfriend on probation who twice got drunk and totaled her car, who wrote checks in her name, who liked to come to work with her, but after we said he could no longer come, things went along just fine, better than fine. When Kiki left to move back to the Midwest, I felt as if an irreplaceable piece of my daughters' childhoods had gone away.

Ilse lived an hour away from us, but when I asked her to come for an interview, she said fine, and when I asked if she might possibly come that very day, she said no problem. A few hours later, she was in our house, looking around, asking questions, showing us a portfolio containing her grades and drawings, and—mostly— kneeling down to talk to the girls, gentle, playful, funny. You wanted to be around her; she had a kindness to her, a presence at once calm and charismatic. Our younger daughter, Sylvie, who was one and a half, ran toward her, then away. Ilse laughed, held out her hand. Sylvie clamped her hands over her eyes and smiled. Ilse sat Chloe next to her on the piano bench and played a Debussy waltz, the music so lovely that Chloe stopped banging on the treble keys to listen. We asked Ilse questions about her previous experience as a nanny. Her answers were smart and sensible, but she also had a spark to her, a wry sense of humor. And she was beautiful, with curly brown hair, wide eyes, a quick smile. Most of all—I remember thinking this—she inspired trust.

We took down the names of her references, and as soon as she left, I called them. One mother worked for a national au pair company. "When I needed an au pair," she said, "I called our contacts in Germany and asked them to send their best nanny. They sent Ilse." "Do you have any reservations about her?" I asked. Was there a pause here, quick as a heartbeat? If there was, I didn't hear it. "No," the woman said. I called the second reference. Responsible, she said.

Warm, good with limits, artistic, smart, professional, funny, trustworthy, interesting. "We've had," I said, "a few issues with our previous nannies having to do with their personal lives. Is she . . . I mean,
would you say she's stable?" A pause then, the tiniest hesitation.
Later, I realized I should have phrased the question differently, left
it more open-ended. "Yes," the woman said.

It is hard to remember back to those first few months. I know I
felt immense relief. I know that Sylvie fell fast in love with Ilse and
sometimes called out for her if she woke crying in the night. "Here's
Picasso," Ilse would say when I came home to find Sylvie at the
easel, and Ilse and Chloe on the floor making elaborate castles out
of cereal boxes, wrapping paper, and glue. Chloe liked Ilse, too,
though not as much, missing her Kiki, wanting her parents. I remember that Ilse began to teach them German words, brought
them a steady stream of cakes and tarts, though she'd said she didn't
know how to bake. She got Chloe to preschool on time. She gave
me full reports of their days. Sometimes, before I went off to teach
or write, she and I talked in the kitchen and she told me about her
childhood in Communist East Germany, how she'd run free through
the village, how her brother had taught her to swim by dropping
her in the lake. She told me about her mother, tenderly, and about
her father, who had a temper, and about her nieces, one of whom
she'd never met. You must miss your family, I said, and she said yes,
she did. Once, as I talked about giving birth to the girls, she said
that she thought the woman should be allowed to hold on to the
man's penis and squeeze with each contraction so that the father
would also have to feel the pain. In some deep, barely conscious
part of me, I registered this response as odd.

Each night, the minute six o'clock came, Ilse was out the door,
urgent, pulled. "I wonder if she's having an affair," I said to Jim.
"Something's making her rush out of here." She had told me she
lived alone and didn't have a boyfriend. When her thirtieth birthday fell on a weekend, I worried about her: Would she spend it

alone? My friends made me a cake, she said on Monday. Was it a nice day? Something passed across her face, then, a shadow, a glimmer. Yes, she said.

"I HAVE SOMETHING TO TELL YOU."

"What is it?"

"I have a daughter."

"You—" I stare; she drops her gaze. "You what?"

"I have a daughter."

"Really? That's—why didn't you, I mean—"

She is crying, and suddenly, inexplicably, I am crying too. "How old is she?" I ask.

"Four months."

"So she was . . . when you started here, you had a one-month-old baby?"

Ilse nods.

"I don't—I have no idea what to say, this is . . . what's—" I breathe out. "What's her name?"

"Alison."

"Who takes care of her when you're here?"

"My mother."

"Your mother's not in Germany? I thought you lived alone. You live with your mother?"

She swipes at her tears. "Are you going to fire me?"

"No," I say. "I mean, I don't think so, I just . . . Why? Are you going to quit?"

"Of course not. This job is a blessing for me. I am so lucky. Nothing has changed. I just . . . I had to tell you. Do you want to see her?"

For a moment, my confusion blooms again: Is the baby waiting in the mudroom, in the car? Then Ilse takes a picture from her pocket. The infant, wrapped in pink, is wide-eyed and curly-haired, like her mother.

"Oh," I say. "She's beautiful."

A daughter like I have two daughters. A mother like I am a mother. At that moment, I feel moved for Ilse, even as I am already aware that I no longer trust her the way I did before, and that I will have to reshape my notion of everything about her and, most centrally, her relationship to my children and to me. So, too, do pieces of the past few months begin, swiftly, to fall into place: the German cakes her mother baked; Ilse's hurry to leave; the comment about giving birth.

"Why didn't you tell us?" I ask.

"I needed a job. I was going to have to go back to Germany. You wouldn't have hired me."

It is illegal to ask applicants about their family situations in a job interview, and we did not ask. But if she had told? Would we have hired her? Probably not.

"So why did you tell me now?" I ask.

"It was Easter," she says. "I am not a person who lies or keeps secrets. You have to believe me. And you'd told me that story."

"What story?"

"The one about how they came for the Jews and I was not a Jew so I did not say anything, and then they came for the Communists and I did not say anything . . . and then, you know, they came for me and there was no one to speak out."

I had told her the anecdote in the context of a professional matter I'd felt I needed to speak out about, despite my fear of doing so.

"I'm not sure I understand," I tell her now.

"I felt I knew you then," she says.

OF COURSE, KNOWLEDGE of another person is always hard to come by, a slanted, partial, ever-shifting thing. Did Ilse know me? Partially. Did I know Ilse? Less well, it would turn out, than I'd thought I did. Less and less well, until my ideas of trust, my ideas of knowl-

edge, my faith in my own ability to read a situation and gauge its stability were all badly bruised and shaken. And alongside this, keeping us going, a host of other things: loyalty, empathy, gratefulness, a
desire not to rock the boat, to stay with the known; a sense of our
privileged life and her difficult one. Affection, and, increasingly,
passing in many different directions (between my girls and Ilse, between her baby and my girls, between Ilse and me), love.

And something else. How can I put this? She . . . somehow I
think she captured my imagination, or perhaps there's always been
someone like Ilse inside me, part of me, long before she walked into
our lives. Before I met her, I wrote two novels about single mothers;
in the first, the mother is forced to give up her daughters; in the second, she raises her daughter alone after the child's father commits
suicide. Had I not found a life partner, I would have had a baby by
myself. As for Jim, he is a Prisoners' Rights lawyer, with a deep instinct, put into daily practice, to help people in need.

How to summarize the year that followed? It could be a novel:
Ilse's Saga, Ilse calls it jokingly. It will be—is already becoming—the
true-life story of Alison, who is walking, talking now, in German
and English. In a nutshell: At first, nothing changes, except that on
Fridays, at our invitation, Ilse's mother, Eva, begins to visit with the
baby, the occasions full of warmth. Then, in August, Eva's visa runs
out, and Ilse takes her mother and Alison back to Germany and re-
turns to the States alone to finish her Masters. Her plan is to retrieve
Alison after she receives her degree.

While she is still in Germany, she writes a letter to the baby's father (the father? Oh yes, there is one: Sean, Irish-American. Ilse
lived with him for a year until just before the baby was born. We
know very little about him, just that Ilse is no longer with him, that
he is "a loser" who provides no support, though his parents have
been caring for Alison two days a week). In the letter, Ilse tells Sean

that she has returned to Germany with Alison and that they are staying there.

I am not a person who lies.

She comes back from Germany alone, bearing two teddy bears and a box of German chocolates. "How are you?" I remember asking anxiously.

"I'm all right."

"When you left her, it must have been so—"

"I have to do this," she says firmly. "For her future. And my mother is like a mother to her."

In the 1930s, my own grandmother, widowed by her first husband, left her two young sons in Spain with her mother and came to the United States to check out a potential husband her sister had found for her. After several months, she decided to marry my grandfather, a widowed Sephardic Jew like herself. Eventually, after nearly a year, her sons came over with a chaperone on a boat. I can see my grandmother in Ilse. They have a similar pride and canniness, an instinct to survive. Their lives have forced them to develop this instinct in ways my own has not.

No NUTSHELL BIG ENOUGH. I am in my study working when a knock comes on the front door. I open it. Before me, a stranger holds out an ID and an envelope. "Does Ilse Mueller work here?"

I feel a powerful urge to lie. Instead, I nod.

"I have a court summons for her."

I swallow. "I'll give it to her."

The woman shakes her head. "No. I need to deliver it myself."

I go upstairs. Chloe and Sylvie are splashing and giggling in the tub. "You need—you've got to go downstairs," I say softly to Ilse. "A woman is at the door with a court summons."

"What's a court summons?" Chloe is four by then, full of questions.

"A letter," I tell her.

When Ilse stands, I touch her arm for a second. Her face, drained of color, has gone completely still. Then she dries her hands on a bath towel and goes downstairs.

"What kind of letter?" Chloe asks.

"For Ilse."

"Who from?"

I sink down and start lathering her hair. "Tip your head back, sweetie. Time to rinse."

In THE MONTHS TO FOLLOW, this: In order to have leverage in court, where Sean is fighting for custody, Ilse retrieves the baby from Germany; Jim finds her a family lawyer; we agree to let her bring Alison to our house for two of the four weekdays she works for us; I find the baby a home daycare for the other two days. Chloe loves having Alison around. She lavishes her with attention, and somehow Chloe and Ilse's relationship, marked before by low-grade tension, improves. Sylvie, in contrast, is grief-stricken, heartbroken, losing attention from both Ilse and Chloe: "Want that baby to go *away*."

Meanwhile—whoops—Ilse has moved in with her downstairs neighbor, Mark, a man she was not, to our knowledge, dating until she returned from Germany with the baby.

"How well do you know him?" I ask when she delivers this news.

"I'm getting to know him. He's very nice, a good person."

"What makes you think you can trust him? I mean, you—" I shake my head. "You made a not-great choice before, with Sean."

"I have to trust people. I can't always think everyone is bad. And I need the financial stability."

"Can't you wait a little and just date him and see . . ."

Stay out of it, my own mother advises me. Don't get involved. As long as she's doing her job.

She *is* doing her job, except on the not infrequent occasions when she misses work to go to court over, first, custody rights, and then, when she is granted primary custody, over visitation rights. Chloe and Sylvie are happy, mostly. There is singing in the house when I come home. Alison comes two days a week, and often the mood is merry, three little monkeys, though sometimes it is chaotic, and the baby, as she grows, turns out to be a mover, a dismantler, and she swipes at the girls and, once in a while, draws blood. We call Alison *Hasi*—"little bunny" in German. Alison stands, walks, starts to speak. We pass on clothes to her. Chloe continues to adore her, and Sylvie begins to like her, though always in a complicated way. On Fridays and Saturdays, when Ilse has classes, Sean has temporary court-granted visitation rights, under his parents' supervision, and he provides (or perhaps his parents provide) $100 a week in child support.

Then one Saturday, Ilse goes to pick the baby up, and there is some sort of fight. A sister-in-law pushes her, calls her a bitch. The next Friday, Ilse does not bring the baby for the visitation. A few days later, the apartment where Ilse, Mark, and Alison live is broken into. Jewelry is taken, along with Ilse's papers and computer. She is sure it was Sean. The police take fingerprints; they come and go. A private detective friend of Jim's finds out that Sean has a criminal record. Seven criminal charges, burglary, breaking and entering. Oh, and he is, Ilse tells us, a drug addict.

Now I am falling, flailing. "What? What does he use?"

She shakes her head. "I don't know."

"How can you not know?"

"I've never done any drugs. Some sort of powder, I think."

"Was he using drugs when you lived with him?"

She nods.

I am not a person who keeps secrets.

"Might he come here?" I ask Ilse under my breath, for during many of these conversations, the girls are around, Chloe listening even when she seems to be at play. "And h-u-r-t somebody?"

"No. He won't come here. And he's not violent. Pathetic but not violent."

"But you told me he said he would k-i-l-l you if you got involved with another man."

"He would never hurt the—" She juts her chin toward the girls. "If I thought he would, I wouldn't—"

"Keep the doors locked," I say, and without my asking her to, she begins to park her car behind the house, out of sight. At night, before I fall asleep, I start to have lurid visions: of Sean kidnapping the girls, or arriving high at our house with a gun, or climbing through a window in the middle of the night. Am I overreacting? Underreacting? These are my kids. I am high-strung. Still, these are my kids. I have no idea. "Overreacting, I think," Jim says. "But it's not a good situation, that's for sure."

Then this: Sean makes a telephone call to Rita, the woman who cares for Alison two days a week in her home, a few miles from our own. He asks her questions about Alison without identifying himself; Rita tells him she does not wish to talk. Sean calls back, then shows up at her house with a video camera and starts filming from outside. When Ilse reports this to me on the phone, her voice is trembling, and when she arrives at our house the next day, she says she has gotten a restraining order against Sean. From campus that day, I call our town police to ask them to be on the lookout for Sean. When I call Ilse to tell her that I've done this, she blows up at me for the first time.

"You're neurotic!" she says. "You should have checked with me first—you need to think before you act! This could make him even angrier. We don't know what he'd do. And my visa, the police might decide to take it—"

Suddenly, I am yelling, too. "You're calling *me* neurotic? My friends have been telling me to fire you for months! I don't want an addict with a criminal record anywhere *near* my children. Do you understand that? Is that unreasonable? He came to Rita's. He knows our address. I—do—not—want—him—at—our—house!"

"I'm sorry," she says quickly. "I am so sorry."

Because she really is? To keep her job? A bit of both?

"Are the girls listening to all this?" I ask. "To you screaming at me?"

"They're okay," she whispers, and her voice breaks.

"Let me talk to them," I say.

THE NEXT DAY, Jim posts an ad on Craig's List: *Seeking live-out, experienced nanny, trustworthy.* . . . People start answering; some of them sounded promising, though the thought of so much as setting up an interview fills us both with dread. Ilse is, after all, a central person in our daughters' lives. When someone loves your child, mothers them, knows them—their moods and rashes, jokes and fears, their particular, idiosyncratic selves—a situation that may look intolerable from the outside can become, well, livable. In the end, we never get to interviews. Supervised visitations are reinstated; Sean calms down. Our lives return to what has by now, during this particular period, become normal for us. One day, I ask Ilse whether she thinks she will marry Mark, and she blushes and looks down.

"You already did, didn't you?" I say. "When did you do it?"

"A few months ago."

He seems to be a stable man, a good man, and she is on her way to a green card. She can apply for jobs without having to be sponsored. He seems to care for her, love her. I get up, give her a congratulatory hug.

"Why didn't you tell us?" I ask. When will I ever learn?

"You wouldn't have approved. Anyway, my life at home and at work are totally separate," she says, as Alison scatters crayons across my kitchen floor.

AT THE END OF THE SUMMER, after a year and a half with our family, Ilse will stop working for us. Her mother will come from Germany again to care for Alison while Ilse does an internship for her degree. Chloe will start kindergarten and an afterschool program, and Sylvie will attend a preschool/daycare program until three o'clock. I will take an unpaid semester's leave from teaching—to work on a new book, yes, but also because I want more time with the girls, and because I am exhausted, and because I cannot stand the idea, right now, of bringing a new babysitter into our house. For a good part of their days, Chloe and Sylvie will be at places where if a teacher is missing, a sub is called in, where the distance between home and school is two miles long. I imagine writing in my study with my daughters not in the adjoining kitchen, and the feeling is both freeing and wrenching—no voices to jar me from my inner world, but also, when I come in for a snack or visit, no hands on my face, no chatter of the day. I won't be able to keep track of them the way I can right now, and they will lose much of the floating, unstructured time that is, to my mind, at the heart of early childhood. I will miss coming in and finding Chloe talking to an invisible friend, Sylvie kneeling by the dollhouse, Alison looking up and saying to me, in a bell-clear voice, "*Hel-lo!*"

Together, Jim, Chloe, Sylvie, Ilse, Alison, and I have made a shape together—fragile, tangled, and frightening at times, but also a shape constructed of the things that matter most to me: minds meeting, bodies growing, the complex interplay of love. "Only connect," E. M. Forster wrote. I am glad we did not jump ship, although I know that I would feel differently if danger actually had entered our house. I am warier now than I was before. You have to trust people, Ilse told me. Yes, I might have answered, yes and no. And what of myself? Would I lie and withhold to protect my children and create a better life for them? If I needed to badly enough, yes: I think I would lie and withhold. I might have been her; she might have been me. At the center, for both of us, our girls. They are growing beautifully, all three.

TILL FAITH DO US PART

Jacquelyn Mitchard

llison was not our first nanny, but she was our last.

And that is not because our children have all grown up. In fact, we still have an infant.

We parted—you might say we were driven apart—not by incompetence, or a salary dispute, or an unfair increase in duties, or a move, or any of the other, more common reasons. We had a ball together and the children adored her.

We were driven apart by ideology, a schism that always existed between us, but which began to signify only during the last few months Allison worked for us, after the whole country seemed to line up along lines of religious affiliations.

I'm what you might call a literary Episcopalian. I weep when I read aloud the gospel according to St. Luke before dinner on Christmas Eve. I attend church for the peace, power, and glory whenever I can. My children are baptized Roman Catholics, because of their father's family traditions. The younger ones have gone to Sunday school; the bigger ones can sometimes be cajoled to mass on holidays, and of the seven, our baby hasn't yet revealed his religious preference. I'm not sure what I believe about the origins of Christianity or any religion. I think I would like to have met Christ in order to ask; and if others are correct, perhaps one day I will.

I'm definitely a liberal, and not an evangelistic Christian. But I tolerate and (usually) enjoy the stories and traditions of other faiths.

And I tolerate, if I don't always enjoy, others' insistence that there is one path and that all of us must walk in it. Privately, I believe what my mother always told me: many candles, only one light. That is how my children's childcare helper and I peacefully coexisted, although she is a deeply conservative Christian, and always found my casual relationship with God puzzling.

Despite that, Allison was very good at her job. In fact, she was almost too good at her job. She made cracks in our family's foundation, without ever entirely meaning to do so, because, as it turned out, what was a covenant to us was a job to her. We were foolish to have allowed the former, and foolish not to have recognized the latter. This is how it happened, and how religion played a role.

⁂

WE KNEW FROM THE MOMENT we saw her that she was the one for us.

A country girl, with skin that bloomed and dark hair that fell in natural corkscrews to her waist, she was forthright, genuine, funny, and dear. We needed a childcare provider because I work at home and my husband was in the process of a huge rebuilding of parts of our house, and taking care of the kids' needs was beyond the reach of our four hands then. She was fresh out of college and needed a job. She wanted to work with children, but not in a school. We were willing to pay; she was willing to take on five kids, then aged six months to fourteen years.

And so Allison came into our lives.

We knew that she was a born-again Christian raised in a very stern denomination. But she also was engaged to marry an Asian man of another faith, which, to us, bespoke flexibility. So, we believed that we could bypass the obstacles through politeness and the avoidance of certain topics—as a healthy artery bypasses another that is obstructed. For there were myriad beliefs we *did* share with Allison: a strong commitment to limits for children, compassionate but consistent discipline, an aversion to televisionitis, and liberal helpings of music, fun, and healthy exercise.

Allison moved into her job like a general taking control of an unruly battalion.

Beds that looked like birds' nests were made each morning before school. Big kids learned to separate their laundry. Little kids learned to make their own lunches and be responsible for their own backpacks. Coats did not touch the floor. Each of the five children (baby Will wasn't yet born) soon had binders, with their vital statistics typed on a laminated sheet in front (quick, tell me your kids' social security numbers!) and pocket folders into which their best schoolwork went each year. After we wrote a letter that was taped to the outside, these were stored in "Mem" boxes—along with their first soccer jerseys, first shoes, and baptismal clothes.

We believed that until the raw spring day she left us, by mutual consent, nearly six years after the day we first saw her, after she'd stood beside us through the births of two of our children, and through the nearly fatal illness of another, through great joy and excruciating pain, after she'd become virtually a member of our tribe. It was a schism we'd felt coming for several months, and the fault was not all hers, not by any means. But the culminating incident was, and it cut so deep that there was no turning back.

No turning back, despite the memories. When we nearly lost our baby daughter through a contested adoption and our baby son through a surrogacy that went awry, Allison was the square-bottomed boat that kept us all afloat. Together, we traveled to Massachusetts and to Europe, on work and family vacations; I had the pleasure of treating Allison, who grew up on a tiny Midwestern dairy farm, to her first Broadway musical, and her first bite of Chinese food. I remember summer nights, spaghetti on the boil, when all of us boogied in the kitchen in the little house we then owned on Cape Cod, to the eighties music Allison so loved, and which I still cannot hear without thinking of her. I remember her tenderness with my now nine-year-old daughter, Fiona, when our pet ferret had to be euthanized. I remember her gentleness in helping our now six-year-old daughter, Georgia, overcome her overwhelming fear of water, and their shared laughter when a humpback whale calf blew water all over both of them. I remember her rocking our toddler, David, after he burned his palms on the glass of a new fireplace. I remember the vigil she kept with us when one of our sons struggled to recover from a life-threatening ruptured appendix.

Sometimes, Allison went on the road with me if I was on a book tour or doing lectures so that I could bring one of the younger children, and we would turn to each other and say, "Who has more fun than we do?"

It felt like forever. My husband intended to revive his business as a master carpenter, which he'd suspended when we married and had a child nine months later to the day, or perhaps turn to real estate.

I'd promised Allison she'd have a job as long as we needed anyone to fill her job, and that by then, given the size of our family, she could take care of *me.*

Was she perfect? No. She had a way of making small tasks seem like painting the ceiling of the Sistine Chapel, probably to assure us that she was worth every cent we were paying her. She could have a sharp tongue when riled. And her grief over wisely but very sadly ending two engagements in two years—one to the Asian guy, one to a young man with whom she'd grown up—sometimes made her short-tempered. She liked to gossip, and when little things she'd said about my husband and me filtered back to us, we tried to ignore them. She made it clear, sometimes, that we were not raising our children as she would raise her own, that we let them "get away" with too much that her parents would not have tolerated.

Were we? Oh, goodness, no! During the last two years Allison worked with us, there was huge stress over my up-and-down fortunes as a writer, about money, about our elder son's continuously ragtag way of life, over a plan to relocate the family, a credit card theft by a relative—in other words, some days, my husband and I were like Chinese fighting fish in a glass bowl. It was hard on Allison, as were the various bumps and lumps of our older kids' adolescence she couldn't have been expected to understand. There were a few occasions when we bickered, when I accused her of taking a morally superior attitude and she accused me of being judgmental. But we always apologized and moved on. One thing is true: My husband and I should have been wiser than to confide individually in Allison, but both of us were often rubbed thin by the other's quirks, and Allison seemed to understand each of us with a practical and giving equanimity. However, Allison often insinuated herself in the middle, and then feigned an innocent objection to being "put" there. We'd fallen into the trap so common with a childcare helper. She was the third person in the marriage, an ear for the grumblings from both principals, ever ready with her own sidelong comments. And there was also this: We were too busy, and too often for our comfort, the younger children cried for Allison, when they ought to have cried for Mommy-on-the-road or Daddy-busy-with-the-house-sale. We noticed, but were not alarmed. At night and on weekends, the children nestled into the circle of their parents' unity and love. And that unity and love, though tested, healed solidly around hairline cracks.

Still, one trend troubled me, from the beginning.

The youngest of our three older children, Ross, was particularly close to Allison, who was, by the time she left, in her mid-twenties, in part because she alone, in our hopelessly unsporting household, shared his love of organized sports. We didn't know one team from

another, but Ross and Allison eagerly discussed each day's triumphs
or defeats for their favorites, which was wonderful. Allison, with
her teasing and her readiness for a game of cards, was like the big
sister Ross never had; we relished their comradely relationship. We
did, that is, until Ross began talking about the benefits of serving in
the military, though he'd always wanted to pursue a career in acting,
until he began to talk about bombing adversaries in the Middle East
back to the Stone Age, about the importance of nuclear weapons
systems, and, as the 2004 election approached, how President Bush
was a strong leader who had done a lot of good things, none of
which Ross could enumerate. After President Bush was re-elected,
and "Support Our Troops" ribbons festooned Allison's car, the atmosphere around the house subtly changed. Though we'd never
discussed politics, Allison clearly felt that her fierce opposition to
abortion and about the virtues of the "values-based" life had been
validated by the election. She was quietly elated by the outcome of
the vote, though she'd often described herself as "apolitical." According to Ross, after the election, Allison felt "more comfortable"
in the United States than she'd felt in a long time. We, on the other
hand, were seriously considering Australia. Ross seemed untrou-
bled by the election, as well. "Nobody trusted Kerry," said our son.
"They thought he was a wimp." But his parents hadn't. We treated
Ross to a no-spin lecture on Senator Kerry's military service history
versus President Bush's. He pursed his lips, clearly unsure whether
to believe his liberal parents or his conservative pal, Allison.

Even then, we considered this swerve to the right to be a quirk,
stoked by Ross's hormones and the rough-and-tumble personality
style he and Allison shared, not a life pattern that would change
Ross's basically tender nature forever. We paid it little mind, and
tried to focus on the good Allison brought to our home every morning, and there was plenty of it, and it was repaid. We were lavish
with gifts; she was lavish with time. We supported her dreams of a
home and family; she planned secret surprises with the children for

our anniversaries. Even when it became clear that we might leave our Midwestern home and move east, Allison let us know that she might consider coming along, though we thought it would be almost impossible for her to leave her close-knit tribe of brothers, sisters, uncles, and aunts, with whom she spent every weekend day and night.

And then, before that move was even under way it happened, a breakfast table remark that changed everything, forever.

Not long after the Easter bunny had come, my youngest daughter, Georgia, aged six at the time, bit into her jelly toast and told me, "Allison says you don't believe in God, Mommy."

Whatever I was doing at the moment dissolved into invisibility.

Quietly, so as not to alarm Georgia, I asked, "Why's that?"

Georgia had a gospel at the ready. She explained, "God wanted Jesus to come down to earth to die hanged on the cross so that we could go to heaven. And Allison says you don't believe that. She says you don't think God wanted Jesus to die for us, and that means you don't really believe in God. And so, you might not go to heaven, Mommy. And I'll miss you."

My heart was knocking at my ribs as I sat down at the kitchen table. I knew that Georgia's theology was shaky at best. But it was clear that she was troubled. I knew she comprehended Jesus as the baby in the old crèche we placed gently every year on the mantel, gradually moving the stone figures of the Wise Men closer as advent passed. I could imagine, in her little mind, the thought of a vengeful father so careless of his little boy that He would allow him to die for the sins of people He didn't know. I said, "Well, first of all, Georgia, Mommy does not believe that God wanted Jesus to die. Bad people wanted Jesus to die, and God was just as sad as He could be. And Jesus was a grown-up man when he died, almost as old as Daddy. Also, God loves every person the very same, no matter how they believe. And so, if God loves everyone, he loves Mommy . . ."

"That's not what Allison says."

"Well, that is what Mommy and Daddy believe."

"Would you let me die on the cross to save everyone else, Mommy?"

I paused.

"No, Georgia," I said, "I know that Allison believes what she believes with her whole heart. But it is not the same as what we think. Mommy and Daddy would die for you, but we would not let you die to save the whole world."

Georgia sighed. "I guess you don't believe in God, Mommy," she said.

I was stunned. The words, "But we *do*! Only not in the way Allison does!" almost sprang to my lips, but I clamped down on them. This hadn't been a subject for a child in the first place, and I wasn't about to further exacerbate a subject that should never have been raised, and by our nanny!

And so I didn't intend to bring up my imminent descent into hell on Monday morning, but the day conspired against me. A part-time but longtime employee, who helped us with housework, had long wished to stay home with her husband, just retired from his job. But she had reconsidered her decision, and was hurt that we'd found someone else to replace her. Allison was upset, and she told me in no uncertain terms that I'd been disloyal. I felt absolutely awful. I asked Allison what she thought about our plans to move—and her place in that. She muttered something. I asked her again. She told me that she'd planned to stay on until we left—if we left—but that the job had become nerve-wracking for her. I apologized for that.

Air heavy with anger fell between us like a wet sheet.

And finally, I asked, "Did you tell my daughter that I don't believe in God and that I'm going to hell?"

Allison drew back, as if I had struck her. "No," she said, "I told her what I believe is the truth about God."

"Did you think that a more appropriate response to her questions would have been to tell her to ask Mommy or Daddy?"

"No," she replied, "because you go around all the time saying you're not sure about this or that about God, and I am."

"But this is my house."

"And I have a right to my own opinions."

"You don't have a right to present them as fact to my children."

"To me, they are fact."

"So, you're saying you don't respect my views, or the fact that I disagree, on that subject."

"I'm saying I should have a right to have my views respected, too."

"I do respect them. I don't want them taught to my children."

"I can't say something I don't believe is true."

"Can you say nothing?"

She stood silent.

"Can you?"

My husband tried to intervene. But I was furious then, in tears, as was Allison. She no longer wanted to work for us, and though my husband hoped she would consider staying, I no longer wanted to employ her. In the end, she left in anger, her severance and vacation pay in hand, neither of us sure whether she had quit or been fired.

Brokenhearted, I fell asleep, prepared for a night of tears and anger from the children.

It didn't come.

Although, over the months, they have mentioned that they miss Allison very much, and we have said we miss her, too, and we do, they seemed to sense that the ideological differences between our family's ethical structure and Allison's had grown from a narrow stream to a great divide, especially in the political climate that prevailed after George Bush's triumphant return to office. And, fortunately, although I know that Ross still believes that my temper got the best of me, all the children understood that their parents, however flawed, need to be the overriding source of wisdom in any family.

We considered hiring another helper.

We decided against it. After talking long into the night about it, we chose to put our money away and our shoulders to the wheel, each of us taking more time with our children. My husband's business became taking care of his family.

Allison had done more than make a passing comment about our religious beliefs. She had dented the trust between my husband and me, making it easier for him to say that he "wasn't the only one" who thought my moods were sometimes irrational, and making it easier for me to say how annoying it was that he changed his mind so many times over every decision. Allison had become the "other wife" for both of us. That was wrong. But it was as easy to slip into a destructive pattern as it would have been to slip on a silken glove.

Yes, life is harder now. I miss Allison not only when I want to giggle and gossip but also when I do the seventh load of laundry some days.

The house is quieter without Allison's music and laughter.

And yet, it is also more peaceful.

The children need to do more chores, but ironically, as Allison often said, they probably needed to anyway. My husband and I sometimes miss the permission slips and the spelling words, but every day, we are a better unit. We learn more about managing our family's needs, and with no one else to turn to, we turn to each other. We aren't as efficient at running the ship. Both of us have lost sleep, and even weight. But we do what we do with abiding commitment. It isn't our job; it is our life. My longtime and beloved office assistant, Cara, often brings her own toddler daughter to work and helps quietly to pick up the slack. She's glad to do it, as she's more than an employee, she also is our children's guardian and a person gifted with the grace to see a situation clearly without interfering in it. She offers her opinion when we ask her, and information when we need it, but she has her own happy life and family and would no more question our choices for our children than we would question hers.

We thought Allison might send a card when our son graduated high school. I sent a letter apologizing for all the hard times and pointing out that I would never forget the good ones. I received no reply. I did not expect to, yet it made me sad. But the sadness passed.

Such a strong and long relationship should not have come to such a poignant and abrupt end, and that end should not have been influenced as much as it was by the world outside our home. A childcare provider whose own upbringing had been more flexible might not have had Allison's strong work ethic. She might also not have had her innate sense that one system of belief, and only one, was right. But the nature of relationships that stop short of family and far exceed the boundaries of job is always dicey, no matter how much both sides agree in theory, and is ever subject to change. I think it is the family who is most often shocked to learn how much resentment there always is toward "the boss," and how much more they have depended on the one they pay to care than she has on them.

We will never regret knowing Allison, nor the lessons of self-discipline, courage, honesty, and charm she left with our children. Nor will we mourn losing her, although when she left, she took a part of our past with her. For in losing her, we regained a part of ourselves—perhaps the best part—that we didn't realize we had misplaced.

THE BEST LAID PLANS

Elissa Schappell

*L*et's just say that my husband's and my plan for childcare was at best murky, and at worst completely misguided, moronic, and steeped in denial. I had this notion that after my daughter was born I'd be able to blithely go about my life, particularly my writing life, just as I always had. I imagined sitting at the kitchen table with my computer, deep in thought, Satie on the stereo, and my child happily playing in a playpen beside me. Wasn't this what Alice Munro had done, and Grace Paley?

I'd imagined Rob, who was starting up a new literary magazine and thus could make his own hours, would work for a while, then we'd meet for pressed sandwiches and iced tea, after which one of us would pack up the baby and head to the park, butterfly nets, harmonica, and soap bubbles in tow. Then, later that evening, after the baby was asleep—having drifted off to the poetry of Marianne Moore, *Gulliver's Travels*, or *The Little Prince* (in *French*)—I'd take a long bath, flip through the latest novel, or perhaps read over what I had written that day.

Ha. We had no idea that being inducted into parenthood was

not unlike entering a war zone. A sort of "Apocalypse Waaaaa!" *I love the smell of diaper cream in the morning. . . .*

After a few months' time it soon became apparent that no creature—save perhaps only the most grub-like of babies—is content to lie in a pen for the amount of time I require to actually write a decent sentence. No matter how chockablock that Pack 'N Play is with plushy animals, rattling toys, and music boxes; even if that baby can read the *Wall Street Journal* or build block towers that rival the Taj Mahal; no matter how much of a genius or nutball they are, no self-respecting baby is going to sit still with you typing at a desk—occasionally breaking into sobs and clutching your head—when clearly you could be dandling them on your knee.

The baby wanted to be held, the baby wanted to be nursed, the baby wanted, inexplicably, to pull my hair, rip off my glasses and throw them across the room. The baby wanted attention and the baby deserved it.

The idea of working when the baby slept was far flung, because that time was devoted to doing laundry, returning phone calls, perhaps bathing, and—imagine—sleeping.

No, we needed help. It occurred to me, to paraphrase Jane Austen's *Pride and Prejudice*: It is a truth universally acknowledged that a mother in possession of a good baby must be in want of a nanny.

A nanny, of course! Exhausted, blithering, unwashed, and seething with confusion—*how did this become my life?* I finally came around. A nanny it was.

It also became clear that while Rob and I split parenting fifty-fifty, and would choose our nanny together, the actual day-to-day dealing, parent-to-nanny, would fall to me. This was terrifying.

I had no clue as to where to begin. I didn't even like to call a plumber or an electrician for help when I needed it. When I went into labor I put off phoning the doctor because it was a Saturday night and I didn't ask for help in case she was, say, at the movies or out to dinner with friends. But clearly to not get help was madness. Still, I was at a complete loss as to who this nanny person would even be. The only nannies I knew of were from books and movies.

Yes, I very much liked the idea of having the sort of colorful nanny I'd read about in books—books were always my greatest source of comfort, and heaven knows I sought comfort. There was Eloise's "Nanny"—an unflappable, loving, stout British woman in a bustled skirt with whalebone pins in her hair. *Oh Nanny, oh Nanny!* Or, the much skinnier and brightly attired Julie Andrews as both wundernanny Mary Poppins, or Maria the ex-original-guitar-playing-nun turned nursemaid in *The Sound of Music.*

Yes, Mary Poppins, that was who I wanted. A nanny who could turn a simple trip to Gymboree into a wild choreographed rooftop dance with chimney sweeps, by whose magic a jaunt to the park would morph into a psychedelic romp on carousel horses. Or Maria. Maria could run up playsuits for my child out of old curtains. Dress her in buckled shoes and capes and little hats so she'd look like she was awaiting the arrival of a steamer ship from Europe in the early 1900s.

On the downside, however, would my English nanny cavort with cockney buskers who resemble Dick Van Dyke? Did I want my daughter imitating the estimable Miss Poppins by leaping off the roof holding on to nothing but a talking umbrella? And what sort of nanny gets off on teaching children to sing lieder and march around in a circle for ten bucks an hour?

As to questions of character, forget the fact that Maria seduced her employer away from his fiancée—shades of Robin Williams, Steven Seagal, and Michael Kennedy danced in my head. How *do* you solve a problem like Maria?

No, no, perhaps a British nanny wasn't for me. As soon as I learned that British nannies are rarely paid by the week (pish tosh!), but instead kept on a very handsome (read: enormous) monthly "retainer," well, it then became quite clear, crystal clear, that I would not at any time be hiring a British nanny. That was a fantasy to rival working at home with the baby ensconced happily in a holding pen.

No, I wouldn't get off easy by hiring someone who came from England where there is a titled aristocracy, a clear social hierarchy, and a history of domestic servitude. Here we have no clear caste system; supposedly anyone is able to obtain the American Dream if they are willing to work hard or if they win the lottery or a large nuisance suit (the newer American Dream)—and as for domestic servitude, we Americans have a deep and shameful past of slavery and other forms of cruelty to the poor or the non-whites among us.

My whole life I'd thought of myself as a liberal without a racist bone in my body. When my public school district was desegregated and families began pulling their kids out of the school in droves, my parents wouldn't. It was ridiculous. After all, they said, people should be judged by their character not the color of their skin. I wasn't stupid enough to think there weren't differences between the races, of course there were, but, naively I suppose, I just never thought much about color. Either you liked someone and you were friends, or you didn't; it didn't have anything to do with skin color. So why was I suddenly so thrown by having to confront what felt like to me racism? Because thinking about hiring a nanny in New York City, where a large majority of nannies are not white, meant thinking about race.

The idea of employing someone who in her home country worked as a nurse or a scientist or a school principal but here couldn't get a green card, was awful. Clearly, in America, childcare is most often the province of the disenfranchised. I knew that. Still, the thought that this person I hired might see me as the White American Devil Oppressor was horrifying. Yet, not hiring someone who might very well turn out to be the most perfect caretaker for my child, someone kind, smart, loving, just because they might perceive me to be the White American Devil Oppressor was also galling.

Thoughts like this kept me stuck in place, and indeed we put off hiring a nanny until we started to come apart. The deadlines and desire to work became overwhelming, and we bickered endlessly. If we didn't hire someone I'd never have time to write and get my work done which meant not getting paid, which meant doing without things like, oh, shelter and food. I could nurse this child for only so long. I felt that if we didn't hire someone, I'd never read a book again, or see a movie, or go to a museum. I felt in danger of being consumed by mommy-hood, losing myself—the self I knew—completely. I reasoned that if I had time to do these things—the things that defined me before I became a mother—I would indeed be a better parent. More present, more patient, happier, and, well, flat out nicer to everybody. We live in hope.

I polled friends and acquaintances as to what sort of nanny they thought would be best for me. It seemed that everyone, even my doorman, had an opinion about who I should hire, all of which were crashingly stereotypical.

People said, *Hire an Irish nanny. They work the hardest, have a sense of humor, and are good disciplinarians.*

People said, *Hire a Filipino nanny. They are gentle, patient, and often Buddhist, so they will work on holidays if you want them to.*

People said, *Hire a Caribbean nanny. They don't take guff, and belong to a vast network of caregivers, so your child will never want for play dates.*

People said, *Hire a Hispanic or non-English-speaking nanny. That way they can't gossip about your private life.*

People said, *Whatever you do, do not, do not, do not become your nanny's friend or therapist.*

People said, *Whatever you do, you must be professional.*

Who could have guessed this would be my biggest problem?

First off, I couldn't bring myself to say the word "nanny" any more than I could say the word "house cleaner" (sounds like it could be a robot), or "maid" or "cleaning woman." Still, I do employ someone to come and clean my house, and my feelings of guilt (couldn't I really do this myself if I weren't such a weakling?) cause me to refer to her as, "My friend who is saving my sanity and protecting me against encroaching armies of dirt and disease."

Plus, *nanny* sounded like I was putting on airs. On the other hand, *babysitter* didn't sound right either, conjuring as it does a pimply adolescent huffing PAM and watching pay-per-view movies, or doing algebra homework on the sofa and eating brownies.

How could I hire someone when I couldn't even bring myself to name the job I wanted her to do? Perhaps the light-hearted title of *baby wrangler* would work, or the more psychological, though slightly sinister, *child minder*? Although the professional sounding *assistant human child-rearing technician* had a certain appeal.

It was hopeless, so, as in all seemingly hopeless and ego-deflating situations, I turned to books. This time of the self-help variety; the authors of *What to Expect When You Are Expecting* would no doubt be able to guide me. However, it was imperative to remember that the last time I followed their advice—the diet they laid out for pregnant mothers—I gained nearly forty pounds. All advice was to be taken with a grain of low-sodium salt.

Clearly, the first step was getting some actual contestants. On the advice of a few friends I was clued into the secret source for nanny listings, the newspaper *Irish Echo*. Through it, I made some calls and set up some appointments. The next day the women began to appear at my door. Surprisingly, or not, not a one was Irish. Every single one was from the Caribbean.

I wasn't upset, exactly, but I'd be lying if I said I didn't feel confused, and didn't experience a little bit of a pang. While I knew I plainly couldn't afford a British nanny, and didn't necessarily think I could handle a Mary Poppins bounding around our tiny apartment, bossing us all around, I had started dreaming, since learning of the *Irish Echo*'s existence, that perhaps I might be able to swing a young Irish nanny, an apple-cheeked Colleen with a big laugh and a big heart who could take care of us all. I wouldn't have to worry about having another adult, someone who might already be a mother or grandmother in my house, watching me, possibly judging not only my housekeeping, but my pathetic mothering skills.

If I hired an Irish girl I could avoid the guilt and the uncomfortable feelings I was dreading.

Since I was striving to be professional I did things by the book; I asked the potential nannies the questions dictated by *What to Expect the First Year*. What was your last job and why did you leave it? When my baby starts getting more active and getting into mischief, how will you handle it? And I watched how they interacted or didn't with my daughter. But when I got to the question where I was to inquire, Are you in good health? and then "ask for evidence of a complete physical exam, and a recent negative TB test" . . . I faltered. This was not me. Why not just ask if they'd submit to a squat test?

Then Jesamine appeared. And I just felt it. No, she wasn't Irish or apple-cheeked or a girl but I felt the same little twinge of recognition I'd felt when I met my husband. It was like, Oh, there you are! She removed her shoes before entering the house and sat right down on the floor and started to play with the baby, who took to her immediately. She paid equal attention to her as to us. She told us she was from the islands, had a husband and a son who was slightly older than my daughter. She was smart, funny, and forthright and, I thought, kind. When I called up her reference, her past employer raved about her. She'd taught her daughter to read, she was fun and conscientious. She was perfect.

I WAITED FOR JESAMINE to show up the first day, my palms sweating, my mouth dry, as though I was waiting for a prom date. Maybe I had made a mistake. Maybe she wasn't the right one, maybe I was wrong to think I could have someone work for me. Then she arrived on time, smiling, seemingly full of energy, and ready to start the day. After she'd changed her shoes and stowed her purse I—again as per *What to Expect*—presented her with a contract and gave it to her to sign, hemming and hawing about the fact that I was a writer, and a nitwit, and if I didn't write things down I'd never remember to ask her to do them—which was in part true.

She very gamely looked over it. My friends had said I should ask her to clean the entire apartment, and do the laundry—she'll have time while the baby sleeps, they said—as well as excavate the Diaper Genie, do our grocery shopping, and once or twice a week, perhaps cook for us.

This seemed preposterous to me. I was slightly alarmed that I knew and liked people who actually asked their nannies to do these things. I couldn't ask Jesamine to do things I wouldn't do if I didn't have to, like launder our dirty clothes and decant the loathsome (if ingenious) Diaper Genie. Plus, I knew that although her child was two years older than my daughter, Jesamine must be pretty darn tired, too.

However, I did need the housecleaning help (the place was truly going to hell), and it was—routinely, it seemed—part of this job, so I sought out a sort of wobbly middle ground. I asked whether she wouldn't please vacuum the living room, especially the rug where the baby played, pick up her toys, and if she had time, do her laundry. And, if she did the baby's sheets would she please make up her crib?

"DOES THAT LOOK GOOD?" I squeaked. The contract also laid out vacation time, sick days, and personal days. I would pay her for any time we took off, all our vacations as well as her own. I would pay her, and pay her, and pay her.

Jesamine looked it over and taking a pen out of her purse, signed the two copies—one for her, and one for me. She handed them back to me.

"This one's for you," I said. I wanted her to feel protected by this contract as much as I did.

She took it, smiling, I thought, a bit ruefully, folded it up and stuck it into her purse.

It never occurred to me at the time that nannies have no union, no one to fight for their rights when they are abused, fired without warning, or cheated. Despite being the de facto parent, they have zero recourse when they are wronged, and no rights when it comes to seeing children they have, in effect, raised. I can only imagine the nightmare if all the nannies went on strike. Cities and towns paralyzed, a gridlock of strollers, children attempting to leap from speeding cars to reach women who look like their beloved caretakers. Bewildered parents howling in the streets, "Where is Music for Aardvarks? For the love of God, what the hell is a *Go-gurt?*"

"Okay," she said. "I think we'll go out for a walk now."

"Great," I said. "I'll come with you."

If she was shocked by my response, she was good not to show it. Though she did, unmistakably, look at me a little quizzically. After all, wasn't I hiring her so I could work?

It was hard enough to convince most people that sitting in a chair in front of a computer all day writing was work. (Perhaps it is the pajamas.) By inviting myself along on their first outing I was undercutting whatever excuse I had for getting a babysitter.

"You know," I explained, "in case she gets fussy, I don't want you to have to deal with it." My daughter rarely fussed, and when she did she was easily soothed. Still, I didn't want her to make a bad first impression. I wanted Jesamine to think she'd landed a plum job. I didn't want her to feel like she'd made a mistake.

I wanted to say, "It's not that I don't trust you," because I did trust her. In truth, I bet she was a better mother than I was. What was more to the point was that I didn't know how to separate my feelings about what she was doing for me—taking care of my child—from projecting my own feeling that what she was doing, the job she had, was a bum deal. After all, I loved this child madly and I didn't want to do it.

"Okay," she said smiling, but looking a little concerned. After about five minutes outside, in the stroller, my daughter conked out. Pretending not to notice I continued to walk along with them, prattling on and on for a good fifteen minutes, until Jesamine said gently, "I think we'll be fine."

She was a little insulted maybe?

"Really?" I said.

"Yes, really."

So I went home. As I poured myself a cup of coffee, I realized with horror that I had offered Jesamine nothing to eat or drink! What kind of a hostess, I mean, *employer* was I? No one enters this house without being offered some sort of libation. How rude of me.

The next morning, when Jesamine arrived I was ready. I offered her coffee—she didn't drink coffee, thank you. I offered her juice—she was okay with water. I offered her cereal—she looked at me like I was nuts. "I had breakfast at home," she said. "Waffle?" I whispered foolishly. I put out bowls of fruit—she brought her own food. I tried to engage her in conversation about her family, her husband, her homeland, and she was always polite, but she was keeping her distance. I wanted to know her, and she wanted me to act like a boss. After all, this was a job not an ice-cream social.

Under Jesamine's care my daughter was happy and thriving. Not only my daughter, though, I was thriving as well. As Jesamine already had a child, and had worked with children for years she knew so much more than I did. I learned how to deal with a stuffy nose or a cold by rubbing eucalyptus onto a bit of linen and pinning it to her romper, I learned that a frozen bagel relieves the pain of teething, and that it was okay to leave the baby in the foyer asleep in her stroller, that children can sleep anywhere. I learned never to put away a child's dinner dish that still had food on it, but to keep it handy so when they complained about being hungry, I had food ready and waiting.

She kept the living room rug and its environs spotless and tidy, and my daughter always had clean clothes, which was more than I could say for my husband and me.

This didn't mean everything was perfect. No. Jesamine lived in Brooklyn so it took her at least an hour, usually more, to get to our house on the Upper West Side. This was after she dropped off her own child (who suffered from asthma) at daycare. Most mornings she was late, sometimes a half hour or more. Because I worked at home, and didn't have to leave for an office job or the floor of the New York Stock Exchange, I felt I couldn't really complain. Still, I felt like this meant she couldn't take me or my work seriously, and this was a problem for me, as those days even I had trouble taking my work seriously. Because I am religiously opposed to confrontation with anyone save the people I am related to by blood or marriage, I would never say anything directly to her about it except, "I understand it's hard for you, but it's hard for me, too." Even then I felt like a jerk. My child didn't have asthma. I wasn't commuting. I wasn't working a job with no benefits and little pay.

It was a problem, but considering the experiences others around me were having—a nanny who was arrested for shoplifting, a babysitter who in frustration occasionally hit kids, and a nanny who had been discovered, via nanny-cam, to be locking the baby in her room for the majority of the day—I knew I was beyond lucky. The fact that Jesamine was late four days out of five, the fact that I felt guilty about the time I spent not working when she was there, the time I spent out having lunch with people, or shopping (I would sneak in and hide the bags in the closet, so she wouldn't think I was frivolous) seemed small in comparison to my need for her stability. Also, we seemed well suited because what I wanted was a part-time nanny—nearly impossible to find—and she wanted part-time work so she could be with her own child and husband. The only down-side of this, I think, was that the arrangement conferred on her the status of not *really* being a nanny. This meant that a lot of the other nannies (especially the turbo commando-nannies who worked from six A.M. to bedtime) seemed to treat her like she wasn't a *real* nanny. Yes, she seemed well liked, had play dates with other nannies, but she wasn't now, nor would she ever be, a capo in the nanny mafia.

Which I think suited her. She didn't want to be a full-time nanny. And it suited me. I didn't want to feel, or have to admit, that I had a real nanny.

Then, it just so happened that we both got pregnant when my daughter was three, prompting my husband and me to move out of our two-bedroom apartment on the Upper West Side and head out to Brooklyn. In the fall, our daughter would start preschool and Jesamine would have her second child. Our relationship would be ending. It was sad, but we promised to stay in touch.

THIS TIME AROUND, my husband and I had a plan for childcare. We would divide the days that we picked up our daughter from pre-school, and after our son was born we would hire some help. Until then we were the nannies. For the first few weeks of the school year there were a few mothers at my daughter's school who did indeed think that *I* was the nanny, and not the mother at all. The nannies, however, *never* made this mistake.

Perhaps it was because the nannies and I really talked to each other, as we stood in the hall waiting for the kids to be dismissed. Unlike the new parents, the babysitters were often chattier and a bit more friendly, perhaps because they were unencumbered by myriad anxieties, perhaps because they'd gotten a full night's sleep. In some ways (and maybe I was deluded), I felt closer to the nannies than to the other parents, especially the wealthier, more politically conser-vative stay-at-home moms.

When my son was born that winter my husband and I decided that we couldn't and wouldn't make the mistake of waiting five months to hire someone to help us. Knowing Jesamine was expecting her own baby soon, we would have to find someone new.

Since moving to Park Slope we'd spent a lot of time at a local bookstore, and it was here that we met Lucy, who was working behind the counter. We soon learned that in addition to being well-read, and making excellent lattes, Lucy was a poet. She lived in a group house a few blocks away from us. When she said she'd be willing to babysit if we ever needed it, my husband and I offered her a full-time job on the spot.

It seemed like a quintessentially Park Slope situation, finding a lesbian poet babysitter at the local groovy bookstore. And again, despite hiring Lucy to perform the duties of a childcare professional, I could fool myself into thinking she wasn't *really* a nanny. Certainly not a nanny like Jesamine or the other nannies I knew before. She had no experience raising children, had no children here or abroad, and wasn't working to help support a family. Not to mention that she was white and came from the same area of the country as me. She could have been related to us. If you squinted, I could pass for her older sister.

If I found it hard to ask Jesamine to do things because she wasn't just like me, if I failed to understand that my treating the job of taking care of my child seriously was imperative to the success of the relationship, I now found it hard to ask Lucy to do things simply because she *was* like me. Had I not gotten lucky and fallen into a job in publishing shortly after moving to New York, had I not met my husband and moved in with him, I could have been Lucy.

With Lucy there would be no contract. It wasn't only that I'd decided that the whole business was—given my personality—ridiculous and awkward (I'd never stuck to the sick days or personal days thing—I'd given Jesamine however much time off she wanted or needed with pay and without question) but also because my son had colic, and I felt I couldn't ask her to take on anything more than dealing with him. Trying to calm a colicky baby didn't simply demand a varied and intricate set of holds and moves, it also required vast resources of incredible cheer and an iron constitution. When Lucy was finally able to get him to sleep, his sensitivity dictated that she freeze in whatever position had seduced him into sleep. So, she didn't pick up, she didn't clean, often when it was time for her to leave, the house looked far worse than when she had first arrived, but this was okay. I couldn't get annoyed if I had never asked her to do any differently. It didn't seem fair, when my son started to become easier, to sleep more, and scream less, to suddenly introduce a list of new responsibilities. In fact, when he slept I often insisted that Lucy, too, should try and nap.

Where Jesamine demurred when it came to my offers of breakfast and coffee, and seemed eager to start her day of work by taking my daughter out of the apartment and off to a play date or any number of classes, Lucy was happy to sit down and have coffee with me. Some mornings I put on a second pot of coffee on just for her. If I were having my breakfast when she arrived, I would insist she eat too, and would sometimes make her toast, or a bagel, or a bowl of cereal. It became part of our routine. I asked about her life and she told me. I worried about her health and her finances. I wanted her to have a girlfriend worthy of her. I wanted her to be happy.

Where I learned about mothering from Jesamine, I suppose I was now trying to mother Lucy. Not only because if she was content she'd be a better caregiver to my children, but also because I was so fond of her. Because I aimed for her contentedness, and because I didn't want to be an uptight bitchy boss (the kind the nannies at my daughter's school complained about all the time). When she wanted time off, even at the spur of the moment, I gave it. When she seemed depressed, I sent her home with a bottle of wine. When I came back to the house with a special sweet, cupcakes, or pie, I insisted she take some home with her.

She was in my house when I got an upsetting phone call, or a check didn't arrive. On a few occasions when we went away—to the beach, a writer's conference—she came along, spending part of the time babysitting, the other part going to the beach, or at the workshop sitting in on lectures and readings. When she didn't travel with us, she stayed in our house taking care of our cats and plants. She knew intimately what my life was like. When I was blue she hugged me like a friend, and I felt adored. On my birthday she gave me gifts, and a card decorated with fairies.

Then, after eight months or so it became clear she was unhappy. I am sure she tried to hide it, but she grumbled about taking my son to swim class and gymnastics. She seemed happier to hang out at the house and drink coffee and talk to me. Which I could understand. Still, I felt resentful: What was I paying her for if not to take care of my son? She did arrange some play dates with other babysitters, but generally she was resistant. It was awkward, she explained, because apart from being babysitters, she and these other women really had nothing in common. They were mostly older women from the islands, or au pairs from Poland or Brazil. There was little for them to talk about. She was losing patience with the kids, didn't even seem to like them on some days, although I knew in my heart she did. Still, when she complained about them, I listened. I didn't fire her. I thought, "Well, they can drive me crazy, too." But I'd be lying if I didn't say it did bum me out. Nevertheless, I liked her very, very much, and my kids loved her. So, I thought, it will pass.

When, a few months later, she blurted out, "I can't stand it. I'm burned out. I can't do this anymore," I wasn't shocked. She explained that she was tired of the kids, tired of the monotony, the lack of intellectual stimulation. I understood. But when she said, "You couldn't have thought I would keep this job for more than a year?"

I thought, stupidly, *I guess I did.* Though obviously I shouldn't have.

When she said she wasn't actually quitting (she didn't have another full-time job), but just wanted to cut her days back to three or four, I thought that this didn't seem very smart, telling your boss you are tired of the kids, hate the job, can't believe that your boss ever thought you'd keep the job, but that you *aren't* quitting. . . .

I thought, *She ought to have lied to me.*

That was when I realized I hadn't treated it enough like a job myself. Yes, I wanted her to arrive at a certain time, but I was flexible. I shouldn't have been casually picking at cinnamon toast and reading the *New York Times* when she arrived. I shouldn't have asked about her personal life, shouldn't have made her such a part of our life. But how could I not? That idea, "Don't become your nanny's friend or her therapist," had perhaps been true.

What would happen to her if she went out into the world to get an ordinary job? In terms of being an employer I didn't do her any favors by letting her call in the morning and announce she couldn't come to work, or saying, Sure you can bring your girlfriend to work today, or Sure you can drink beer in the middle of the day and socialize with your friend when you are supposed to be babysitting.

I couldn't go back.

Through some sort of divine intervention of the babysitting gods, over the weekend, out of the blue, Jesamine called to tell me she was going to start looking for a job and would I be a reference? I rehired her on the spot. I called Lucy and told her she could have her wish of working part-time. Because Jesamine was a mother, and needed the money (she'd have liked to work five days a week) I told Lucy I could employ her only two days a week. This would give her time to find a job that suited her better, and more time to herself. I knew this wasn't what Lucy wanted, but it was what I wanted. And after all, wasn't this about what I needed, what was best for my family, my kids?

It would be a good balance. I was grateful to have Jesamine back. Her stability, warmth, and professionalism were gifts. There would be no contract. Now that we lived in Brooklyn her commute was much shorter, and thus she arrived at work on time, happier, and considerably less harried. I felt terribly lucky.

Now, however, I was aware of how precarious the situation was. My son was charming and beautiful and funny, but inexhaustible, too, and boundlessly curious. I knew that Jesamine had two boys, so she would have no trouble dealing with my son's occasionally wild behavior (okay, normally wild behavior). But still. So I asked her to do nothing more than be with him, and pick up my daughter from school some days. There'd be no cleaning up, no vacuuming, and no laundry. (Though it must be said, never did she leave the house untidy.)

A short time later, Lucy applied to graduate school and got into a poetry program at a great university. The day she left Brooklyn we all got teary. We knew we would miss her.

It was good to have Jesamine back full-time. I felt comfortable with her in a way I hadn't before. Maybe it was my being more comfortable as a mother. Maybe it was the knowledge that came from raising children but I now knew hard it was to take care of a child, how being a nanny required more focus, ingenuity, energy, and patience than most jobs I could think of. I realized it was okay—no, it was necessary—to make clear what I needed and expected, because clearly everything worked more smoothly when we weren't attempting to connect through ESP. Maybe I realized that despite the color of her skin and her upbringing, Jesamine and I were more alike than Lucy and I were.

Whereas before it seemed that we were two people at different places in our lives, two people who liked each other but couldn't really relate to each other's experience, now we had much on which to bond. Our older kids were both in school and negotiating new relationships, our husbands both worked too hard, we both had sons who were handfuls, bright and inquisitive. We both had lost fathers. Both of us were hoping that our thirties would hold great things for us. I didn't ask Jesamine to tell me what to do with my children, or expect her to mother me, and thus our relationship—mother to mother—felt much more equitable. I didn't offer to cook for her, but when there was food in the refrigerator and she wanted to eat, she knew it was hers for the taking. And when on occasion she'd now sit down at the table with me and share a cup of tea, it felt good. I knew how lucky we were.

I certainly hadn't planned on any of this. Perhaps it was best not to listen to anybody else, friends or the writers of self-help books, but to trust that in the same way a parent knows her child best, as a parent in need of a nanny you will know the best nanny for you.

Part Three

A Spoonful of Sugar: Taking the Bad with the Good

DUMPED

Pamela Kruger

The intercom in my apartment rang. I expected to hear my doorman announce a delivery. Instead, a woman spoke nervously. "I just wanted to let you know that your nanny is working for another family. I thought you should know."

"What?" I was trying to process what she said. It didn't make any sense. My nanny, Mary, was in Jamaica visiting her sick father. I was sure this stranger must be mistaken. "Do you mean *Mary*? Mary is in Jamaica," I said.

"Yes, your nanny Mary is working for another family," she said.

"Who? Who is she working for? Who are you?" I sputtered.

"I don't want to get involved," the woman said. "I just thought it was so wrong." Then she hung up.

Stunned, I literally just stood there for a few minutes before it occurred to me to buzz the doorman back. By the time I did, it was too late. The woman had vanished, and the doorman couldn't describe her other than to say she was a Manhattan mom, pushing a baby in a stroller.

Immediately, I replayed my last conversation with Mary. On a recent Friday, she had told me, quite somberly, that her father had a heart condition, and she had to leave the next day to see him. It was ten days since she'd left, and I hadn't heard from her. I'd assumed she would be back in a few days. Was her dad being operated on, or was he recuperating? Mary had been unclear but had seemed so melancholy that I didn't press for details.

I hadn't once considered the possibility that she might be lying. Until now. Mary was my first nanny. Recommended to me by the baby nurse I had hired after giving birth, Mary instantly impressed me during the interview. I was your classic nervous, first-time mom, second-guessing every move I made around my daughter, Emily. I was so afraid of making mistakes that I didn't dare change Emily's diaper by myself until she was about two weeks old, when the baby nurse had long since left and my husband returned to work. Divorced and in her late thirties, with a big smile and gentle laugh, Mary radiated calm and was warm and comfortable around Emily. When I saw her cradle my then four-month-old in her arms, talking softly to her without a hint of self-consciousness, I decided to hire her without interviewing anyone else.

But I never felt comfortable around Mary, and this caller stirred up all of my doubts. In the eight months that Mary worked in my home, I don't think we ever had an extended conversation. I knew little about her life; she knew virtually everything about mine. The imbalance made me uneasy, but anytime I asked Mary an even mildly personal question, such as what she was doing that weekend, she would give a monosyllabic answer, leaving me to feel like I was prying.

Some days, I thought she was just shy. Other times, I wondered what she was hiding. She'd leave with Emily for hours, and when I'd ask where she went, I would get answers like "To the park" or "Walking around." For *five* hours? What could they possibly be doing for five hours? Was my daughter one of those babies in the park, ignored, strapped in her stroller, staring into space, while her nanny gabbed away with friends? There was the time my husband came home from work and found Mary chatting on the phone, while Emily was in the next room, wailing in her crib. How long had my daughter been crying? Had long had Mary been gabbing on the phone?

"Trust your instincts," the experts say. But what was I supposed to do when one day my instinct said, "Fire her," and the next it told me, "Relax, you're just another neurotic, guilt-ridden working mom"? Also, this was 1997, a time when nanny-cams were first gaining popularity. It seemed that every week another TV news-magazine show featured a nanny captured on hidden camera beating a baby or abandoning it in a crib all day. At the end of the segment, the parents always appeared, tearfully recounting how their babysitter had such wonderful references and seemed so lovely around their kids. To me, the message was clear: Don't trust your nanny.

Periodically, I would make half-hearted attempts to spy on Mary. Once I hid a tape recorder on my daughter's bookshelf. I felt embarrassed and guilty when I listened to a forty-five-minute tape of Mary singing and jabbering away with my baby. I tried to cultivate friendships with moms whose nannies were friends with Mary. While she was playing with Emily in the living room, I'd be holed up in my bedroom on the phone with another anxious mom. In hushed tones, we'd share our worries and whatever tidbits we'd picked up about each other's nanny. I'd always end the call saying, "Please, if you ever see anything amiss, tell me. I want to know."

That was how I learned that Mary took Emily on a play date on a day that she had a 102-degree fever. The mom had come home to find my then eleven-month-old sitting in a corner, looking lethargic and flushed. I was livid and angrily confronted Mary. She apologized, saying she didn't realize I'd be so upset and that she was just taking Emily out for a little fresh air. Could this be the "red flag" that the TV news shows warned parents about, I wondered?

"If you're so worried, let's find another nanny," my husband would say. He didn't agonize over it. His self-worth as a parent wasn't tied up in this relationship, as mine was. Of course, he wasn't in charge of hiring and managing our nanny. Although my husband and I have always had a fairly egalitarian marriage (I'm one of those women who is constantly told, "You don't know how lucky you are!"), I'd insisted on making all of the decisions when it came to childcare, and my husband was happy to comply. It made sense: Working from home, I spent all my time with Mary. By contrast, David left for work so early and returned so late that many days he didn't see Mary at all.

But the truth is, I also had emotional baggage, which made me want to seize the control—and also fear it. When I was a young child, my family had a live-in housekeeper who babysat often for my two siblings and me. I never warmed to this woman, but when I was eight, she developed serious psychological problems that were deeply disturbing to me. She repeatedly warned me to stay away from my much adored big brother, then thirteen, saying he had a "tail." I'll never forget the night she came into my bedroom, waving a tabloid article about a ten-year-old girl who had been impregnated. "Do you want that to happen to you?" I quietly listened to her rant, too innocent to grasp the horror of what she was suggesting but clued in enough to be frightened by my caretaker's simmering rage.

I told no one about these incidents. Although she never laid a hand on me, for me she was a real-life boogieman, a creepy and sinister presence lurking about my home, ready to unleash her awful fury if I crossed her. I did my best to avoid her and stayed close to my big brother, who had absolutely no fear of her. Unlike me, he recognized that she was just an employee who could be dismissed and he grew to disdain her. So when my brother complained to our mother that our housekeeper had violated some house rule or blatantly favored our younger sister, then four, she would turn her wrath on me, refusing to make me lunch when my mother wasn't home. "You better tell your brother to stop telling lies about me!" she threatened.

As it happened, within a few months, she was fired when she had one of her outbursts while my father was at home. With her gone, I felt safe. My stories about her poured out, and my parents let me know in no uncertain terms that her behavior was appalling and that they would have fired her sooner had they known. Still, for many years, I would open my brother's bar mitzvah album to study the photograph of her; with her strange, bug eyes and dark secret, she looked so obviously off balance to me. How could my mother have not seen the warning signs?

As an adult, I realized that it was a more trusting, naive era, when six-year-olds were allowed to ride their bikes to the park alone, and no one dreamed that a neighbor, relative, or babysitter could be abusive. But I couldn't shake the feeling that my mother, as the parent at home primarily responsible for managing the household, had failed me by leaving me in this woman's care. So, when I became a mother, I felt an extra urgency to monitor the nanny closely; I had learned that bad things could happen, and I was determined not to miss any of the "signs."

But whenever I seriously thought about firing Mary, I'd talk myself out of it by considering the facts: She was so reliable and, up until that point, never missed a day of work. More important, Mary seemed to genuinely enjoy Emily. She'd point out all of Emily's little quirks—the way Emily lifted her pinkie when she drank from a bottle, or how she rubbed the corner of her blankie against her cheek when she was going to sleep—habits that only someone smitten with a child could possibly find interesting. Most crucial, though, was that Emily was so obviously happy around Mary. She gave her big hugs and nestled her head on Mary's shoulder. Wasn't that what really mattered? Hadn't we all made mistakes on the job? And who was to say that I would be able to find a better nanny than Mary, who was willing to work a part-time schedule to boot?

Getting that phone call from my Deep Throat, though, pushed all of my fears about her to the surface. Suddenly, I felt like the insecure wife who had been waiting for indisputable proof that her husband was cheating on her. I was kicking myself for being so dumb, but also still holding out hope that my worst fears wouldn't be confirmed. Maybe there was some kind of misunderstanding; maybe this stranger was wrong. Without any clue as to what I might say, I impetuously picked up the phone and dialed her home number in the Bronx. Despite my suspicions, I was nonetheless shocked when she answered the phone.

"So, you're back," I said.

"I just came back yesterday. I was going to call you," she said, speaking very quickly and so softly that I had to close the window in my bedroom to hear her. Mary proceeded to tell me that she didn't feel well and needed the rest of the week off.

"I know what's going on," I said coolly. "I know you got another job." It was an old reporter's trick. Pretend to know what you only surmise. At first, Mary stuck to her story, but when I told her that a mother in the neighborhood had told me about her new job, Mary said defiantly, "Well, you only hired me part-time. This is full-time."

Her matter-of-fact attitude made me furious. Mary gave me no advance notice of her "trip" to Jamaica and sent me her "cousin" to fill in—an elderly woman who, on her first day on the job, fell asleep on my couch. I found my one-year-old toddling around in the kitchen by herself when I came home from an errand. For the last ten days, while Mary was working for another family—had she gone to Jamaica at all?—I had been forced to cobble together childcare and work nights so I could meet my magazine deadlines that made no allowance for nanny crises. If Mary wanted a full-time job, that was understandable. But she'd lied and left me to scramble! When was she going to get around to telling me she had found a new job? Was she planning on disappearing from my daughter's life without a good-bye to Emily, let alone me?

I don't remember exactly what was said. I do know that I yelled and accused her of being deceitful and told her never to use me as a reference. Mary, for her part, became indignant, insisting she had been a good nanny. "Did I ever hit your daughter or hurt her?" she pressed, as if this were some acceptable yardstick. "Never!"

In the weeks that followed, I couldn't stop thinking about Mary. As I had with past intimate relationships that had gone bad, I became obsessed with reviewing the details, looking for clues. How could I have entrusted my daughter to a woman who had always aroused my suspicions? How could I have left my baby with someone who cared so little about her that she was willing to walk away without saying a word? If this was an eerie repeat of the questions I had asked of my own mother years earlier, I didn't recognize it at the time. All I knew was that I felt ashamed and was convinced that I had failed miserably as a parent. There were lessons to learn, and I was desperate to learn them before I hired my next nanny.

But in talking to other mothers, I quickly found out that many of us had been dumped unexpectedly by our nannies. One friend's full-time nanny of three years—whom she considered "part of the family"—suddenly stopped showing up for work. No note, no call, no explanation. Her kids were so devastated that my friend would never hire another nanny again, patching together after-school and other programs instead to keep her child supervised. I also discovered that "going back to the home country" was an infamous exit line among nannies, the equivalent of "Let's just be friends," or "I'm not ready for a commitment." It meant, the relationship is over. "There just isn't professionalism in this field, so people don't think they have to give notice," one friend said. "It reflects cultural differences," said another friend, who has a sitter from the West Indies. "People from the Caribbean will do anything to avoid confrontation." Regardless of the reason, I was relieved to learn that I wasn't alone. If so many other women had similar nanny problems, it meant that there was something wrong with Mary, not me. In my mind, even the woman who had "stolen" Mary from me was another potential victim; I felt sorry for her.

Newly reassured that I wasn't a bad mother, I became convinced that my mistake with Mary was that I hadn't listened to my gut from the start. Now, no matter how much a prospective caregiver grinned and cooed at my daughter during an interview, I wouldn't hire her unless *I* felt a rapport with her. If I clicked with a nanny, I figured my daughter would eventually feel comfortable with her, too. Over the next few years, I had some wonderful babysitters and stopped consulting experts, books, and other parents for confirmation of my mothering skills. Still, it wasn't until a few years later, when I hired Ellen to be a fill-in babysitter, that I finally grasped how Mary might have seen our relationship.

In her mid-twenties, Ellen was one of those sought-after, college-educated nannies that went into the field simply because they love children. Normally, she worked for wealthy CEO types, but she was between jobs, confused and trying to figure out what to do with her life. She didn't want to commit to a full-time job. I didn't want a full-time nanny. My husband and I had just adopted our six-month-old daughter, Annie, and I was taking time off from work. We agreed that Ellen would work for us part-time until she decided on her next move, or I lined up permanent childcare, whichever came first.

But during that period, which expanded to several months, Ellen and I spent so much time in conversation that I gained new insight into the nannies' perspective. Ellen told me about employers who expected her to be at their beck and call; they'd come home hours late from work without warning or apology, or suddenly announce they were going on vacation and expect her to come along. There were the mothers who micromanaged her or resented it when the children became attached to her. And Ellen worried constantly about the children getting bumps and bruises, fearing that an employer would assume the worst.

I thought about Mary, wondering how it must have felt to work for someone who was wary of her from day one. I never voiced my anxieties to her but, surely, my behavior exuded it. Until Ellen, it hadn't occurred to me that as her employer, my every move was being scrutinized, and that Mary might sense what was behind my whispered conversations with other moms. Could it be that she was evasive about her time spent with Emily because she feared I'd misinterpret or become one of those hovering mothers, questioning her every decision? I had placed more trust in the other working mothers whom I knew only in passing than I had in my sitter of eight months. Should I have been surprised if she felt more kinship with other nannies?

I'm not sure whether it was because Ellen had one foot out of the nannying world (she was fairly certain she'd return to school or move into a new career), or that she was working for me only temporarily, or that the two of us were spending so much time together, but as she and I grew closer, she confided in me about what other nannies were saying and doing. I learned, for instance, that one nanny regularly referred to her boss as "The Bitch" and complained that she was a control freak. Ellen also told me that another nanny had come over to my house for a play date, then deposited her two babies with Ellen while she disappeared upstairs to "use the bathroom." After ten minutes, Ellen became uneasy and called for her. "I think she was snooping," Ellen said.

I felt in a bind. Was I obligated to tell the mothers what their nannies were saying or doing? Before I knew Ellen, I probably would have felt that as a mother, it was my moral and ethical duty to speak up, just as that tipster on the intercom had done years earlier. But now my loyalty was no longer automatically and completely with other moms. I felt sympathy for the employees but guessed that I probably knew only half the story. Perhaps that acquaintance was a bitch. Maybe that other nanny did poke around my medicine cabinet, but did that mean she wasn't a loving and responsible caregiver?

No longer certain, I chose not to intervene—or interfere, as the nanny would no doubt see it. Short of concerns that a child might be in danger, I now regard such matters as the exclusive domain of the parent and the sitter. Theirs, after all, is a personal relationship entitled to the same respect and privacy as any other bond. They need to talk to each other, not to some distant third party. Perhaps if I'd realized that way back when, that stranger never would have had cause to ring my buzzer.

WILDFIRES

Ann Hood

ildfires surrounded the Black Butte Ranch during the weekend of Hillary's wedding. Evacuation routes hung from trees, bright orange, pointing the way to safety. An AM radio station gave updates as the fires moved in on us, growing closer and closer.

Afraid to unpack, we left our luggage by the door of the condo we'd rented on the property. Without the haze of smoke and the bitter taste it brought with it, we would have had a beautiful view of the Cascade Mountains, towering Ponderosa pines, the silvery leaves of aspens. But when we stood on the deck, we saw only smoke growing denser as the fires moved toward us.

As a distraction, my husband and I took our nine-year-old son, Sam, to the swimming pool. The nervous wedding party and other guests lounged poolside under the thick gray skies. I jumped into the water beside Sam. When my head popped out, I saw ash floating on the surface. Ash showered down on us. There was ash in people's hair and dusting their tanned shoulders. I thought of Pompeii, of worlds coming to an end.

Hillary, the bride, our former nanny, appeared, a giggling and golden blonde, dreamy-eyed and hopeful, even as fire threatened. She was not thinking that plans could go awry, that catastrophe loomed around every corner. She was optimistic, her new life about to unfold amid this ash and these mountains. Why shouldn't she be optimistic? Why shouldn't she believe the fires would change direction and spare her and her fiancé?

I bent my head so that no one would see me cry. I was at a wedding, I reminded myself. I was surrounded by happiness, by happy people, even if that part of me, the happy part, had disappeared.

A year earlier, my five-year-old daughter Grace had died suddenly from a virulent form of strep. Hillary had been her first and longest nanny. She had been there the day I went into labor with Grace, and the day that I brought her home from the hospital. She had carried Grace all around Providence, Rhode Island, in a backpack, the two of them chattering to each other as they went out for adventures. And Hillary had flown to my side when she learned that Grace had died. Without hesitation, she had traveled from her home in Portland, Oregon, and stayed with us, her pockets full of pictures she had of Grace.

My crying grew stronger. For me, Grace and Hillary were linked in a special way. But now here was Hillary about to be married, and we had lost Grace. I caught sight of Hillary, her head tossed back in laughter, and the ache of my loss overcame me. I dunked myself back under the water. Eyes open, the blue shimmered around me. Above, the bits of ash floated like confetti.

HILLARY CAME INTO MY LIFE on a bright summer afternoon in 1996. She was tall and skinny with a tattoo on her ankle. She had hair dyed bright red and cut real short. If Princess Diana was an art student, she would have been Hillary: They shared the same nose, the same posture, the same awkward smile. Hillary came that day to talk to us about the position of live-in nanny that we had posted on the jobs board at the Rhode Island School of Design.

We had already had a disastrous live-in, a man who taught in a sports program at a local community center. Mark slept all day and his idea of babysitting was writing letters or watching television while Sam, then three, entertained himself. One morning, as I headed by car from our home in Providence to teach a graduate writing class at NYU, I realized I had forgotten my wallet. Back at home, the wallet in hand, I heard Sam upstairs crying. Following the sounds of his sobs, I found him still in his crib, wet from tears and urine, while the nanny snored, oblivious, down the hall.

Even after I woke him up and handed Sam to him, I worried that this was what had been happening every Tuesday when I left for New York with him in charge. Our arrangement was a good one: We provided room and board in exchange for twenty hours of babysitting a week. Surely, I decided, someone else would want the same deal.

Two days later, we asked him to leave and Lorne, my husband, posted our ad. Before he even left the employment office, he had met a twenty-eight-year-old returning student, an Apparel Design major from Portland, Oregon. She was here only for the summer, she explained. Then she was leaving for an internship in Paris. Since we had asked the sleeping nanny to leave by June 1, Lorne reasoned, that still might work out. They arranged a time for her to come over to our house to talk.

As Lorne walked out the door, another woman ran toward him. She was also twenty-eight, also a returning student, also an Apparel Design major, and also from Portland, Oregon. But she was going home for the summer, and was interested in beginning in September. Her name, she told him, was Hillary.

WHEN I WAS A LITTLE GIRL, I had a fantasy. It was not to be a ballerina or a movie star, or even a writer. My fantasy was to live in a big house like the one on the TV show, *Please Don't Eat the Daisies*, and to have a lot of children and a big dog and a messy office where I would try to write novels. I liked the happy noise in that fantasy. I liked the chaotic household, the wry, witty mother, the mischievous children.

When Hillary came into my life, I thought I was on my way to realizing that fantasy. After many happy years living in New York City, I had been lured to Providence by Lorne. Handsome as a television sitcom star, he also had an amused attitude and an appreciation of me, the slightly distracted, head-in-the-clouds writer. To complete the picture, when Sam was three and I was pregnant with Grace, we rented a huge, slightly run-down Victorian house.

The house had thirteen rooms, three floors, and several staircases. Its poor insulation caused the curtains to blow about on windy days, even with the windows shut. The walls were painted pink or blue or purple with colorful scrolling trim. It had fireplaces that didn't work, soaring ceilings, and a bookcase that slid forward to reveal a secret door in Sam's room. In short, it was the house of my dreams.

The day that Hillary knocked on the heavy bright-green front door of my dream house, I was thirty-nine years old and seven months pregnant. I loved my husband. I had found happiness in motherhood and adored my son. We had learned that this new baby I was carrying was a girl, whom we would call Grace. Like Hillary on her wedding day seven years later, I saw only possibility ahead of me. I was hopeful and optimistic. I opened the door of my house, and Hillary walked in.

On her second day with us, Sam told Hillary: "I'm going to suck your toe."

Then he bent and did just that. He sucked her big toe.

Later, Hillary would tell us everything going through her mind in that instant: I don't even know these people and I don't know what to do right now. Sam confessed to us that she had been wearing her clogs all day, and her feet were sweaty.

"Hillary," Sam said, "you need to wash your feet."

But he said, "Even so, I'd suck your toes again."

The night before her wedding, the fires still raging, the barbecue they'd planned was moved to an area considered safer than the original site. People were asked to come forward and give toasts. Sam was one of the first to do it. He told the story about sucking Hillary's toe. Everyone laughed at the audacity of his three-year-old self and the confidence in him still.

Sam turned to Hillary and said, "You get married tomorrow. I still have time before then." Then he said to her fiancé, "Watch out!"

I wanted to speak, to put into words what Hillary meant to me. Many things ran through my mind, but I couldn't speak. It wasn't just the smoke that caused the back of my throat to ache; it was the tears that I kept forcing back. At one point that evening, I literally lost my voice. From somewhere in the crowd, I heard a woman calling. "Grace! Gracie?" And then the delighted giggles of a little girl. Foolishly I ran toward that voice, that laughter. Everyone was wearing name tags, and I stumbled into a woman holding the hand of a little girl whose name tag said GRACE in big loopy letters.

The woman looked up at me, but I turned and walked away before she could say anything. In a tumble of memory, I remembered how Hillary's aunt had had a baby shortly after we'd had Grace, and that she had named that baby Grace. Here they were, mother and daughter. Grace. Gracie.

Quietly, I slipped away from the party, and back to our condo, the orange evacuation signs leading the way.

A WEEK AFTER HILLARY MOVED IN WITH US, I went into labor. She found me in our foyer, doubled over in mid-contraction, waiting for Lorne to get the car. We hardly knew each other.

"Wow," she said, wide-eyed.

Two days later, I was home with Grace. Hillary's presence became immediately important. She had a soothing calm about her, a way of knowing what I needed before I even knew it.

That night, I awoke in horrible pain. Funny, I remember thinking, I'm having an appendicitis attack right after having a baby. But I soon realized that this was something else. At dawn I was in the Emergency Room where the doctor discovered a piece of placenta still left behind. He removed it and I was sent home, but by that afternoon my fever began to soar. Only Hillary was home with me, and she found me on the bathroom floor, wild with fever, scrawling my will on the back of a grocery receipt.

She called the doctor and got me antibiotics, then put me to bed, where I fell into a deep sleep. When I woke up, Hillary was sitting there with a toasted bagel topped with melted cheese. She brought Grace to me so I could breast-feed her. "I'm right here," she said. The last words I heard before falling back to sleep.

MIRACULOUSLY, UNEXPECTEDLY THE FIRES changed course. Hillary's wedding day had blue skies, sunshine, that drop-dead stunning view. Lorne and Sam and I sat together, crying, as Hillary got married. We didn't have to tell each other what we were thinking. We all knew: Grace should be here. A line of little girls in colorful dresses led the wedding party, and I had to turn away from them to gaze out at the mountains beyond.

Later, from afar, I watched this other Gracie playing tag, eating strawberries, sitting on her mother's lap. I fought the urge to run from there, back to our condo with its new-wood smell and dangerously high deck. The stars hung heavily above us, and I looked up at them as if there really might be a heaven and Grace was gazing down at Hillary's wedding. But I didn't really believe that, and my disappointment mingled with my grief.

I overheard some women saying that Hillary wanted to start a family right away. Immediately, they said. I remembered Hillary cradling my baby daughter, holding her on her lap, the hats she made for her and the way she would smash garbanzo beans for her lunch to be sure Grace had protein. Soon, I thought, Hillary would have a baby of her own.

HILLARY MADE BIG SALADS for us at dinner.

She painted the dingy walls on the third floor warm colors with names like buttermilk and mink.

She gave us presents for our half-birthdays.

On Saturday mornings she made waffles with warm maple syrup.

When my father was dying in the hospital, Hillary made pots of black bean soup and left me notes to find when I came home.

She put quotes from *Eloise* beside the telephone.

She planted pansies in our backyard.

She spent hours with Sam and Grace, teaching them to draw. Even Grace, a little over a year old, would hold a crayon and fill a blank paper with spirals. After Hillary graduated and moved away, Grace kept drawing. Grace wanted to go to RISD when she grew up. She took special art classes, and brought home projects that looked like someone much older than she had painted or drawn them. Grace moved slowly. She took her time. In the morning, as I tried to get Sam and Grace to school on time, Grace would still be looking for her shoes.

"Come on, Grace," I'd yell.

"You can't rush an artist, Mama," she'd tell me.

Hillary did that. She made Grace an artist.

AFTER THE FLUSH OF THANK-YOU NOTES and wedding pictures, Hillary grew silent, adjusting to her new life. Back at home, we struggled to do the same. As time passed, our ache for Grace grew larger, more painful. I spent days sitting alone, simply missing her.

One night at dinnertime, our telephone rang.

"I'm pregnant!" Hillary told us. She was due in June. The baby was a boy. They had already picked out the name Henry.

We gushed together over the phone. Sam and Lorne shouted their congratulations. After we hung up, we all sat back down at the table, silent. I thought of that red-haired girl at my door. Now she was an elegant and sophisticated woman, about to have a baby. Life was moving on, without Grace. As much as we had been forced to stand still, we couldn't really.

WHEN HILLARY CALLED TO TELL US that she was taking Henry to New York City to see Christo's "Gates" in Central Park, we decided to meet her there.

It had been three years since Grace had died. Slowly, we had gone back to work, went out with friends again. Our loss still filled our home, every corner of it. It still filled us. Time doesn't heal, I had learned, it just keeps moving. And it takes us with it.

That blustery day in New York, when Hillary stepped forward with her baby, she looked as if she had been a mother forever. To me, she had. From the easy way she placed him in the snuggly to making sure he ate the right foods at lunch, I saw her younger self taking care of my baby.

"I didn't really get it," Hillary told us later that night. "I didn't really understand what losing Grace meant. Until I had Henry."

I nodded, remembering those wildfires at her wedding. I never actually saw them. I just knew they were out there. Once, I would have believed that of course they would stay away. I would have believed that danger could be averted. That days that are supposed to be happy are happy.

One of the pictures Hillary brought us when Grace died is Grace at age two. The picture is fuzzy, but you can tell that she is smiling as she lifts her fingers to her lips and blows us all a kiss.

IN HIS MEMORY

Andrea Nakayama

By the time we met Matthew we had interviewed several nanny applicants. None were acceptable. There was the woman who seemed hip and energetic and only became suspicious to us when she revealed that her life was devoted to Jesus. There was the twenty-one-year-old girl who looked twelve and sat limply on the couch, barely taking notice of our babbling one-year-old son, Gilbert. And then there was the woman we called Gladys after she left. She was a stout and jolly grandma, sweet but skittish. She was visibly shaken when my husband, Isamu, relayed that he had a brain tumor. "Thank God it's not the baby," she said, earnest and teary.

In April of the previous year, the tumor had materialized in Isamu's right frontal lobe. It was diagnosed on April 15, tax day. I was seven weeks pregnant with Gilbert at the time. Pathology after surgery revealed it to be the most malignant form of primary brain tumor. With tremendous effort and an aggressive grouping of treatments, both allopathic and integrative, the tumor appeared to retreat. Keeping it at bay was as time consuming as caring for a small child. Gilbert was born in the midst of this, and we welcomed him with both joy and ease. Haunted by death, the small inconveniences of life—the lack of sleep, the unaccountable cries of a newborn, rashes, new teeth—were not so daunting, even to the new parents that we were.

Before Gilbert's first birthday we brazenly left our reliable community of friends in San Francisco to move to Portland, Oregon. We knew no one, but could afford a quality of life unavailable to us in the Bay Area. Then the cancer that had seemed miraculously and deceptively under control for over a year made a vicious comeback. Just three months after moving, it sprouted new roots. The new cerebral growth, so close to the brain stem, was inoperable. Gilbert's first birthday party that December was canceled as we focused on fabricating a plan to tackle the recurrence.

Through it all, I worked at my job in book publishing from my home office in the third-floor attic. Isamu juggled his time between computer-science work, research on cutting-edge cancer treatments, and his many meetings with health care practitioners. And for more than several hours a day, a nanny cared for Gilbert. We learned to coexist in the house like blood running through a body, each aware of its necessary course, flowing together at different points during the day. Mothering our son, working, and care for Isamu and concern about the renewed urgency of his health took more energy than I had. My days were scheduled down to the minute. My attention was splintered. Clearly we needed help. *I* needed help. Then the nanny announced she was moving to Australia and we tacked "hire new nanny" onto the lengthy to-do list. Finding the right person was daunting. Not an easy challenge under the best of circumstances.

Matthew arrived at our home in Portland on a wet and brittle evening in the middle of December, his brown hair soaked, his round glasses spotted with rain. It was a half hour or so later, while we sat in the living room talking, that he told me he'd applied for a poetry fellowship in Texas for the fall. His large frame was folded on the wood floor. His hands looked gentle, almost feminine, as he used them to delicately stack blocks with Gilbert. If we hired him as a nanny for our son, and if he was also accepted to the writing program, he would be leaving Oregon and his position in our home in August. Though I liked Matthew immediately, I pondered whether he was the right person to join the delicate situation in our family. It wasn't that Matthew might leave us in August. For us, August was a lifetime away. The future was only tentative. Hope was all we had.

MATTHEW POSSESSED MANY of the qualities that were important to us. His sister was the nanny for a family we knew. He came with glowing references. He had childcare experience working in a KinderCare facility. He was warmhearted and witty and interesting and mature. He engaged Gilbert immediately, looking him in the eyes and speaking to him directly. His own baby face was bright and open. At twenty-six he was a dedicated writer of poetry and was looking for work that would pay the bills without distracting his ambitions. It's a unique and wonderful thing about raising a child in a city like Portland: The cost of living here allows for the educated twentysomething population to slow down and consider what they might want to do with the rest of their lives. While they explore and pursue, many are happy to embrace jobs in childcare. But most of these people are women.

So, although I was desperate for help, I also found that I was somewhat dubious about hiring a male nanny. Especially a twenty-six-year-old straight male nanny.

Would he have what it took to nurture our baby? Change the diapers? Lay him down for a nap? Feed him lunch? Make his snacks? Patiently play and hold and support? Entertain? Endlessly entertain.

My feminist awareness nudged me not to discriminate. My social experience whispered caution. Since my own attention felt fragmented, I worried that Gilbert was not getting all the mothering he needed. My hope was to find a nanny who would supplement *my* job as mother.

Could a man do that?

Could *anyone* integrate into our family during such a difficult time?

Isamu was upstairs resting during most of Matthew's interview. Within the warmth of the house, he had retreated to the lair of our bed after dinner. He was just learning to submit to the exhaustion that could consume him. The treatment he had most recently completed, a focused delivery of radiation admitted through thin rays in a procedure called gamma-knife surgery, had zapped him of all energy. Maybe it was the treatment, maybe it was the tumor itself. The recurrence was in the cerebellum, the part of the brain responsible for coordination, muscular movement, posture, and equilibrium. He had stopped riding his bike months earlier, given up driving shortly after, but he didn't expect to need help walking. Who could expect such a thing at the age of thirty-three?

As I spoke with Matthew I was disturbed that Isamu might not weigh in on this nanny applicant. Though I had become disconcertedly accepting of his decreasing motor capabilities and had taken on many of his previous physical responsibilities, such as driving, hauling out the trash, carrying Gilbert in the backpack, I still relied on his partnership and was not prepared to forgo his opinions when making decisions regarding our son. Neither was he. Toward the end of Matthew's interview, Isamu did make his way gingerly down the stairs. Never defeated. Always looking out for Gilbert and me. Gallantly avoiding bracing his hand against the wall for balance.

Isamu questioned Matthew. Why did he work with children? What experience did he have with toddlers? How might Matthew treat his son if he didn't want to nap, if he threw a wooden spoon across the room? Isamu was a protective father.

Eventually they talked about Seamus Heaney. Isamu was reading the Irish poet's translation of *Beowulf*, a copy of which sat on the coffee table between them. Heaney was one of Matthew's favorite writers. That night, Isamu knew Matthew was the right nanny for Gilbert. He knew because through his conversation he was able to discern that this was a person he could trust. And on that night, a friendship was born.

After further deliberation on my part, I retired my preconceptions and concerns about employing a male nanny. Matthew, the poet, pastry chef, and sometime actor was hired. I'd learn that he was all that we needed and more.

MATTHEW ARRIVED FOR WORK a few days later. Quickly he developed his own routine and rhythm in our household. In the mornings he walked Gilbert around town, carrying him in the backpack, rain or shine. They rode the bus, infinitely exciting to a toddler. He took him to the park, to visit the ducks, to the library, or to pre-school playgroups. There they'd convene with the other children and mothers it would take me a couple of more years to meet. People noticed them: the tall male nanny, or "manny" as Isamu and I took to calling him, and the chattering red-headed boy bounding with energy.

Many assumed Matthew was Gilbert's father. Matthew was quick to correct them. He was concerned that Gilbert's notion of his role in our household might be confused. All of our roles were in a state of flux. Isamu had been too reserved and self-sufficient to allow for me to care for him in the way I now had to. And Matthew could now do the things that were increasingly challenging for Isamu. He could chase Gilbert around in circles, pick him up when he fell, wrestle with him and carry him lovingly in his arms. Difficult things for a father to give up, but Isamu grew to fear that if he lifted Gilbert, he might topple over while holding him. He sacrificed his own delight for our safety and well-being.

Matthew switched Gilbert from two haphazard naps a day to a single longer one scheduled after lunch. It was time for that transition, but I had been too preoccupied to make it happen. While Gilbert napped, in Isamu's and my bed or on a small futon along my side of the bed, Matthew sat in a chair in our room and read his books of poetry. If the naps were long, he would venture downstairs to clumsily fold some of Gilbert's small clothes and return them to their drawers. Or he'd start cooking dinner, dicing and sautéing and learning the art of cooking good vegan food to meet our dietary restrictions and culinary expectations. He did all this with agility, lightness, and humor, a dishtowel thrown jauntily over his left shoulder, music from Isamu's extensive collection on the stereo. He was a natural with Gilbert and not a novice in the kitchen. In his first weeks in our home he tried his hand at some vegan refined-sugar-free desserts. They were difficult to resist, until Isamu told him that he needed to limit his intake of sweets. We were operating on the principle that sugars feed tumor growth. "Great," Matthew joked, his voice tinged with sarcasm, "here I was trying to give your sweet tooth a treat and I find out I'm actually killing my employer!"

It was during these culinary exercises, while Gilbert slept, that the friendship between Matthew and Isamu blossomed. In the rectangular cut-out window between the kitchen and the dining room, where Isamu sat with books or a notepad in front of him, the two men had conversations about literature, music, spirituality, and bacon. Matthew asked the questions that nobody else did: Are you scared? What do you see as the connection between Stereolab, Chet Baker, and Bob Dylan? How does it feel when you know you're in love? Don't you miss drinking whiskey?

*   *   *

FEBRUARY 14 WAS ONE of those beautiful days in Portland, when hints of spring force their way through the winter torrents. The sun shines high and bright and the heads of early bulbs push through the deeply drenched earth. It was the first of these days, our first Valentine's Day in Portland. And it was the day I realized how anemic our household would be without Matthew.

Isamu was on a new regimen of drugs—new to him, yet a staid course of treatments for his type of cancer. He had already exhausted the most advanced medical technology and pharmaceutical experimentations and developments. His tumor had built up its resistance. It was growing, wreaking havoc on his body. There was nothing to do, advised Isamu's physicians, except the deficient standard treatment of chemotherapy.

The chemo was administered intravenously. Its side effects were fatigue, a temporary drop in bone marrow, loss of appetite, and as is usual, nausea. On that Valentine's Day, Isamu had an appointment with his acupuncturist, Dr. Kou. There's not much acupuncture can do to help fight a brain tumor. But Dr. Kou was doing an amazing job of maintaining Isamu's red and white blood counts, usually depleted by chemo yet a necessity for continuing treatment each month. Their twice-a-week appointments were critical. Matthew prepared Gilbert for our rapid departure and at three-thirty I ran down the stairs from work, scooped Gilbert from Matthew's arms, and carefully loaded Isamu and Gilbert into our new Subaru station wagon.

We left. Matthew stayed. For another hour or so he helped with household chores and the preparation of dinner. It was this additional assistance that riddled me with guilt. Having a full-time nanny felt excessive. Paying someone to help during the hours that I was not working felt extravagant. But we were aiming to eat a consistently healthy and clean diet and Isamu needed to have his meals by five-thirty each night to ensure that he could take his many supplements and get to sleep at an early hour.

Preparing my family's meals was something I loved to do. I had always enjoyed cooking, especially for Isamu. He was a sensual man and he relished good food. But there was no longer any time for me to cook. I didn't just feel inadequate as a mother, I felt deficient in every family function I prided myself in. But if I didn't have Matthew's help I wouldn't have been able to be with Isamu during many of his medical excursions out of the house. Nor would I have had quality time with Gilbert each afternoon. It was a time of learning to accept limitations. I embraced Isamu's as they arose. I badgered myself about my own. Not only did I lack the time to prepare meals, but I couldn't stop the brain tumor from growing, I couldn't protect Gilbert from witnessing his father's decline.

Not five minutes from home, Gilbert cooing in his car seat in the back, Isamu alerted me that he was feeling sick. Pull to the curb, he directed. Quickly. I hit the automatic door lock at the moment Isamu did. The locks clicked in a ridiculous battle. It lasted just a few seconds. He vomited all over the inside of the door and the floor and himself before we could open the lock.

After the purge, we proceeded to Dr. Kou's office, humbled, resigned, and mildly amused by the absurdity of the circumstances. Once parked, I carried Gilbert on one hip and assisted Isamu with my free arm. They both leaned their weight into me and held a conversation of sweet gibberish with each other across my body. Always enjoying each other. Once in the office, we helped Isamu to strip from his clothes, loaded them into a plastic bag, and off Gilbert and I went toward home while Isamu got needled in his boxers.

Matthew was surprised to see us so soon. Gilbert and I usually played in the park, went for walks in the stroller, or did some grocery shopping during Isamu's afternoon appointments. The music was blasting and Matthew was writing in the oversized journal he kept, giving Isamu and me a window into the day with Gilbert. I apprised Matthew of the vomit situation. He lowered the music and gently lifted Gilbert from my arms. He graciously offered to stay until I got Isamu home. He was tender with me. Aware of the burdens I was shouldering without patronizing me. Ready to assist but not coddling me.

I loaded the clothes into the washer and scrubbed the car with rags and an old sponge. Before leaving to drive back to Dr. Kou's office with a fresh pair of jeans and a T-shirt for Isamu, I peered out the oversized window in the kitchen, looking out onto the backyard. There sat Matthew and Gilbert, on a south-facing wooden bench on the deck. They both stared off into the distance, eating homemade popsicles, sitting side by side in their comfort. I was riveted. Stilled for a moment, watching theirs. There was a quiet understanding between them. Nothing needed but the company of the other and the sensation of cool juice popsicles on a hot early spring day.

That Valentine's Day I felt more love than I expected on a day like that: love for my husband and all that we had been through so intimately together, tackling each new development in our lives with a collaborative equanimity and deep passion for his precarious life; love for our son and all that he had to behold and endure; and love for Matthew, our dear nanny, the man who entered our household so seamlessly and took on his position in our family while Isamu was dying, not as an employee might, but as a brother would, with patience, sobriety, and allegiance. He had been with us for only two months yet he grasped the delicacy of his role. He was Gilbert's nanny, sustaining normalcy where it was absent. He was my right arm, doing much of what I couldn't do, in the house and with my son. He was Isamu's last friend.

Matthew and the smell of dinner greeted us at the door when Isamu and I returned home from acupuncture. Isamu was freshly clad, with two needles sticking out of the top of his head, purposefully left by Dr. Kou. I was exhausted yet stoically I assisted Isamu up the stairs. Matthew took Isamu's free arm and encouraged him to release his weight onto his body, relieving mine. "Hey," he assured Isamu, "I dealt with plenty of vomit and people who couldn't walk up stairs in college." They laughed and joked about youthful drunken ventures all the way up to the bedroom.

By APRIL, ISAMU'S HEALTH went from bad to worse. He was falling more, struggling against severe fatigue, and vomiting nearly every day. I scaled my work hours back but still didn't have enough time for all that required my attention. At night I went to sleep in between Isamu and Gilbert's slumbering bodies, feeling the heaviness of the needs of the two people I loved most. They were primal needs. Gilbert woke in the middle of the night to nurse. Isamu woke in the middle of the night to pee. He'd sit at the edge of the bed for a moment, waiting for his equilibrium to return. My fear of him falling down the stairs on his way to the bathroom was enough to keep my sleep light. As soon as he righted himself I was out of bed, at his side, ready to walk with him to the toilet, hold his body upright from behind. Gilbert woke me again at five-thirty to nurse. At six-thirty I was out of bed. I needed to shower and dress before Gilbert awoke, cook our breakfast of fresh grains, feed Gilbert and myself, dress him, and help Isamu in any way he needed. By eight-thirty, when Matthew arrived each weekday, I was ready for the additional support.

Since Isamu couldn't make it up the narrow staircase to the third-floor office anymore, he was now more often with Matthew and Gilbert when they were home. The three would sit on the living room floor and play together. Sometimes the focus was completely on Gilbert. At other times Matthew and Isamu would pick up on their ongoing conversations about music, books, spirituality, and relationships. Matthew restrained himself from catching Isamu when he stumbled around the house, having learned to appreciate his pride. And sometimes, when it was Gilbert's naptime and Isamu could not extract himself from bed, the three of them would hole up in our bedroom together. One large male nanny stretched along the length of the bed, his glasses perched on his face, one red-headed toddler cuddling between the two men in his daily life, and one small, part-Japanese man, his body slowly withering around his strident spirit, his black-rimmed glasses atop a pile of books alongside the bed.

That April was the second anniversary of the brain tumor. April was also when Matthew told us he'd been accepted for the poetry fellowship in Texas. But it wasn't until late June that I contemplated hiring a replacement for Matthew.

How could Matthew be replaced? It was overwhelming to even think about.

THROUGH SOME ACQUAINTANCES I contacted Jess. The only day we could arrange to meet was July 4. There were more of us in the house than usual that day. Isamu's brother and I helped him down to the dining room for lunch. He sat in his usual chair across from me. Suddenly his neck muscles lost their strength. His head fell off to the left side. He continued to eat, spoon to mouth, food dripping from the utensil as he tried to navigate its new destination. His mother, brother, and I sat glumly at the table, slowly eating our own lunches, more out of habit and respect for Isamu's efforts than hunger.

There may be nothing more difficult than watching someone you love deteriorate. Except perhaps being trapped in your own deterioration. The only counterpoint to our sorrow was the sound of Matthew and Gilbert laughing in the kiddie pool in the backyard.

Jess arrived promptly at two. We'd need some privacy for the interview. She and I left the full house, Isamu resting on the couch, in search of a café open on the Fourth of July. While we were gone, there was much activity back at home.

Isamu indicated to his brother Mako that he needed to go to the bathroom. His increasingly thin legs could no longer carry him across a room without the risk of collapsing under him like those of a baby foal taking its first steps. The trip to the bathroom required the help of both Mako and Matthew, the two practically carrying Isamu on nearly useless legs from the couch to the downstairs bathroom where Mako held Isamu while he urinated. They didn't quite make it to the toilet on time and Isamu needed clean pants. Mako and Matthew made the quick change and returned Isamu to the couch. What's happening to me? Isamu asked them.

Matthew and Mako quickly retreated from his proximity. They didn't want to scare the new nanny applicant with the desperation of the scene. When Jess and I returned from our interview, Isamu was just where I had left him. It was a stage set, with the ill husband resting peacefully on the sofa. We said hello and proceeded to the backyard to join Matthew and Gilbert. Gilbert fed Jess raspberries as he picked them from the bush on the perimeter of our property. She was enchanted.

I brought Jess in to speak with Isamu. I seated myself on the couch. I rested Isamu's legs atop my thighs. Jess sat in a chair across from us. I asked Isamu if he had any questions for Jess. He opened his mouth to speak. Sounds came out. No words. His forehead scrunched. What now? In the time I had been gone to interview the new nanny, Isamu had lost his ability to talk.

Later that afternoon Isamu had a grand mal seizure on the pale blue couch. His legs were still atop my thighs. Gilbert was snuggling on top of his chest. Matthew swept Gilbert into his arms and darted to the backyard. He spared our boy the trauma of seeing the abysmal.

The seizure went on so long, I thought it was the end of Isamu's life. I thought, so this is what the death I've feared for over two years looks like. But it wasn't. He lived for two more weeks, one in the hospital and the last at home. Gilbert still climbed atop his body, nuzzling the slowly growing stubble on his chin. It took all Isamu's strength to reach a limp arm up to touch his son. As if his spirit, already drifting away, was making a few last appearances to stroke the cheek of his beloved child.

Matthew kept Gilbert's schedule as normal as possible. The rest of us circled and tended to Isamu. Matthew and Gilbert walked to the park. I bathed Isamu's body with warm washcloths and soapy water. Matthew and Gilbert ate pretzels and peanut butter and popsicles. Mako and I learned the art of delicately rolling Isamu's body to change his sheets after they'd been soiled. Matthew and Gilbert played in the backyard, within earshot of Isamu, occupying the hospital bed we had set up for him in the kitchen nook, his head tilted toward the light coming from the back door.

For that brief time the fact that Matthew was leaving was far from my mind.

MATTHEW ARRIVED FOR WORK as usual at eight-thirty on Friday morning, July 19. He was the first person outside the family to learn of Isamu's death, less than two hours earlier. He went to see Isamu's body, pausing with respect at the entry to the room, choking back tears, before leaving for the day.

After that, Matthew worked for another two weeks. During that time I hired Jess. I am consoled by the fact that even though Isamu could not speak to Jess, he was able to meet her, to take in her generous spirit. She was the right person to journey with us through the next stage of our lives—an unknown place that included what I had most feared. "What's the worst thing that could happen," I had often asked myself while we lived with the looming presence of the brain tumor. He could die. And now he had. There is no way to move on from the death of a father or husband. All we can do is build the strength to move past the pivotal occurrence, to find it within ourselves to continue to live. It can't be done without support. And I couldn't have done it without Jess's.

I'm fortunate that Jess is still Gilbert's nanny. She champions him and buttresses my role as a single working mother. When she first entered our downsized family, Matthew helped to show her the way things worked. Then he left for Texas.

Matthew has returned to Portland in the summers and during winter breaks. He sends letters and cards to Gilbert throughout the year. Recently, Gilbert and I returned from a trip to find a note from Matthew addressed to Gilbert. Accompanying the note was half of a butterfly shell. The shell is delicate, paper-thin in some places, the thickness of a frail fingernail in others. It's golden and rich with countless elliptical lines covering its surface, the lines mimicking the shape of the half shell. Matthew explained in his note that he had found the shell at the beach. This half was for Gilbert. He would keep the other half himself. Wherever they might be, they'd each possess one half of the same shell.

What does Matthew's gift mean to Gilbert? It's impossible for me to know. Gilbert is young—just five. He was only a year and a half old when Isamu died. It's all very matter of fact for him. At this point there isn't any interpretable feeling or emotion involved. He can blurt out "my dad died" in the middle of the grocery store as easily as he can say that his sneakers are red.

What do *I* think Matthew's gift means? It's my feeling that Gilbert's memories of his father are tangled up with Matthew. They are now only sensory memories—an inner knowing that he was loved, held, and cherished by the arms of a man in his early life. Perhaps a cognizance of his tiny fingers on chin stubble or the comforting warm breath of someone other than me on his dozing baby face.

We say that Gilbert's dad is in his heart. He's also carried through several corporeal forms—Gilbert's grandfathers, his uncle Mako, who is more dear to him than anyone, and his nanny, Matthew.

It's been more than three years since Isamu died. He and Matthew left our everyday lives at the same time. Matthew comes back.

THE COMPANY OF STRANGERS

Caroline Leavitt

hree days after the birth of my son, Max, I contracted a rare, deadly blood disease, a form of postpartum hemophilia. I grew so sick I was in a coma. Two weeks, five emergency operations, and hundreds of transfusions later, I woke up, surrounded by a circle of doctors and Jeff, my husband. I was hooked up to transfusion tubes, cautioned not to move, because if I did, I could hemorrhage and they weren't sure they could tamp the flow. I looked around, horrified and astonished. On the wall was a huge photograph of my baby and scribbled underneath it said GET WELL SOON MOMMY, I MISS YOU.

"Where's Max?" I said, anxiously.

"He's at home," Jeff said quietly.

"At home? With who? Did my mom fly up?"

"She did," he said quietly. "But she's in her eighties. You know she can't do it all." He touched my arm. "He's with Ellen," he said finally. "A nanny."

*   *   *

I NEVER APPROVED OF NANNIES. I admit now, with great shame, that I used to disdain those who did. During my blissful pregnancy, I'd watch the parade of nannies in the park and shake my head. They were raising other peoples' children, a modern-day convenience that enables parents to continue to work, and the nannies knew more about those babies than the parents themselves did. They were a sort of "bond market" in that you paid them to bond with your child. But wasn't there a better way? Why would you want to miss a moment of your baby's life by handing him or her over to another person to raise? Why risk having your baby bond with someone more than he or she might with you?

Personally, I couldn't wait to be with my baby all the time. My husband, Jeff, worked at home, and though I was a novelist, I also worked for a video company in the city because of the spectacular benefits they offered us, including a substantial paid maternity leave. My mother-in-law, busy tending a rapidly ailing husband, would come when she could, and my mother would fly up from Boston. I was going to spend every moment I could with my newborn. I'd make my son's baby food, I'd sing his lullabies, I'd be the first and last loving face he'd see every day.

I knew how important those first early months were, how tight the connection. I had stacks of baby books, describing how newborns could almost immediately pick their mothers out of a room just by a scent, how mothers could recognize their babies' cry almost instinctively. I knew bonding gave babies self-esteem, it gave them a model for their future relationships—and it gave their moms a reason to never mind waking up at all hours of the night to diaper their charges and rock them back to sleep.

A nanny! it drove me crazy. Those precious first months that I knew were so important were being played out in the company of a stranger! Instead of with me! That small window of opportunity was slamming shut for me—and being opened by a paid stranger. Panicked, I gripped the sheets.

"We have to have a nanny," Jeff insisted. "I need to be here and I need to be there with him and I need to work, and it's not so easy for your mother. How else could I do it without a nanny?"

I settled against the pillow. "Insurance is paying for it, right?" I said.

Jeff grew quiet again. "We're managing," he told me.

In the weeks that followed, I swam in and out of fevers. I had CAT scans and MRIs. My veins were surgically glued shut and I was given memory blockers so I wouldn't remember the more gruesome aspects of the procedures—and I didn't.

But I always remembered Max.

Max wasn't allowed in the hospital: He was too little, and I was too sick, but Jeff brought me a color photograph of him, an exquisite boy in a daffodil-printed onesie, gazing up at me, and I kept it by my bed. A week later, Jeff and my mother brought in a video. "The next best thing to being there," he said, and wheeled me into the nurses' training room so I could watch. I wept when I saw my baby being bathed in the bathroom sink. I wept when I heard him burbling. And I wept even harder when I saw Ellen, the nanny, tall and exotic looking, with dreadlocks skipping across her shoulders, tenderly tickling his belly. I knew it was irrational but I wanted to cry to Jeff, Do you love her? Does Max? But I was too afraid. What could I do if they did?

I tried to feel grateful to Ellen for caring for my son when I couldn't, for making it easier on Jeff, who was stressed and exhausted and worried, juggling work and virtual single-fatherhood and a desperately ill wife. "Tell me everything that's going on," I begged Jeff, and when he did, spinning stories about taking Max to the park, about taking him to the zoo, about singing to him in the new rocker someone had given us, my heart crumpled because I wasn't there to share it. Every night, when Jeff called me from home, I made him put the baby to the phone. "Let me talk to him," I said. I swore I could hear his breathing and I babbled into the phone, "Honey, Mommy's here!" I sang the Beatles', "I Will," the same song I had sung to him every day I carried him.

"Did he perk up?" I asked Jeff.

"Of course, he did," Jeff said, and I tried to make myself believe it.

I didn't have time to stay jealous of Ellen, though, because the agency Jeff was using couldn't allow any one nanny to stay for more than two weeks at a time. Baby nannies were booked months in advance. Almost all of them had other jobs lined up, and the nannies we got were the ones who were between positions, who were willing to give up a week or two of their off time to take on an emergency job and care for our Max.

New nannies appeared like different seasons. There was the nanny who put Max on such a strict schedule that she wouldn't let my mother see him whenever she wanted; Jeff fired her on the spot. Then there was one who watched TV all day and wanted Max to sleep on the couch because she was too obese to make it up the stairs. He let her go, too. I knew about all these nannies through the stories Jeff and my mother told me, through the snapshots Jeff took. *I know as much about them as I do my baby*, I thought, and I slid down into the hospital bed and worried: What would happen to Max, having so many different nannies? Would he think that caretakers leaving him was natural? Would he think I'd leave him, too? "We have to find just one nanny," I told Jeff. "It can't be good to keep switching them."

"I told you they're all booked," he said. He sat down on the plastic chair next to the bed, rubbing his eyes, and I saw, suddenly, how exhausted he looked, how overwhelmed. "I'm doing the best I can," he said. I took his hand and held it. And then I felt, riding on top of my worry, a strange guilty pulse of relief.

The nannies were coming and going. No one was replacing me.

*   *   *

WE BEGAN TO HAVE other problems. My hospital bills mounted, and when they topped a million, the insurance company began to balk at payment. Creditors were calling Jeff all day long, and in a final, shattering insult, his boss suggested that if Jeff couldn't give his all to his job right now, perhaps he shouldn't be there at all, and then he promptly fired him. "How are we going to pay for the nannies?" Jeff whispered.

When I was growing up, my mother stayed home with me, and when she went back to work, as a schoolteacher, she was home to make my afternoon snack. "Everything for you," she always said, and she said it again when she heard me crying about the cost of the nannies. "Don't you dare say one word," she said and took out her checkbook. I was too ill, and Jeff and I were too worried about money to issue the protest we surely would have made under normal circumstances.

∽

IN ALL, I WAS IN THE HOSPITAL for almost three months. When I came home, I came home to two strangers: a nanny named Maria and my son. I was still very ill. I had to stay in bed for another month at least. I couldn't lift anything, including the baby. And I was terrified. I knew from the books that a three-month-old baby was beginning to perceive his parent as separate from him, but how could that be, when I had *always* been separate, away in the hospital while Max was at home? Had I totally missed out on what every parenting expert says is the crucial time?

What did I know about either the nanny or Max? I knew Max was beautiful and smart and was always smiling. I knew Maria was Hispanic and had a wonderful thick accent. I knew she made vegetarian lasagna and went food shopping with my mom, and she made Jeff laugh, something I should have been happy about, but which instead threw me in a panic. They were doing fine without me; Maria was seeing to it. "She's smart and funny. She even does the laundry!" Jeff had assured me. "And she can't wait to meet you!"

Jeff helped me into the house and settled me on the couch. "Hello!" called a voice and then a dark-haired, middle-aged woman came down the stairs, carrying a baby.

My baby.

"I'm Maria," she said, but I looked past her at my son.

"Max—" I breathed and held out my hands. The nanny, smiling, carefully put Max on my lap. "We're going to have to make up for lost time," I said haltingly. I lifted up his delicate little hand. "I'm so glad to meet you," I said, and Max began to scream.

"He's just tired," she said apologetically. She stepped to the side and Max's eyes followed her and he screamed louder and she bent and picked him up.

The screaming stopped.

I looked down at my lap, devastated, but Maria patted my leg. "We were just talking about you!" she said, nodding at Max. She gazed at Max and then cocked her head, as if she were listening, then she vigorously nodded her head. "This baby, he talks to me," she told me. I blinked at her, astonished. "He says he missed you so much," she said. "He says that he knows you have been sick, and he was beside himself trying to help, but what can he do, a little baby?" She smiled. "I tell him, you just grow. That's what you do. And that's what he's doing."

Part of me thought she was crazy. A baby whisperer! But part of me wanted to believe her. She had told me that Max understood my absence and whether it was true or not, it was exactly what I needed to hear. I glanced over at Jeff, who was grinning. If, after firing so many nannies, he trusted her, then I would trust her, too. "I'm glad you're here," I told her.

I quickly grew to love Maria. Every morning, afternoon, and

evening, she carried Max into my room for a long visit, filled with stories of what they had done, and what they were planning to do next. She kissed and cuddled my baby and her face lit up with delight. She lifted Max high and made him laugh, all things I couldn't yet do. And she included me in every part of her work that she could, bringing Max in so I could watch her feed him; setting up a small bassinet by my bed so I could watch him sleep. I loved the way she put words in Max's mouth. "He told me he's not afraid of anything," Maria told me, cuddling Max. "He told me you shouldn't be afraid of anything either." She squeezed my hand, dipped Max down for a kiss, and left the room to give Max his bath. I heard the rush of water. I heard her talking with my mother who was getting the towels ready, and I felt suddenly alone again. Would I ever be well enough to take care of my baby? To give him his bath? To hold and tickle him? I thought of Maria's baby whisperings and, suddenly, I whispered to myself, "This mother, she's not afraid of anything. She's strong. She's getting healthy," and to my surprise, I felt better.

I wanted Jeff to tell the agency we wanted Maria until I was well, but she announced she had to leave. "I'm getting too attached," she said. "If I don't leave now, I never will." Her eyes filled with tears, and then mine did, too. "I can't bear to leave both of you," she said. "I can't bear it, either," I cried.

BARBARA CAME NEXT. Tall and quiet and from Haiti, she rarely spoke to me, except to contradict all the advice Maria had given. "Oh, this feeding schedule is a disaster!" Barbara said, shaking her head. "And a nap schedule! You don't dictate naps to an infant!" She didn't come into the bedroom with Max as often as I wanted and I had to call out to both of them, "Please! Come see me!" And when she did, reluctantly bringing Max, silent, I felt awkward, as if

I had imposed on her. I tried to talk to Max, to touch his baby hands, the side of his face, and he whined. "He's cranky," Barbara said, standing, carrying Max close to her chest. "Time for his bottle," and then she whisked him away.

And then one day, I woke up, unable to move my left leg, and had to go back to the hospital. I struggled down the stairs, leaning on Jeff, terrified that I was leaving Max again, that this time, they wouldn't let me come home so soon. Barbara met me downstairs, making a place for me on the couch. "Listen," she said. "I didn't know if it was my place to tell you this, but I'm praying for you." I nodded at her. "And this," she said, and fit a book into my hands. *Vitamins for Health*, it said. "I thought to give you this the first time I arrived here, but I didn't want to impose. I wanted to keep our relationship professional, but now I can't." She turned and dug in her purse and handed me a bottle, and when I looked up at her to thank her, I saw, startled, that her eyes were wet. "I've been so worried for you that I was afraid you'd see it in my face," she said and took my hand.

I WAS BACK IN THE HOSPITAL and I asked the doctor if I could take the vitamins Barbara's book had suggested. "Can't hurt," he said, and I called Jeff and asked him to bring them to me. Every morning, along with my other meds, I took three vitamins and I whispered to myself the way Maria might, "This mama is strong." I don't know if the vitamins had anything to do with it, or the whispering, but the combination gave me hope, and that certainly helped. Slowly, surely, I began to get well and, two weeks later, I came home again.

This time, I was well enough to walk. I was supposed to lift small weights, in practice for lifting Max! Things were returning to normal. My mother, who had been away from her home for months, needed to go back to Boston, but she hugged us all. "I'm just a phone call away," she told us. "Keep the nannies," she whispered. "Don't worry about the cost."

Of course, I worried. I knew my mother had money, but that money was for her own necessities, not mine. What if she got sick and needed a nurse? What if she wanted to move to a retirement community? And I worried about bonding with my son, too. Would he ever know that he had just one mother? Someone had given us as a baby gift a copy of *The Ugly Duckling*, a story about a baby swan separated from his mother, raised by ducks, who endures ridicule and sorrow, right up until he finds his real mother, and every time I read it, I cried. Would Max know me as his real mother? Or was it too late?

Finally, four months after Max had been born, the doctors told me I could now pick up my own baby. I could walk around outside with him. "We'll wean the nannies away," Jeff said. "Have them half-time so you can see how it goes, so you can depend on them if you need to." I shook my head. "I have to do this on my own," I told him. "It has to be just me and Max for him to bond."

"Are you sure?" he asked.

I wasn't sure. I was terrified I would have trouble taking care of my son, but I was more terrified of not being able to build a bond with him. Max still looked past me when I approached, he still sometimes cried when I touched him. A week before we were going to go nannyless, Barbara sat me down with a notebook and said, "Ask away," and I asked her everything, taking notes like this was an exam I had to pass. When to feed him. What to do if he cried. What to do if he wouldn't eat. Then she leaned over and hugged me.

After barbara had left, the house felt quiet. I thought of being here without my mother, without the nannies. I thought of all the bills we still had to pay, and all the money my mother had spent on nannies. And I thought of Max. "I think you and your son need some time to yourself," Jeff said gently. I walked into Max's room alone. I stared into his crib and thought, *This is it*. And then, I bent down and gently picked up my son, the first time I had since he had been born. "Hi, honey," I whispered to Max and he rested his head against my shoulder and I cried and cried and cried.

THE FOREVER OF REMEMBERING

Meg Waite Clayton

his story starts on a Friday evening at a kitchen table in Santa Monica, California, me on the phone with a pediatric-neurosurgeon son of a friend of my mother's. "Unilateral coronal craniosynostosis," he is saying, and he is explaining it to me: A baby's skull, unlike an adult's, is made of several plates of bone that meet at the baby's soft spot—plates that grow together after the child's brain is grown. In my four-month-old son's case, the bones on his right side have grown together prematurely, leaving his skull unable to grow on that side. His brain, undeterred, has grown disproportionately on the left, leaving him with the beginnings of a lopsided head. The solution—this is when I first start crying, when I hear this—is to cut my baby's head open, cut off the front half of his skull, reshape his forehead or perhaps cut it into tiny pieces they will wire together, and replace it forward on his head, for him to grow into. Optional surgery, but not really, the neurosurgeon tells me. My son's brain will be fine even if we do nothing, but without the surgery every time we walk into a grocery store, people will turn to stare. "His brain will be fine," the surgeon repeats. "He'll understand they're staring at him."

A week later, I am at a thrown-together, best-friends-only private baptism, despite my Episcopal priest's assurance that "we"—unlike the Catholic Church I grew up in—don't believe little babies are barred from heaven just because they haven't been splashed. And then I am at the doctor's office, being read the awful list, the your-son-may-die stuff. And then it's the day, May 10, and we are handing our son over to the nurse who will take him into the operating room. I have been warned how devastating this will be, but my imagination has failed me. Somehow, I imagined this moment to be like when I'd handed my happy, healthy son over to the nanny the first time, wondering if she was, underneath her all-American-girl exterior, a direct link to the black market in baby adoptions or Jacqueline the Ripper or simply incompetent. But this is nothing like that. When I cried on that first drive back to work, I was not imagining a scalpel slicing through my baby's pale skin, or the saw cutting through his bone, or his brilliant brain exposed to even the smallest disaster of a mistake. Not once that morning did I see little baby-sized coffins.

This is just the backstory, and maybe I could tell this story without it, but I can't think the story without it, so there it is. But the story does have a happy ending. Our son survives the surgery, grows up strong and healthy and handsome, makes the high school tennis team, gets straight A's, plays an extraordinary game of chess. My husband, Mac, and I survive the surgery, too, against all odds. We have a second son, a soccer-playing thespian mathematician, and we move to Baltimore, to Nashville, to Palo Alto. We abandon lucrative legal careers for writing lives. And our nanny, Sonia Aguilar—our housekeeper first, and then the fourth and last nanny we will ever hire—gets a happy ending, too: three children and one grandchild, and a daycare center in her own home.

That all comes after that moment at the hospital, the handing over of my baby. At the time, Sonia is our cleaning lady, whom I prefer to think of as "housekeeper," a term with more dignity, and we are already on our second nanny: a mature, responsible woman who will not be intimidated by the bruised and scarred baby who comes home after the operation, who will never forget to put the antibiotic ointment on his scar, who holds him close and comfortable in her lap. She will last only a few months, though, before returning east to care for her own grandchild, leaving us to hire a perky British girl who will lie about her citizenship, who will record in a journal that she feeds and bathes our son and takes him to the park when the truth is she lounges in my swimsuit in my jacuzzi tub, ignoring the squawking on the baby monitor, that she abandons him to Sonia's care while she goes off with her boyfriend. And we will be left, for the fourth time, in the throes of a nanny search, which—have you ever done a nanny search?—is no easy thing. How do you trust your judgment after you've hired this false Mary Poppins? How can you be sure you'll find someone who is not just smart and kind and loving, but also as unrelentingly careful as you are, who will keep your son's cap on over his sun-sensitive scar, who will tell him how handsome he is, who will not, God forbid, let him fall off a slide or the monkey bars onto his fragile new forehead, his skull with the gap where the bone has not yet filled in?

Mac and I paid a decent wage for a housekeeper on the west side of L.A., at the time, which would not have been enough to live on anywhere in L.A. even working full-time, which Sonia wasn't. It was more than most people paid non-English-speaking, probably-illegal-immigrant-so-just-don't-ask "housekeepers," but it was a pittance. We paid our nannies considerably more, and we employed them full-time and then some—they started at 8 A.M. and stayed until one of us got home from work, rarely earlier than seven and sometimes midnight and beyond. And we had not once considered hiring anyone who wasn't Mary-Poppins pale and English-speaking to fill that post. We interviewed candidates from nanny schools and nanny agencies, candidates who read the want ads, nannies who'd heard about the job from other nannies in the neighborhood—it was that kind of neighborhood; the nannies knew each other, but no one else much did. We spent evenings reading nanny résumés in the library, a room that was all bold patterns screaming for attention, set perfectly off balance by an insipid earth-tones-and-aqua couch, a room without coffee or end tables because we'd tired of the painters and crown-molding installers and all of it before we reached the coffee-and-end-tables aisle.

That's what we are doing the night we decide to hire Sonia as our nanny—we share the library couch with a stack of nanny-candidate résumés and a plate of cheese and crackers, wine glasses on the floor. The library is sparkling clean—this was a Sonia cleaning day—and the sheers, vacuumed free of dust, are billowing in the warm evening breeze; even the desk, a huge, leather-topped, not-quite-antique partners' desk I'd found dusty and forgotten in a corner of an antique warehouse storage-room looks almost respectable.

Mac, grinning a toothy, Bugs Bunny grin though he is much more handsome than that sounds (turn-around, drop-dead good-looking when he is not smiling, and utterly, boyishly charming when he is), asks if I'm hungry. "Sonia left a chicken," he says. Sonia cooked a chicken for us every week: pale, flaccid things that were still red and raw at the bone, things Mac left for me to throw out because it amused him that I could stomach neither sticking a still-warm Tuesday-night chicken back into the oven nor suggesting to Sonia that she cease these offerings—not even in her job description, but dinners she made because she thought we ought to eat dinner at home at least this once a week. Which we did. We had cheese and crackers and wine every Tuesday night after I threw the chicken out.

"This one doesn't look too bad," he says. He's talking not about the half-cooked thing in the kitchen, but about a nanny candidate whose résumé he's handing me.

I sit there on the awful couch in the too-loud room with the cheese and crackers and the wine and the thought washing over me that I almost cannot bear to go through this again. I think of the day we found the partner's desk, when I'd imagined someday yanking one of those stuck drawers out and coming upon a five-dollar gold piece, or a daguerreotype of a baby in christening lace, his perfectly formed forehead framed by a white bonnet, or old love letters from Robert Browning to that woman who wrote the poem about the moose that I love even though I can't remember her name or much about the poem except the moose, and I have no idea, really, who Robert Browning is or if he was even alive at the same time as the poet—Mary Someone? I'd had this idea that someday Mac and I would abandon our high-stress, high-finance jobs to sit across from each other at that desk every morning and . . . and write poems about moose caught in headlights, and drink strong, politically correctly–grown coffee, and laugh.

And the idea bubbles up again—not the idea of quitting work to write, because I don't have the confidence to see that as more than a dream yet, not quite yet. But the idea about Sonia.

I try to swallow, but my Adam's apple has grown unwieldy. It's the stupidest idea I've had since I got engaged to my college boyfriend during winter break of my junior year. Mac will think it's a joke.

"Or this one," Mac says, pulling another sheet from the pile, another fine candidate from the same agency we paid big fees to assure us that Nanny #1 was well-trained and experienced, Nanny #3 was here legally, Nanny #2 would be a long-term prospect, that she wouldn't have a new grandchild who needed her care.

"I was thinking . . ." I start, and Mac peers at me expectantly, his haircut making his ears stick out like a ten-year-old, leaving him goofy-looking in a way that only enhances his boyishness.

There's a rustling on the baby monitor, and I imagine my son growing up to look like his father. And then quiet.

"I was thinking . . ." I say again, and I try to play out this scenario like we used to play out legal theories when we worked together, when any thread of a possibility was something to be explored. "I was thinking we should make Sonia the nanny."

Mac smiles, the beginning of a laugh, then purses his lips. He always knows when I'm about to cry, though he never can imagine why; it's one of his many talents, that he can always tell what a person is going to do even though he has no idea why. I have no idea why either, but I can feel the tears crawling up my throat, trying to make their way by my oversized Adam's apple, which is climbing down into my empty stomach, making it swell.

"You know, Sonia doesn't speak English," he says cautiously.

"I know." My voice not quite steady.

He looks down at the stack of résumés. "And you don't speak Spanish."

"No."

"And neither do I?"

"I know."

He sets the résumés on the cushion beside him, scoots a little closer. "We can't figure out how to tell her not to bleach the towels," he says. "Or how to cook a chicken."

I look to the swaybacked old desk, completely dust-free, wanting to say something about that but knowing it will sound ridiculous, that the fact that Sonia can dust a house to a polished shine and leave a window so clean you'd think it wasn't there has nothing to do with, say, how well she might teach our son his alphabet or his numbers in a language she doesn't even speak.

"Or even not to *bother* to cook a chicken," Mac says.

I feel a smile somewhere behind my teeth, under my tongue.

"And her passport, I'm afraid, went into the same washing machine as Nanny #3's."

"But she'll *love* him." My voice a pathetic wail Meg Ryan could turn into a great comic scene. "She loves him already."

And it registers in his eyes, then, that we do know one thing about this maybe-illegal immigrant with whom we can't communicate: She loves our son and his chapped cheeks and cradle cap, his staring eyes that are already behind glasses. She loves him without even the simple excuse that he is her son. It's there in the way she touches his toes, his cheeks, his long pink scar that is slowly disappearing behind beautifully wispy blond curls.

"She loves him," I repeat, crying full-bore now, and Mac puts his arm around me, pulls me close, pats my head. "Shhh. Shhhh. It's going to be okay," he says. "He's going to be fine. He'll be fine, you'll see."

∞

"DOES SHE DRIVE?" Mac asks two mornings later, after the sitter has strollered our son and set off for the park, leaving us listening to the sputtering Honda that is Sonia's husband dropping her off. I say that I'm sure she drives, we've both seen her drive, though I do wonder how she reads the street signs—YIELD, STOP, MERGE. He says we'll have to provide her with a decent car, and I say she can have the BMW, and he's considerate enough not to point out how ridiculous this is: We will give our only reliable car to the nanny for her occasional use, leaving Mac to his daily commute in a ten-year-old Alpha, me to my longer one through some pretty bad neighborhoods late at night in an old Mercedes convertible that caught fire at La Cienega and the 10 freeway well after midnight one night before we started dating. (The police dispatch officer, who'd promptly told me to get back in the car, responded to my "The engine is *on fire!*" with something like "You are not in the Midwest anymore, Dorothy. Get back in the car and lock the doors.")

"We'll have to get her on the insurance," Mac says as Sonia's husband pulls to a stop. I try not to look at the dented front bumper, the scrape across the back passenger-side panel.

"Mrs. Clayton! Mr. Clayton," Sonia says, startled to see us. I'm usually gone long before she arrives, and even Mac is generally heading out, having left a check for her on the kitchen counter. She smiles uncertainly: Has she done something wrong? Is she being called to task for the half-cooked chicken? Is she going to be fired?

"Everything is fine, Sonia," I say. "We think you're doing a great job." It sounds like my negotiating skills at work: The contract looks great, we just need to change everything but the signature line.

"We just have something we want to talk to you about," I say.

She might understand "fine" and "job," and maybe "talk," but she hasn't put these words together well enough to be reassured. I look down at the piece of paper in my hand. I've had my bilingual secretary write out the sentences I think I'll need—"We'd like you to be our nanny" and "We'll pay you what we were paying Ellen"— but this isn't one of the phrases I anticipated needing.

"*El . . .* vacuum?" Sonia says uncertainly. *"Necesita . . ."*

"No problema," Mac says, a phrase he picked up from his own secretary, the wonderfully ebullient Raquel. He motions with a hand—will Sonia come into the library? She hesitates, then follows us, standing even after I sit. Mac, raised in the South, is constitutionally unable to take a seat until all the women are comfortable, and no one could describe Sonia as anything close to that. He motions to the near wing chair. "Please," he says. "Have a seat."

Miraculously, she does.

"Sonia, Ellen is leaving," I say in Spanish, reading the first sentence on my cheat sheet, crinkled where I've gripped it too tightly. Mac looks at me, thoroughly astonished. I smooth the paper. "My secretary . . ." I start to explain—to him, to her. I'm more prepared for this than he has imagined. I'm going to make this work.

"We need to hire a new nanny," I read, again in Spanish.

"Nanny?" she says.

"I know you don't speak English and I don't—" I look down at my paper. Again, not a sentence I've written out.

"We think you would be a wonderful nanny," I say, giving up on the Spanish. "All you have to do is love him. We can do the rest—

the alphabet, the numbers, the college applications. We can do that ourselves.

"I know you already love him," I say.

It's a sign of my incredible presumptuousness that it hasn't occurred to me that Sonia won't be thrilled with the opportunity to be our nanny. She says several sentences, not a word of which I understand, but I get, anyway, that she's not leaping at the job. I haven't heard "*sí.*"

The front door opens then, and at the sound of baby giggles, Sonia's face lights up. The stroller fills the library doorway, and Sonia coos in Spanish. Our son isn't speaking yet, but he takes in every word she says.

Mac picks up the phone, dials. "You're on, champ," he says to Raquel. "I think she understands we want her to be the nanny, but we don't understand her, and the little guy isn't old enough to translate yet." This is why Mac is so much more effective than I am. He delegates to someone who knows what they are doing. I try to do everything myself.

He hands the receiver to Sonia, says "Raquel." Sonia's face lights up again—she adores Raquel and, unlike me, she isn't shy about showing it. She doesn't worry, that, say, she'll end up liking someone who doesn't like her back, that she'll look the fool. It's a moment I'll come to remember when approaching awkward social situations—how amazingly quickly one generous smile can spread.

Sonia listens to Raquel, then speaks, listens, hands the phone to Mac. Mac listens, says, "I see . . . hmmm . . . right," while I say, "What?! What?!"

"We hadn't thought about that," he says. "Can you ask her what would work for her? Hours-wise, pay-wise, commitment-wise." He listens for a minute, then says, "No, you're a better negotiator than I am. Look at the salary I'm paying you."

While Sonia and Raquel speak, Mac explains: Sonia has a family, a husband and a daughter. She loves our son and would love to care for him, but she knows the long days our nanny works, and her daughter needs her, too, her husband needs her, too.

I sigh. I'm an associate at a big law firm; the many things I can do in my life don't include being home regularly at five o'clock, or even at six, or seven, or eight. But Mac and Raquel and Sonia work it all out: the hours, the pay, the responsibilities. She can start at nine—Mac never leaves before nine, anyway. And he will be home by six every evening. We won't ask her to babysit on weekends, we'll find someone else for that—someone who will eventually be Sonia's daughter, Claudia, though that is years later.

And when I hand my son to Sonia that first morning, she runs her hand gently over his head like it is the sweetest little skull she has ever seen. *"Mi amor,"* she calls him. *"Mi amor."*

It's a small thing, Sonia's comfort with my fairly-well-healed-now son, but it will make me weep three years later when he comes out of his second operation, a one-hour cosmetic touch-up that stretches on and on. An hour that turns into five hours and endless panic, that turns into forever before an exhausted young doctor finally enters the waiting room, before he explains that our son's skull inexplicably failed to regenerate well after his first operation, before he describes the new forehead they have constructed for him with artificial bone. Before I begin to weep uncontrollably at the thought of the eggshell-thin skull my son has had all these first vulnerable years, at the thought of what might have happened if we'd left him in the hands of anyone less careful than Sonia all that time. It's then—we've moved to Baltimore and Sonia and her family have moved with us; the second operation is done at the University of Virginia, three hours away, and we are home recovering—that I ask Sonia why she and Hugo left El Salvador. I'm a fiction writer, and sometimes I can't keep straight what is fact and what I have spun from fact, but I'm left with the impression of a bomb exploding, of a child screaming in her bed in a house engulfed suddenly in flames. I am left with the image of a young mother and father grabbing their daughter from that bed, of Sonia and Hugo rushing Claudia out and away, turning from the safety of an open field finally to watch their home collapse. It's an astonishing story; as I listen, I wonder how I have known Sonia for years already and never known this is part of her life. But it doesn't surprise me, or if it does it's like that inevitable surprise I'm always striving for in fiction, that "of course, I should have seen that." She has lived the same unbearable fear of losing her child that I have; she, too, is left forever living it, forever searching through empty spaces for the unscarred face of a child in a photograph, long since grown into a full, rich life.

NANNY DEAREST

Daphne Merkin

nhappy childhoods, as those who've had experience of them know, tend to stay with you, immune to displacement by the therapist's wand or later joys. Like fogs, they hover somewhere behind the appearance of better weather, threatening to cast their dreary atmosphere over the momentarily sunlit. You can, for instance, forget so much else that has happened more recently, and yet still be able to re-create the bleakness of those long-ago Sunday evenings, when Ed Sullivan's ritual goodnight wave at the end of his weekly show—the one that seemed to project directly from the middle of his peculiar hunched-over body rather than as an extension of his arm—signaled that the television around which the six of you huddled in pajamas and leather slippers from Indian Walk (red for the girls, navy for the boys) was about to be firmly turned off. The gray-blue light of the pre–color era TV screen would wink out, like a fading firefly, and then there was nothing to be done but go up to bed and acknowledge that the weekend, which you hadn't liked all that much in the first place, was officially over and would be followed by the advent of the school week, which you liked even less.

Given this immediacy of recall, it is all the more curious that I find it so hard to summon up Jane, the woman who was hired to look after me and my five siblings, find it so hard to put the various images of her together into a lasting impression of a singular person whose life touched mine at all its crucial points. That was what we called her, Jane, blunt and American, although she was in fact born and raised under the name Adrienne in Holland. I don't know when or why she Americanized her first name, but it always intrigued me that she held on to her surname of Van de Ven, so that she became Jane Van de Ven, as though half of her belonged in a "See Spot Run" primer and half of her wore wooden clogs.

∽

I COULD BEGIN ANYWHERE, pull out any detail from the vast inventory of yellowing sorrows that make up my childhood and not one of them would be of much help in filling out Jane's stringent cookie-cutter outlines. None of these images—and I will dutifully cobble together a few—would serve, that is, to leave a sufficiently weighty imprint, some warm doughy impression that would make her feel real to me in memory and thus real to you in depiction. Jane was in the habit, for instance, of wearing incongruous pastel-colored baby doll pajamas summer in and summer out, drawing my mother's chilly glare of disapproval at their abbreviatedness, although she was in fact the most chaste and least sex-kittenish—least feminine, really—of women and, I believe, died a virgin. She had taut legs and frighteningly visible muscles in her arms, well before the Age of Fitness had dawned, biceps you could win a boxing match with. At night she liked to smoke while sitting straight up in bed and watching TV, hour after hour, the ashes piling up in a little blue-and-white dish she kept by her bedside. She read in exactly the same fashion as she watched TV, sitting straight up in bed and smoking while she grimly paged through a novel she had picked up from around the house, never slumping against the pillows with what I considered to be a true readerly surrender. I don't know what powers of imaginative empathy or even simple identification she had to draw on, whether she ever saw herself through the eyes of a character she was reading about, envisioned herself leading someone else's life. It wasn't that she lacked discernment—she noticed the sort of little things about people, mannerisms, and gestures that suggested some kind of psychological attunedness—but it seemed to me that she read very much from the outside in, refusing to get overly involved. This posture of disengagement fascinated me as much as it puzzled me: What was the point of reading if you didn't get overly involved?

Which brings me to the crux of the difficulty in writing about Jane: I never learned during all those years how to read her from the inside out, never learned what made her, as they say, "tick." Jane woke me almost every grade-school morning and turned off the light every night when I was still young enough to have a bedtime. Yet she exists for me now as more of an absence than a presence—like a blur at the very center of a portrait where a likeness should be, a snapshot that failed to develop, a character who never quite came off the page. I cannot, for instance, remember her ever reading to me; or her taking my hand as a little girl in a companionable way, other than to drag me away from a playground swing or to pull me along faster than I was going on my own steam; or her leaning down and saying something sweet to me. But she must have, even if only once or twice. The thing is, she left so few traces. We are all born to die, of course, and in the end the fewest of us leave indelible marks, existing mostly in the memories of others. But even the erased memories are a clue to something, if only to a need or insistence on the part of the person doing the erasing. Why, then, do I insist on erasing Jane? What is making me so uneasy, back there in the far reaches of the past?

∽

JANE VAN DE VEN CAME to work for my family in the fall of 1953, half a year after my older brother was born and seven months before I, the third daughter and fourth child in a tightly spaced lineup of six—there were less than nine years from the first of us to the last—joined the group. It was during that brief, zealously domestic period when it was fashionable for even upper-middle-class American mothers to look after their children themselves. They might not do the actual drudge work of mothering, the picking up of toys and changing of diapers, but they tended to be around and available, to dole out the eggs and toast at breakfast as well as the steak and peas at dinner. My mother, to be clear about all this right from the start, harbored no such ideas about the virtues of hands-on childcare or, indeed, about feigning interest in the intimate but also tiresomely repetitive tasks that went along with being a full-time mother. True, the word "bonding" hadn't yet achieved the preeminent pride of place that it would by the time I had my daughter, but I don't think my mother would have much cottoned to the notion even if it had. For one thing, both she and my father were Europeans, transplanted German Jews who had found each other at a Manhattan dinner party that had been hatched precisely with this matchmaking intention in mind. For another, my father was a Jurassic forty-two when he married my thirty-year-old mother, a man long used to his pampered bachelor ways. He had particularly little tolerance for the clamorous demands of a pack of kids and particularly large expectations for himself as being the main object of my mother's attentions.

Jane was the second such person to be hired, part of a household staff that included a cook, a laundress, a cleaning woman, and a chauffeur. An earlier full-time nanny—who was actually referred to as "Nanny," as Jane was not, and was properly trained in her calling, as Jane was not—had been hired before the birth of my sister

Debra, the second eldest. This woman wore a gray bun, red lipstick, and a starched white uniform, and although she overlapped with Jane for a while, she left while I was still too young to have any memory of her. But it seems to me in retrospect that she was closer to the idealized, credentialed nanny of my fantasies, someone who might have been hired to look after young royalty. Indeed, she gives off a dignified, almost regal air in the black-and-white photos where she is shown standing proudly, a slim, beautiful older woman with her two identically dressed charges, one of them sitting up in a Silver Cross carriage. Still, under her impressive bearing Nanny seems to have exerted her own malign influence, apparently having favored the younger of the girls in her care to such an extent that my oldest sister insists to this day that the disparity in the affection grievously affected her development.

I was, you might say, Jane's first "baby"; she became the designated caretaker just as I came into view. And while I suppose this might have translated into a greater solicitude for or attachment to me than to the three children who came before or the two brothers who came after me, in fact it meant nothing of the kind. Jane was a boys' kind of nanny, to the extent that she was a nanny kind of person at all. She vastly preferred my two younger brothers to me and didn't seem much moved by either of my two sisters, but her capacity for rage together with her remarkable lack of interest in my siblings' inner lives and my own was particularly focused on me and the brother who was a year older than I. She herself had been the third of sixteen children in what must have been a tightly run and hardscrabble Catholic household—her father lost a leg during the Allied bombardments in World War II—and I don't think she had the faintest ripple of a maternal instinct. (One summer during high school my sister Debra and I, as part of our first trip to Europe, visited Jane's family home in Eindhoven, in the southernmost part of Holland, where her mother still lived with two aging daughters. I remember being shocked by the cramped house and the undercooked hard-boiled eggs with gluey, bright-yellow mayonnaise that we were served for lunch, food that had been painstakingly prepared so as not to violate any of the kosher dietary restrictions but seemed all the same unpalatably alien.) What, one might ask, was Jane doing taking care of us, with so much impatience and next-to-no signs of love? Why had my mother hired her with such unerring antimaternal instinct in the first place, this colorless cold creature, transfiguring her from her former position as a cleaning woman who worked for cousins in London to the woman who looked after—or, more correctly, intimidated—the six of us, three girls and three boys, all lined up, with freshly shampooed hair, anxious eyes, and tentative smiles?

∽

WHEN I TALK NOW about Jane with one of my sisters, she uses the word "schizoid" to describe her. And certainly there was that quality, a chronic remove, an unwillingness—or inability—to connect (except to my mother, whom she both feared and worshipped, giving me an early lesson in the power of sadomasochistic attachment). I'm sure I tried hard to engage her when I was little, during those quick, silent baths she gave me in the bathroom off my brothers' room, the one all six of us took baths in when we were little. In spite of our living in a duplex, it wasn't that commodious in terms of square footage, at least not relative to contemporary standards or even the size of our family. There weren't enough bedrooms to go around, for one thing, so we three girls and three boys each shared one. Aside from this, my mother didn't believe that children needed their own space—or, for that matter, much of any facilitation—in order to develop a better sense of self. (I don't think she was convinced, when you came right down to it, that a better sense of self was such a good idea to cultivate in one's child.)

I attribute my compulsively hygienic grooming habits to a lingering sense of horror I have about that bathroom, which in my memory always smelled slightly fecal. The bathroom was small but it had a window so it must have been periodically aired even with the six of us tumbling in and out, but I can still see Jane wrinkling her finely modeled nose after one or the other of us had used the toilet to detectably odoriferous effect, and saying, "Stinky." My oldest sister insists that she reused the same bathwater for successive children, which sounds perfectly plausible, given how much exertion it would have taken to let the water out and run it afresh each time.

What I remember most, though, is the cavernous sense of loneliness those grim, assembly-line baths used to induce, just me and Jane, the gray-and-white tiled floor and the silent white-tiled walls. I was a fairly chatty child, given to asking a lot of questions, but somewhere along the way I gave up the effort at meaningful communication with Jane. I didn't splash around or laugh or pretend the bathtub was a swimming pool and duck my head under the water as my daughter later did during her bath times. Instead I would sit in the minimally filled tub, my skinny legs thrust in front of me, and obediently hand my limbs over for Jane to scrub with a washcloth and then stand up so she could swipe between my legs. She used a set of washcloths, actually, one for my top and one for my bottom half, as though I were literally sawed in two. I continued to use two washcloths when I started bathing myself and only stopped living under their bifurcating rule sometime in my late twenties.

Beyond this, I can't remember feeling anything but fear of Jane and caution around her until I reached the age of about thirteen or fourteen. At that point—in part because I reported an out-of-the-ordinary act of physical abuse toward me and must have made a sufficiently good case for myself so that my usually immovable mother said something admonishing—she no longer felt free to bend my will to hers with her superior strength. Jane regularly administered full-scale, over-the-knee British boarding school–style spankings to my siblings and me, sometimes with her amazingly strong hand and sometimes resorting to a Kent hairbrush. I know that being a witness to these fervent spankings—especially those she gave to my second-to-youngest brother, who was the only one of us born with blond curls and who was Jane's clear and away favorite—affected me deeply, but I can't remember being spanked myself.

The particular incident I am referring to, after which Jane ceased muscling me around, occurred one Friday afternoon in early summer out at our beach house. The three youngest of us had been driven there—it was about an hour out of the city, a small enclave fronting on the Atlantic Ocean that was tucked on the upscale, white side of the Far Rockaway bridge (as opposed to the side that was black and impoverished), frequented by a sprinkling of Mafiosi and a growing Jewish community—ahead of the rest of the family. I had been talking to my mother—whom I clung to with all the more frenzy when I was in Jane's hands—on the kitchen phone, when my second-to-youngest brother had grabbed it out of my hand. I tried to grab it back, we started scuffling, and that was when all hell broke out. He was Jane's darling, and no matter that he was bigger and stronger than I was, she turned on me with the ferocity of a wolf guarding her vulnerable young at this show of resistance to my being bullied by him. I don't know why it happened on this occasion and not on another, but something in me resisted her bullying me as well, and refused to submit to her greater will. Jane dragged me out of the kitchen and began banging my head against the wall of the downstairs guest bathroom to the right of the staircase. Again, I can't remember the pain or humiliation of it—it seems to have happened to someone else, someone whom I have but the vaguest sense of inhabiting—so much as I can remember the space in which it took place. The interior of this guest bathroom had been fixed up with gilded faucets, smoked mirrors, a marble sink, and fancy wallpaper by the former owners and although this nouveau riche taste was emphatically not my mother's, she had left the bathroom as it was when she redid the rest of the house before we moved in. I took it all in very carefully, my face bobbing somewhere in the smoked mirrors as Jane exerted her dominance. What I can remember most about that scene is how I focused on the details of the bathroom as though everything depended on them, particularly the two little glass bottles etched faintly in gold that stood to one side of the sink. They, too, had been left behind by the former owners and were probably once meant to hold cotton balls and Q-tips—I can imagine a whole other, more delicate kind of life they had been envisioned for—but now they stood empty. They were fragile, those bottles, and it surprised me that they hadn't broken once my family took up residence in the house.

After that, I became less afraid of Jane, although still wary, and then somewhere along the way I left her behind, in her mousehole of a room behind the kitchen which became effectively her home. She lived in two successive mouseholes, to be exact, over the almost fifty years she lingered on in the apartment I grew up in. First she lived upstairs in a tiny so-called maid's room, behind what was called the nursery; then, later on, she was moved to an even tinier room behind the kitchen, where she sat and smoked and ate skimpy cheese sandwiches and wrote birthday cards in her unmistakable forward-slanting handwriting. She never forgot anyone's birthday, not once during all the years, nor did she forget the birthdays of any of the next generation—the proliferating first cousins who eventually came to number a whopping twenty-one in total. That was touching of her, I suppose, if I were inclined to see it that way. Just as it was touching that, like it or not, I and my siblings and my parents became more like her family than her own original family.

But, then again, you might say that this was exactly where the trouble began: with the family, and the core feelings they evoked of a not-enoughness (of basic warmth and affection) and then again of a too-muchness (of anger and coldness and lack of interest). That was the originating problem, I see it clearly: Jane had annexed herself to the wrong family, either out of instinct or by mistake. Even to think about her now is to remind myself of my limited ability, in spite of years of therapy and my ingrained habit of introspection, to go back to where the pain started and stay with it until it flows out and away and is perhaps gone. My limited ability, that is, to "own" the pain, as the psychobabble of the moment would have it. So it stays with me, obscuring the present as it inevitably does, and when I am asked whether I would like to contribute to an anthology of pieces about nannies, I immediately assume it is Jane the editors are asking about. When of course I should have assumed, given the passing of decades and the facts that have accumulated, that they were inquiring into my adult experience of *hiring* a nanny for my own daughter.

Jane died at the age of eighty-eight one hot July day three summers ago; she was a wizened version of her former self by then, still in my mother's employ, still given to her meager, straight-backed pleasures. When I cried at the funeral home, where she lay in full cosmeticized glory in an open casket—so alien to the Orthodox Jewish tradition I knew—I wasn't crying for her. I don't know what I was crying for, these huge noisy sobs that came out of the blue, in a little side chapel at Frank Campbell, with pitifully few in attendance. One of Jane's sisters and a niece had flown over from Holland but other than that the gathering consisted of my mother, some of my siblings, and an older male cousin who had known her since his childhood. Perhaps I was crying in response to the words of the resident clergyman who guided the brief service. This priest spoke in the most gentle of Father Christmas affirmations, to the effect that Jane (whom he compared unconvincingly to the biblical character Ruth) was an enterprising spirit who had crossed the Atlantic to take care of us and had loved all of us like her own. His belief seemed to settle over the room like a tender-hearted, hope-inspiring balm, in contrast to the sense of bereftness the occasion inspired in me: a lack of grief, more than anything, just a sense of puzzlement that Jane had grown old and vulnerable, and here I was in my late forties and there was a void where an attachment should have been.

∞

UNDOUBTEDLY IN RESPONSE to my own experience with Jane, I became obsessed with the idea of nannies, both real and fantastical. I devoured the Mary Poppins series and when I was in the fifth grade, Mrs. Berle, the school librarian, helped me locate P. L. Travers's address in England so I could send her a letter in which I inquired whether she was planning to write any more books after the fourth and what appeared to be the last, *Mary Poppins in the Park*. I loved reading about the Banks children, Michael and Jane, followed by the twins and then baby Annabel, who resided on Cherry Tree Lane with their harried mother, their irascible banker father, Cook, Katie Nanna, and various uniformed housemaids, until one day the "spit spot"–intoning, wryly affectionate, magic-spinning creature known as Mary Poppins arrived with the East Wind to take firm but loving charge of all of them. They seemed like a shinier and cozier version of my own family, a tribute to a lapsed golden Edwardian moment. And whatever was wrong with Mary Poppins—there was an undeniable crustiness, even chill, to the original fictional character, as opposed to the sweet-as-spun-sugar version of her that Julie Andrews played on screen—seemed minor compared to all that was wrong with, or merely missing in, Jane. Later on, I devoured Jonathan Gathorne-Hardy's *The Unnatural History of the Nanny*, where I read with fascination about the venerable British upperclass tradition of trained nannies, with its assortment of supremely good and horrifying bad examples, the sterling mother-substitutes as well as the evil antimaternal stand-ins. It was here I first learned about Winston Churchill's beloved nanny, Mrs. Everest, who was the mainstay of his youth, "his dearest and most intimate friend," as Churchill described her in *My Early Life*. I thought his nickname for her, "Womany," the most moving appellation anyone could come up with, as though she stood in for all that was most female and nurturing about her whole sex. She in turn wrapped him in endearments like "Winny," "my Lamb," and "my darling Precious Boy." I wondered who I might have become with a Mrs. Everest behind me, worrying about my welfare, the way Churchill's Mrs. Everest worried that her Winny would catch a chill even as he stood by her deathbed. Then there were the nannies who sexually fondled their charges or maltreated them so egregiously—like Miss Paraman, the nanny who looked after the young Lord Curzon, beating him and his siblings savagely and making them parade around in conical caps with words like "liar" "sneak" and "coward" written out in enormous letters by the children themselves—that it's hard to believe no one called the police.

∽

HAVING EARLY ON become aware of the hazards of the childcare arrangements I was subjected to, I was preternaturally attuned to potential signs of ill will in any caretaker I encountered, even in passing. It was impossible not to notice the simmering class and racial hostility that many of the women who were hired to look after children on the Upper East and West sides of Manhattan displayed to their charges, and there was little danger that I would miss out on these signals when and if the time arose for me to hire someone to look after a child of my own. Indeed, the whole "nanny" concept struck me as misapplied to these women, and I never thought of any of the warm-hearted caretaker/housekeepers I eventually hired to look after my own daughter as "nannies," nor called them that. A nanny was what Winston Churchill was lucky enough—and Lord Curzon unlucky enough—to have had.

The other possibility that has been much discussed in the guilt-ridden, politically correct literature written by women who seek to understand their own complex relationships with what I believe these days goes by the official jargony term of childcare workers—which is that one's child might end up more attached to his or her caretaker than to oneself—has also never seriously concerned me. Without considering myself the least bit saccharine in my outlook, I guess I come from a sufficient sense of emotional deprivation in the first place that it has never occurred to me that too much affection might be a problem in the second. Although I knew I didn't want to hire someone who would vie with me for my own child, I also wanted to make sure that any child of mine would feel loved by whoever picked her up from nursery school that day.

In the event, I hadn't counted on the severe post-partum depression that hit me shortly after my daughter Zoe was born, exactly ten months after I had finally gotten married at the age of thirty-four. My marriage, I will add, was fairly rickety from day one and although my ex-husband considered himself an expert on all things having to do with child-rearing based on his experience with two daughters from his first marriage, I had gone ahead and hired a baby nurse to help me get through the first few weeks. I was working in a pressured, high-level position in book publishing at the time and the shift to being a mother of a newborn—the constant receptivity and the primal feeling of connectedness it demanded—was hard to adjust to. The nurse's name was Maria; she was an older spinster of German extraction and infinite Christian faith who had definite ideas—indeed, a thoroughgoing methodology—about how best to get infants to sleep through the night without too much fretting. Her approach involved putting Zoe down to sleep on her stomach with her head tucked into the right-hand corner of the crib the better to provide her with a secure sense of boundaries, as well as a great deal of rocking and patting on her back. Maria was also a big believer in the power of the pacifier, although its use was already looked down upon, together with that of playpens and walkers, in the fashionable ideology of upper-middle-class childcare. I watched Zoe suck on her pacifier contentedly and imagined that she learned how to provide solace for herself—a psychic process that is described by child developmental experts as "self-soothing"—through finding consolation in that rubbery, invincible nipple. It is Maria to whom I give secret thanks for the core of stability I detect in my daughter. I am convinced that those first few months in her calm hands did Zoe no end of good. I ended up holding on to Maria for far longer than I had originally planned and cried bitter tears when I finally parted from her.

In the wake of Maria's departure, I hired a Jamaican woman in her sixties by the name of Desi, who herself had two grown daughters. She moved slowly and with great dignity and adored my redhaired daughter. Sometimes at night, I would sit in Zoe's room, which had been painstakingly decorated in gentle pastels, and watch Desi massage her legs with Johnson's baby lotion. I loved the smell and the way Desi caressed the folds of soft flesh in my daughter's chubby legs. She was more ambivalent about me, but that was tolerable up until the period my marriage dissolved in earnest, at which point Desi became a casualty of my estranged marital situation, virtually from one day to the next. Desi thought it was a woman's duty to put up with her man and make him happy. She certainly didn't understand why any woman would leave any man—for any reason—and she instinctively sided with my ex-husband. At some point it became untenable, with Desi hissing at me that I was "mad" to want to divorce, and I regretfully let her go.

After Desi came Annie, a beautiful young Jamaican woman with gleaming gold and white teeth and a body that made men stop and stare. Although she was only in her early thirties, she had been married off at the age of fourteen to an older man at her parents' instigation, and had left him as well as four children behind when she came to America. She too took great pleasure in Zoe, who after an initial post-Desi period of wariness, warmed up to Annie with renewed affection. The two of them danced and played together like two children and I can still hear Annie's delighted laughter coming down the hall. Annie eventually left my employ when she no longer wanted to live in, but she still calls from time to time asking after Zoe.

There have been other caretakers for shorter and longer periods of time, but I think Zoe has never forgiven me for casting her asunder from her beloved Annie. I can think of only one woman, a South American who worked for me for about a year, about whom I had suspicions in terms of her treatment of Zoe. Not that I ever saw anything specific, but something about Zoe's submissiveness around her and readiness to kiss her on command made me wonder whether she scared her in some fashion when I wasn't around. I'm not sure, on the other hand, whether I invent this after the fact, to explain away the general sense of unease I had about this woman when I returned from a trip and discovered that not only had she suddenly left without warning but that she had taken some of my jewelry with her.

Needless to say, none of these women bore even the faintest resemblance to Jane. But Jane herself seems part of another world, the world of my parents, with its strict hierarchies and children kept out of sight and mostly out of mind. Sometimes it seems to me when I look back that things can not have been so dark and uncuddly as I remember them. Then again, I can find no evidence that they were otherwise. So you see where all this has left me: outside any useful frame of reference, any illuminating context, except my own. There are Jane's outlines, waiting to be filled in, if only so that she will get up off the page and make herself felt as something other than a flickering, ominous shadow in my head. But it may well be too late for that. These days, everything is gone or in the past—my childhood, Ed Sullivan, Indian Walk, Jane herself—and I am left to conjure with ghosts.

Part Four

Till the Wind Blows
in from the West:
Departures

MISSING JUNE

Suzanne Berne

I have always been a worried person, and having babies brought out the worst of that characteristic in me, as my husband will be the first to tell you, which is why we had so many arguments back then. So it's not surprising that when my older daughter was eight months old and I needed to go back to work, what I really wanted when I went looking for a part-time nanny was someone who was not just responsible and kind and good with children, but who would also assure me that I was doing reasonably well by my baby, that she would persevere in spite of my mistakes, and that in the end we would all be fine. I was overjoyed to be a mother, but often bewildered and exhausted—I loved my daughter to the point where I could hardly sleep for wanting to look at her and make sure she was breathing. Now that she is ten, it's embarrassing to admit how little faith I had that she would survive her first year. But as I said, I've always been a worried person.

Fortuitously, a friend from down the street called to say that she had hired a woman to care for her two children in the afternoons, and the woman was looking for more hours. Would I be interested in meeting her? This particular friend was someone I admired for the calm and practical way she mothered her own children—she did not get up several times in the night to check if they were breathing, but held them easily and good-humoredly when they were awake, fed them organic applesauce, and did not look desperate when they cried. She was vigilant but not hysterical. If she approved of someone enough to leave her children in that person's care, then most likely I would, too, and so I arranged for the woman to come by my house the next day for an interview.

She arrived at my house on a brisk, sunny afternoon wearing a yellow sweatshirt with a picture of a duck on it, sneakers, and ironed denim pants. I will call her June, because there was something tentatively summerlike about her—as if at any moment she might become truly warm instead of just shyly friendly—and because she would not want her real name used. She was small and slender and black, and had a soft Southern accent, which reminded me of the accents in Virginia, where I lived as a child. Though, like me, she was in her early thirties, she had a teenaged son and another who was eleven, and two girls of eight and six. She had worked for a time in a daycare center. I liked her from the moment I saw her on my doorstep.

The first morning June worked for us I stayed downstairs. June played with the baby, who did not cry at all with her, as she did with most people; then she folded laundry while the baby napped. Hesitantly, I had shown June the washer and dryer and a basket of clean laundry, unsure whether laundry was part of childcare, and careful to specify that she needed to do only the baby's laundry. I also asked her to wash only the baby's dishes and pick up only things the baby had left lying about. I suppose I was trying to pretend that June was not my employee but the baby's, for whom I was acting as an all-knowing secretary. In this way I might avoid the awkwardness of having another grown woman in my house, doing what I felt I should be doing myself—only, I hoped, better.

The morning went well. June folded the baby's clothing so neatly that I said it would be a shame to take each tiny shirt and pair of pants out of the drawers again. She smiled but looked uncomfortable when I also complimented her on the excellent way she organized toys on the baby's shelves and on her perfect dicing of pears for the baby's snack. It was a great relief to both of us when the baby woke up shrieking.

Satisfied that June was good at childcare, I went upstairs to my desk. A few minutes later, June took the baby out on a walk in her stroller. I stood by the window watching them go. It occurred to me that June might be a kidnapper. What did I know about her, really? Several of my friends had conducted criminal-background checks on their nannies, something I had neglected to do, mostly because I didn't know how, but also because I found the idea insulting to both parties. I found myself wondering whether I had been negligent, until I recalled that June had four children of her own, and did not seem eager for more, as much as she liked babies. So I sat down at my computer and stared at the screen until I heard the front door open and June's voice quietly informing the baby that she needed a change.

In this way, June became a regular part of our weeks. She came for four hours each day, from eight to twelve. Occasionally she brought along her cheerful younger daughter, who liked to sit and read while June played with the baby. In the time June afforded me, I attended to my teaching demands and managed to finish a novel I had been working on for years. Sometimes she sat with me and had her lunch—always something appetizing like barbecued chicken wings and pasta salad, boxed in a styrofoam container—before she was due at my friend's house for the afternoon. I fed the baby while June ate quickly, then she packed up her carry-all bag to leave.

Gradually I learned that she lived in a housing project in Somerville, that she had recently moved from a small town in Tennessee, where her father still lived, that her husband worked at a local restaurant as a fry cook (he was the source of the appetizing lunches), and that he had a large extended family living nearby, about whom June had mixed feelings. She worried about her older son, who was a good boy, but who sometimes got into trouble. I discovered that she was a doting parent, who could not resist giving her children the presents that she'd bought for them for Christmas two months early, then had to go out and buy more.

Though she did not complain about him, her husband didn't seem to pay her much attention, aside from those good lunches. For instance, despite June's objections, his sisters borrowed money and the car and used the apartment as a crash pad. Worse, in my view, they hardly remembered to say thank you for the birthday presents June gave them. And one day she confided that no one had remembered her birthday, which had just gone by.

Birthdays are unnervingly important in my family. Forgetting to celebrate a relative's birthday is considered worse than refusing to pick him up at the airport, a breach of common humanity—even though having your birthday celebrated can be something of an ordeal beyond the age of twenty. Like holidays, birthdays can emphasize more about what you don't have than what you do and should be approached cautiously, especially with someone you barely know. But for all my worries, I was an incautious person in those days when it came to magnanimous gestures, and so that afternoon I used a precious free hour to bake June a cake while the baby napped, and when my husband got home I went out and bought her a present. I don't remember what it was, probably something small, like a picture frame or a vase. The next day, while June was having lunch, I proudly carried in the cake, with birthday candles, and her name on it in icing, placed it in front of her, and then handed her my wrapped gift. The baby crowed at the sight of the lit candles, I beamed. June's face fell. She looked stricken for just an instant, then she recovered herself and smiled her shy smile and thanked me. She blew out the candles and we ate slices of cake, but a chill had settled in the room, which I did not understand. Opening the present did nothing to dispel that chill, though June said she loved whatever it was and made a little show of being pleased.

The next day she called in sick. It was one of my teaching days and so my husband had to stay home from work, but friends of ours were always dealing with similar situations, so I did not think much of it. I don't think it crossed my mind that our little birthday celebration of the day before could have had anything to do with June's absence, and perhaps it never crossed her mind, either. June had been with us for about six months and was very responsible. She was back the next morning and everything went on as before.

Except an odd sort of strain developed between us. June began to talk more openly of her disappointments at home, to confide in me about her husband's sisters, who took things and did not return them, who ate up her food, who slept in her living room for weeks when they were supposed to stay only a few days. I confided in her about my worries about the baby, who had suddenly decided that she did not like strangers, following a round of vaccinations at fifteen months, and began to scream all the time. But at the end of these sessions, neither of us looked relieved. I felt June was talking too much, and that I was listening to her instead of getting my work done. She probably thought I was fussy, which I had the luxury to be, with only one child, a house of my own in a safe neighborhood, an attentive husband, and relatives who always made a big deal over my birthday. That I was also white went without saying.

I discovered that I was pregnant again. I complained to June about my morning sickness and tiredness, as well as about the baby's tantrums, which were coming more and more frequently and lasting so long that sometimes whole afternoons disappeared into them. June complained about her husband's sisters and her children's bad schools.

We depressed each other. I think June believed, and somehow needed to believe, that middle-class white families had everything—

privacy, security, nice houses—the kind of everything that could be bestowed, like presents, but more arbitrarily. Just as I believed that people with "calm" children who smiled instead of screamed when someone said hello to them, had everything. (And how I envied June her calm and reasonable children, whom I believed must be calm and reasonable because of her superior parenting, back in the days when I thought parents were entirely responsible for the way their children turned out.) Probably we each wanted to shout at the other, "Are you crazy? Look how lucky you are!" But the truth was, we were neither of us more nor less fortunate than the other, at least at that time, though our benefits and deficits were quite different, and a few gifts, like a few reassurances, weren't going to tip the balance for us either way.

And yet, it wasn't as simple as that, either.

Added to the strange mix of dependency and confused resentment that was building between us was June's very real affection for the baby, who loved her in return, and whose screaming didn't seem to bother June as much as it did me. June tended to take our pediatrician's view that the baby was simply "spirited," the euphemism in vogue at the time, although June's more tolerable word was "noisy."

I had lost several pregnancies before my daughter was conceived, and my anxiety about her baffling behavior floated atop a secret reservoir of fear that I had "harmed" her during my pregnancy by worrying that I would lose her. Because I'd been a nervous wreck, my baby was now one, too. That was my reasoning. June could not allay this fear, any more than I could allay hers that she was harming her own children by not being able to provide them with all the things I was able to give to mine. Her older son had a brief run-in with the police. Her second son was doing poorly in school. One of her daughters had a first-grade teacher who yelled too much, and then there were those lousy relatives and their bad boyfriends and bad habits, always hanging around the apartment.

It was not fair, after all my troubles, that I should have a difficult baby. It was not fair that June had to live in a housing project and couldn't persuade her husband to banish his freeloading sisters. Well, that's life, you'll probably say. Well, of course. But neither of us seemed able to accept our lives as they were, and so we continued complaining and depressing each other. Meanwhile my due date got closer. The baby screamed louder. She was also talking. Her first complete sentence was, "I'm a little bit anxious."

A fairly sophisticated statement for a child of twenty-two months, which, now that I think of it, should have given me a certain confidence in her future, even though she was parroting her mother. But then, she could have said, "I feel a little sick," which I announced just as frequently. Maybe she was having tantrums all those years because she had complicated things to say and not enough words to say them. Certainly all the testing we put her through failed to produce another, more convincing, explanation, and these days she is a wonderfully intelligent and reasonably calm person, a startlingly beautiful and gifted girl, who promises to become a fascinating adult, and of whom I am intensely proud. If only back then someone could have shown me a picture of who she is now, both her early childhood and my early years of motherhood might have been very different. Unfortunately, there are no background checks one can run on the future.

On the morning of Christmas Eve, three weeks before the baby was due, June gave my daughter a lovely little fleece jacket and booties. I gave June a large bonus, more than we could probably afford, and several gifts, which I had gone to great trouble to buy and wrap, although I barely managed to give my husband anything and for the first time in my life ordered gifts for my sisters and parents through catalogs. I did not closely examine why I was giving June so many gifts, it simply seemed important to do so. This might be all she gets, I recall telling myself grimly.

June exclaimed at the sight of her presents, which she hastily placed, unopened, in her carry-all bag. She did not open the card which held her bonus check, but tucked it into her bag as well. I felt this was discreet and appropriate of her. I did not want to be thanked. I was already too aware of the big balsam Christmas tree in our living room, decorated with pretty glass ornaments (June had told me she had a white plastic tree, which she left up all year), the fir branches we had placed on the fireplace mantel, the bright jumble of gifts sent by my mother and my sisters and my husband's family. Everything looked just the way Christmas was supposed to look—in my family—and I would have given a great deal to have it all over and done with. I hugged June as she was leaving that day, and wished her a happy Christmas. She clung to me for a moment, then said she would see us next week.

I was not entirely surprised when she called the day she was supposed to return to work to say that her daughter had the flu. By then I had noticed that following a vacation or a three-day weekend, June often did not come to work for one reason or another. She always seemed sorry to say good-bye to us, but then equally reluctant to return.

However, she was back by the following Friday, looking nervous. She did not say much when I asked how her daughter was feeling; my questions about her Christmas went unanswered. But as was always the case, she embraced my daughter tenderly and appeared to be glad to return to our house. She liked us, I realized, more than the idea of us.

My second daughter was born the following week. From the beginning she was an easy, uncomplicated baby, who smiled and laughed and seemed delighted to be alive; but naturally a new baby made more work for everyone, though I took care of her, for the most part, and let June continue along pretty much as she had been with my older daughter, whose behavior, unfortunately, got worse. As throwing tantrums was supposed to be a "normal" reaction to having a new sibling, no one seemed very concerned about her but me and my husband, who was finally starting to worry. We read dozens of parenting books and not only was none of the advice helpful to us, none of the children they described seemed like our child. I tried for a long time to believe that it was me, that if I could just find the right way to be a mother, she would find the right way to be a child, until I had to believe something else.

If someday my daughter reads this essay, I hope she'll understand that our fears were for her and her future, not ours, and that if we had to go through it all again to have her as our daughter, we would, because she is one of the great gifts of our lives and nothing could ever replace her. But back then we had no idea what we were facing and we became frightened. We stopped inviting friends to dinner. We stopped letting relatives sleep at our house. We did not talk to people about our daughter's difficulties, afraid of making them seem permanent to ourselves. Only June knew what our life at home was really like. And only with June did my daughter seem to relax a little.

I gave June a raise. I gave her a scarf and a pair of leather gloves. I gave her an advance copy of my novel, inscribed: "To June, without whose help I could not have finished this book. Thank you for everything."

A week later, June disappeared. She came to work on Friday, but the following Monday I got a call from her husband, who told me that June's father was sick and that June was in Tennessee taking care of him. She would be back the following week. I was not teaching that semester in order to be with the new baby, so June's sudden absence did not pose the hardship it would have earlier, except that every day back then was a hardship. But the next Monday also came and went without June, or any word from her either. I called her apartment and spoke to a woman who confirmed tersely that June was in Tennessee. No, she did not know when June would be back.

Weeks passed. My husband and I joked gloomily that maybe June had read my novel and hated it, that she was secretly a literary critic. Again and again I called her apartment, unable to accept that she might not be coming back, at least to work for me. I knew she would not leave her own children for long, especially with relatives she didn't trust. I knew she'd be back. But no one who answered would tell me anything about June, though they stopped mentioning the sick father.

My daughter's grief broke my heart. It made no sense to her that June would vanish without saying good-bye, June who had been her loving friend and uncritical companion, who never looked flustered or tense or angry when she fell into a tantrum, who never hung over her crib, hissing, "Stop it, stop it." It did not make sense to me, either. I could understand, eventually, that June never wanted to see me again. But she had cared about my daughter. She was a mother. She understood the feelings of children. And this was a child so much more sensitive than most, who registered every disappointment, every deviation from routine the way a leaf registers a breeze. A child who also never gave up on her disappointments, but repeated her demands for whatever she'd lost over and over and over.

How could June not visit, one last time, to say good-bye? Could she simply not bear to?

After a while we got used to her being gone. We had a lot of other things to think about. My daughter started preschool two mornings a week that fall. We found someone else to come in from eight till noon. I started another novel. Yet I never stopped wondering what had happened to June, or how she could have left us so suddenly. (She had left my friend and her family, too, of course, but as their children were starting school, they didn't seem to mind very much.) How could June not want to know how our story had turned out and whether our struggle to understand our child had led us to any discoveries? Wasn't she curious about how my daughter was growing up?

Several years went by. Then one Halloween, I was standing with my children on a neighbor's doorstep, when I recognized a young girl coming up the walkway, dressed as a bumblebee. It was June's daughter.

June herself was nowhere to be seen. But a moment later I saw my neighbor's privet hedge rustle and realized that June was ducking down behind it, trying to peer at my girls through the branches. I called to her and she stood up, looking embarrassed. I said I was glad to see her, then told the girls who she was. June smiled in a small agony of apology. My older daughter looked shocked. Whoever she had been remembering over the past years when she said she was "missing June" no longer bore any resemblance to the woman standing in front of her. June and I chatted for a few strained minutes. Then she said she had to go. We never saw her again.

I don't know if June came back to our neighborhood to see my daughter—on a night when she knew we were likely to be out on the sidewalks, when crowds of other people would be around as well and she could pass by unnoticed—or because it was a neighborhood where she knew she could safely take her own child trick-or-treating. My guess is that both impulses drew her. Just as she must have had more than one reason for disappearing without telling us good-bye: Our daughter had become too difficult. The addition of another child was too daunting. We had too many of the things she wanted for herself and her own family and the contrast became painful. Someone offered her a better job. Any of them, all of them. Who knows. She would have been too shy to try to explain.

Frankly, I no longer care very much about June or why she left us so suddenly, though I cared more before I began this essay. She was a woman who looked after my child for a while during a hard time. I will always be grateful for the hours she provided me to get my work done, and for her kindness to my daughter. I will never forgive her for her cowardice, and the sadness she caused.

Perhaps it's because of June that I no longer have patience with people like the young mother I once was, who believed that she could give someone else what that person didn't have, whether it was birthday gifts, or a calm disposition, or the assurance that everything will be fine in the end. My daughter grew calmer on her own, or maybe as a result of one of the many things we tried with her, because we could afford to take her to specialists and we were desperate and inventive. (Though the only truly helpful advice I received during those years came from an elderly child psychologist I met at a party, who said, "Your child will receive all sorts of diagnoses, and they will all sound terrifying. Just try to remember, probably none of them will turn out to be true.")

Meanwhile June has gone on to have whatever life she is now living. Presumably she is still in Somerville; her daughters must be in high school now. She was black and poor, I was white and middle class. You can explain or excuse a lot of things about us given that set of variables, and still miscalculate the truth. Which is that we were both worried during much of the time we spent together and neither of us could do much about it. Except try not to make each other's life any harder, and it seems we both failed on that count.

INFLAMMITIS OF THE
AFFLUENTITIS

Rebecca Walker

I believe we coined the term in the sixth month of my pregnancy, to describe a certain seven-hundred-fifty-dollar stroller. We were in the car, on our way to the grocery store for provisions. My life partner and father of my soon-to-be-born child, a warmhearted Buddha of a man I'll call Vaj, was looking for a way to describe what had become an outright obsession for me: the right stroller.

The last three weeks had been a study in comparison shopping. I had analyzed each and every Maclaren, the entire Peg Perego line, the Graco travel systems, and of course, the au courant Rolls-Royce of strollers, the Bugaboo. After considering pluses and minuses ad nauseam, it was no surprise to Vaj or me that even though I found it heavy, cumbersome, and completely incompatible with our lifestyle, the Bugaboo, with its award-winning design and Scandinavian provenance, was at the top of my list.

But it was so decadent, so showy, so seemingly unnecessary, that I needed to enlist Vaj in the decision-making process. I needed him to tell me how practical and lovely the aubergine-colored carriage was, how absolutely indispensable, so that I could buy it without feeling so darn guilty.

To my dismay, Vaj would not oblige. Easing our generic, American-made SUV into a parking space, he shrugged his shoulders and told me he didn't want to get into it. "No matter what I think," he said, "you're going to buy whatever you want anyway."

Huh?

"Get into what?" I asked, feigning ignorance. Vaj stole a look at me out of the corner of his eye. "You know. The whole inflammitis of the affluentitis thing you get hooked into."

"Inflammitis of the affluentitis?" I repeated back, a huge grin on my face. Vaj is known to call a catchy truism, and I had a hunch this was going to be a keeper.

"Yes," he said. "Inflammitis of the affluentitis, the age-old disease in which affluent people go ballistic with their affluence, and get so preoccupied with their own wealth they buy things they don't need and which sometimes don't even work."

"Inflammitis of the affluentitis," I said again, laughing uproariously. "That is fucking genius. Let's call it I.A. for short. But I'm still getting the Bugaboo!" And then we both burst into peals of laughter, and rolled our shopping cart into the store.

It wasn't the first (or last) discussion we had about class, but it was pivotal. We had discovered the first phrase of our own lexicon, a workable language we would use to discuss our different backgrounds and values, and how they played out in our relationship. I.A. was perfect because it was hilarious without being judgmental, spot-on without being divisive.

After that conversation, Vaj and I began to identify I.A. traits and characteristics wherever we went, fleshing out the dimensions of our new discovery.

I noticed, for instance, that I.A. people tend to congregate in I.A. ghettos, places we believe are "diverse communities made up of all kinds of people from every possible background" but which are really inhabited only by people like us.

We also tend to be dangerously dependent upon magazines, newspapers, and other readily identified cultural arbiters to tell us what movies to see, food to eat, doctors to go to, and neighborhoods to live in. We don't like to think of ourselves as sheep, but that's essentially what we are.

Finally, for the purpose of this essay, I.A. people tend to be wholly convinced of the superiority of their overall aesthetic. They believe the objects they aspire to possess are objects everyone aspires to possess, and if someone doesn't, there must be something wrong with them. Organic vegetables come to mind, and expensive European cars. Outdoor umbrella seating at restaurants, and Manolo Blahniks. Multiple homes, and of course, a staff to run them. A staff that includes, you guessed it, a nanny.

I can hear the grumbles now. What parental unit *doesn't* want a gentle giant to care for their child while they're out swapping lifeblood for college tuition? What sane person would not give anything, like their right arm or at least their spare bedroom, for an unsexy bilingual angel who can cook delicious meals for their family involving grass-fed beef and organic leeks?

But that's another I.A. trait. It is almost impossible for us to recognize the degree to which we buy into objects and trends largely to affirm their value to each other. It is astonishing for the average I.A. person to consider that the other ninety-five-plus percent of the human population doesn't really give a damn about what we think and buy, and when they do, it is usually to criticize our gullibility. (When pressed, Vaj describes I.A. people as living lives "completely driven by the American marketing machine.")

The fact is that the other ninety-five-plus percent of the population have their own list of stuff they think is right and cool and decent and good. And here's what I've learned: Giving someone else your kids to raise, if you don't absolutely have to, isn't on it.

*   *   *

I WOULD BE LYING if I said this didn't come as a shock to me. I am a child of the women's movement, which means I understand the urgent need for female self-determination, and good childcare is arguably a huge part of that. I am also a child of Reaganomics, which means I understand the impossibility of living well on one salary, and decent childcare is definitely a huge part of that.

Natch, I myself grew up in the care of several rotating babysitters, and my mother always told me that having a career and kids would be, if not easy, then at least easier for me than it was for her, because I would have a nanny.

When I finally did get pregnant, the issue of "finding someone" became a central theme. If I wasn't obsessing over it, someone in my family or circle of friends most certainly was. "You should find someone before the baby is born," one dear, childless friend said to me. "The two of them will bond right away, which will make the transition easier when you have to leave."

When I have to leave? I thought to myself, patting my stomach protectively.

But I knew what she was talking about. I had hired people to take care of Samuel, the son I parented with my ex for eight years. I hired them to take care of him when, between lectures in different cities and recording sessions in different countries, we just couldn't. And I can't say I wasn't grateful. Like, I-am-adding-an-extra-hundred-dollars-to-your-paycheck-this-week-because-if-it-wasn't-for-you-my-entire-life-would-be-falling-apart grateful.

But "finding someone" also had its problems.

There was one young woman, I'll call her Kaya, that we hired to drive Samuel to school in the mornings. His school was on the other side of town and depending on traffic, dropping him off could become a two-hour commute—four if you added the afternoon pickup.

Initially it worked out fairly well. Kaya had baby dreadlocks,

drove a shiny new hybrid vehicle, and taught kids about soil con-
servation at various elementary schools in the area. She was beautiful and reliable and Samuel seemed to enjoy her company. My
partner and I enjoyed being able to work or sleep in the mornings
without worrying that Sam would be late for school, or that one of
us would be so worn out from driving we would lose the better part
of the workday.

But from the very beginning it was awkward. Like every other
caregiver I had hired for our son, Kaya was more than a little bit
starstruck. Not by me, I am afraid, but by my partner, a singer and
musician with a cult-like following. In the beginning it wasn't a
problem because our interaction beyond the initial getting-to-
know-you stage was limited: She drove up and honked her horn.

As the weeks went on, though, Kaya began to show up earlier
and earlier. First we saw her leaning against her car by the curb as
she waited for Sam, and then we watched her stroll through our
front yard and sit on the grass. Then one fine autumn day, without
knocking, she walked right through the front door.

What could we do? Sam was in the shower, at least half an hour
away from being ready. Because we both worked at home, to the
untrained eye it appeared we had nothing better to do than hang
out with whomever happened by. Why fight it? We offered her a
cup of tea.

Over that first cup of yerba mate we learned that Kaya was an
aspiring musician, and would be "honored" to learn a few things
from the musician of the house. Could she bring her guitar over one
morning? What was it like to be on the road? Who had we met?
Could she come along one day? As she unfurled her wish list, she
made quite a bit of eye contact with "the musician of the house,"
and even though I prepared her tea and signed her checks, she made
me feel almost invisible.

When you grow up in the toxic haze of fame, that creepy feeling
of invisibility is almost always a sign. The worshipful questions are

signs, too, because they tell you things. Such as that the person speaking has little or no idea that you are an actual *person* with bad days and real emotional needs. Or that the person has an agenda, a plan for your involvement in their life that goes considerably beyond the plan you have for your involvement in their life.

If you have fielded questions like these over a lifetime, it is quite unlikely that a person who asks them will end up in your home, taking care of your child. But there she was.

Because we were desperate for a break, and so truly grateful for the difference she was making in our lives, and because we felt an obligation to be role models of some kind to young African American women with creative ambitions, we tolerated Kaya. We even grew to like her.

It wasn't long, though, before I discerned that Kaya also suffered from depression. Which made her a prime candidate for my own codependent, save-the-world-by-saving-one-depressed-person-at-a-time addiction, a remnant of a childhood spent fruitlessly trying to take care of my often depressed mother, or at least make her happy.

In other words, I couldn't stop myself. Kaya sat in our kitchen drinking tea and telling me she felt ugly, untalented, and unsure of her future. And I leapt into the vortex like there was gold at the bottom. I drew her out, affirmed her positive qualities, recommended medications, therapists, ashrams. In the whirl of it all, I forgot to think about how her mental state might affect my son. I also failed to notice how drained and depleted I was after she had gone.

There were other problems, too. I didn't like that I was no longer the last familiar face ushering Sam into the public realm every morning. I missed hearing about his dreams as we barreled down the freeway. I was losing track of how he was doing in English and Social Studies, his least favorite subjects.

In the end, however, it boiled down to boundaries, and how I needed better ones.

Having a stranger involved in the intimacy of our lives was

wonderful at some times, intrusive and complicated at others. For starters, who were we when Kaya was around? Not ourselves, surely. We were on display: the famous musician and the empathic writer. We were employers, role models, and potential mentors, all of which involved a level of performance we both found exhausting.

It wasn't just that, and it wasn't just Kaya. Every person who worked for us became a de facto member of our family—otherwise, how else could the bond stick—and this made for several unholy alliances; quiet unions in which two sided, ever so subtly, against the third. In which there was always an outlet, another person to turn to when the two of us, the parents, the couple, should have turned only to each other.

None of the people we hired over the years worked for us full-time, but when they did work for us, our family lost the exclusivity it needed to have to be fortified against predictable intruders, both internal and external. We became more like an exclusive club than a family, with one or two constantly rotating memberships.

I STARTED TALKING WITH VAJ about nannies during the first month of my pregnancy. How were we going to afford one, and once we figured that out, should she speak French, Spanish, or Mandarin? I had forgotten about Kaya, and now saw only my full speaking schedule and looming book deadline on the other side of my rapidly expanding belly.

But Vaj didn't oblige me here, either, and instead responded with a discussion about the benefits of pushing oneself to be there for your child even when you feel you can't possibly manage. "That is what parenting is," he told me in the seventh month, in the eighth month, and again in the ninth. "That is what parenting is and that is what intimacy is, showing up and showing up again, over and over until you die. Intimacy is not sending a surrogate, and it is extremely I.A. of you to think that it could be."

"Intimacy isn't about letting your child starve because you're afraid of missing an important moment either," I countered for the ninety-second time. "No," he said, "but intimacy is worth sacrificing for. We can live more simply. We can work part-time. Between the two of us, we can make it work."

Huh?

Even though I knew he was right, my I.A. beliefs were blazing. I just couldn't imagine how I could be the fully realized woman I had always envisioned without striving like crazy at work, and doing the best I could at home. That's what everybody I knew did. They didn't try to make it work. They let somebody else come and work.

But Vaj was still talking, reminding me that there is no shortcut for providing a stable foundation for a child. When I thought about my own life, I had to agree. My childhood ended when my parents divorced and started spending more time building their careers than nurturing their families. From that point on, I craved more from them: time, attention, the monotonous routine of family life. If you had asked me what I wanted back then, I certainly would not have said my own, private nanny.

As it happened, psychobiology took over. My due date drew nearer and nearer, and the idea of handing my newborn son over to anyone, even his grandparents, grew less and less appealing. He was going to go from *inside my body* into the arms of someone I had met only a couple of times? Over my dead body.

Once he was born, the idea took on a whole new level of absurdity. I was going to crack open this incredible cocoon we had built over the last nine months to let in a complete stranger? Someone who could leave at any time and had no long-term investment in the health and well-being of this tiny, vulnerable creature I had just risked my life to bring into the world?

The mere thought brought tears to my eyes.

And so, ten months later, here we are. I've long ago sold the Buga-boo on eBay, and am writing this to the hiss of the baby monitor that has become a permanent fixture by my side. I am dangerously sleep-deprived, two months late in getting my book to the publisher, and I would swim through a swamp filled with crocodiles for a spontaneous and prohibitively expensive trip to Tahiti.

But in a week or two my vacation would be over. If I am lucky and play my cards right, I'll have my son for the rest of my life.

MADAME

Roxana Robinson

n the early 1970s, when I was in my twenties, things seemed very good. I was married to a smart, funny, handsome man. My husband had a job that he loved, and I had a job that I loved. We lived in New York, on Gramercy Park. In the evenings I used to go running there, doing lap after lap around the leafy green square, and it was cool and pleasant, and I felt as though I could run forever. It seemed to me that the world was a transparent and benevolent place, one that I could move through with contentment and accomplishment, like a fish swimming through clear water. When I became pregnant, it deepened my sense of all this. It seemed as though it would take only effort and foresight to attain the things I wanted.

Our apartment would be too small for three, so we moved to a pretty brick townhouse in the West Village, on a quiet garden block. Our house had four floors, and we rented out the basement flat and lived in the top three. The first floor was very formal, and we hardly ever used it. It was composed entirely of two elegant, high-ceilinged parlors, separated by sliding etched-glass doors. In them were two marble fireplaces, a crystal chandelier, our best furniture, and a little closet which we'd made into a bar. On the second floor was the tiny narrow kitchen, the dining room, and our bedroom. On the top floor was the baby's room, the guest room, and the French nanny's room, though we didn't yet have the French nanny.

At that time I worked at an English auction house, in the Paintings Department. I was in the American Paintings Department, where my job was to catalog the pictures we sold. I was to find out as much as possible about each one, so I spent my time studying the history of American art, and learning the work of American painters: This was fascinating to me. In our department we were all Americans, but in the other paintings departments—Old Masters, Contemporary, and Modern—almost everyone was either English or French. Our clients were from all over the world, and on the wall were four clocks, marked NEW YORK, LONDON, LOS ANGELES, and TOKYO.

It was a wonderful place to work. We were all there because we loved art, and we sold some of the most exquisite things in the world. We were performing a kind of alchemy, doing simultaneous translation from the history of aesthetics into the history of economics. We enabled people to translate art into wealth, and wealth into art. Because great art has always carried with it intimations of social standing, this gave the auction house a certain cachet. The cachet was enhanced by our internationalism, our sophisticated cultural complexity, which deepened the connections between art and social elevation.

I loved going there each day, and it never occurred to me to quit because I was going to have a baby. Remember, this was during the '70s, and it was not the fashion to stay at home with your child. It was the fashion to go out and fulfill yourself, and demonstrate that biology was not destiny. On Wall Street, where my husband worked, I'd heard that women competed to see who could get back to the office fastest, after childbirth. I planned to stay at home for a few months, and then go back to work. So I needed a nanny.

I wanted a French nanny: I was in love with everything French. I loved the supple and mellifluous language, which I had always wanted to speak rapidly and fluently, with a perfect Parisian accent. If I had a French nanny, I would be able to offer this priceless linguistic gift to my child, for which she would be forever grateful. Also, if I had a French nanny, my own French would improve. My husband spoke fluent French, and as soon as we had our nanny, our household would become a tiny but distinguished Gallic islet.

I also loved the elegance of the French, their sophistication. I loved the fact that they cared so much about culture, and possessed such incomparable style. I wanted my baby to grow up with all of this. I wanted *je ne sais quoi* to be part of her air. I wanted to add a layer of cultural complexity, European elegance, to our household, like the one there was at work. All this seemed accessible: I had the husband, the house, and the job I had wanted, and soon I would have the baby. I also wanted the nanny.

I don't remember, now, how it was that I found Madame, but I remember how I felt when I did: I had found my dream.

Madame was Parisian, in her early sixties, tall, and beautifully erect. Her thick white hair, parted on one side, lay in dense curls against her head. Her Gallic nose was high and noble, and her eyes were dark and large and liquid. Her teeth were slightly crowded, and her chin recessive, but her hands were exquisite. They were pale and slim, with narrow tapering fingers and oval nails. Right now, as I write this, the French word comes back to me: *les ongles*, and I think of Madame's smooth, shapely fingernails. She often held her beautiful hands folded at her waist, in a gesture both modest and elegant. And her fluid, melodious accent nearly brought tears to my eyes.

Madame had a full bosom, a thick waist, and narrow legs. She wore crisp white blouses and dark straight skirts, stockings, and neat, low, lace-up heels. Over her clothes she wore a three-quarter-length peach-colored cotton smock. The smock made me very happy: It was perfect. It was not a uniform, she was not obliterating her individuality behind the mask of servitude. Nor was it ordinary clothing, a pretense that she did not have a task to perform. It was a practical acknowledgment of her situation. I was grateful that she understood the subtleties and complexities of this issue, and I was impressed by her response.

I had fallen in love with Madame at once, but I followed procedure. I'd asked her for a reference, and she gave me a name and phone number. Responsibly, I called. A man answered. Monsieur was impeccably courteous. He had an accent as thick as Brie, which awed me at once.

Yes, M. confirmed, Madame had worked for his family.

There was a silence.

And, I went on clumsily, you liked her? She was fine?

Because of M.'s heavy accent, I found myself speaking abbreviated English, nearly pidgin, though he was clearly very fluent in my language.

She was punctual, said M.

I wondered if he'd mistaken the word, despite his fluency in English. Had he meant to say punctilious? Should I ask him to clarify, or would that be rude? Punctual was an odd adjective to use.

She was? I asked, floundering.

Yes, he said.

And that was all. I was too timid and too confused to ask any more.

Thank you very much, Monsieur, I said.

It is my pleasure, he answered, and we hung up.

The conversation was bewildering—who knew what he'd intended to say? But I convinced myself that it was insignificant: I had found my French nanny. She was experienced, responsible, loving, and punctual. And she was Parisian. I don't remember interviewing anyone else.

The week before the baby was due Madame arrived at our house with her modest luggage. My husband had not met her—he left these things up to me. When I introduced the two of them, Madame offered him her beautiful pale hand. *"Enchantée, monsieur."*

During the interview, we had discussed Madame's duties. Or rather, Madame had explained to me what her duties would be. At her preceding job, she told me, she had done nothing but look after *le bébé*. No housework, no dishes, no laundry, no cooking—except for *le bébé*. She would keep the baby's room clean, do her laundry and cooking, and wash her dishes.

Bon, bon, I answered, nodding knowledgeably. *Ça va*, I said, *d'accord*, though I had been hoping she'd do more.

At the time I had a cleaning lady who came in once a week, for half a day. Even if I asked her for a full day, then who, as I was nodding and agreeing that Madame would do none of this, did I think was going to do the food shopping for all of us? Who did I think would carry the laundry down three flights of stairs and down the block to the laundromat? For though our house had two elegant parlors and four bedrooms, it had no washer or dryer—our tiny kitchen didn't even have a dishwasher. Who did I think was going to cook dinner every night, and wash the dishes? If the answer to all these questions was me, then when was I ever going to see the baby? The answer to none of these questions was my husband; I knew that without asking. (During the '70s, there was much excited talk from feminists about men sharing household duties, but there was very little enthusiastic response from men about this sharing. In fact, my husband believed in the strict division of labor, and he believed that my sphere of responsibility was the house and everything in it. This was fine with me, as I thought I *should* be in charge of the house and everything in it. There were other things over which we disagreed, but this was not one of them.)

Since I couldn't answer any of these questions, I thought it best to ignore them. In fact, I don't now remember even considering them. I simply thought that I could manage. I think I thought I would do all those things myself.

The baby—my daughter—arrived exactly on schedule. I fell in love with her at once, and for a while after the birth, I stayed in bed, recuperating, and worshipping the new arrival. Madame, in her neat smock, her tidy white curls, attended me.

"*Bonjour*, Madame," she said, smiling, each morning. She was charming—courteous without being deferential, respectful without being fawning.

"*Bonjour*, Madame," I would reply, in my best accent.

Madame and I (we addressed each other as "Madame," which I hoped made us both into Parisians) conversed always in French. This did, in fact, improve my language skills. It also meant that, in a crisis, I would probably not know exactly what was going on, and I would certainly not be sure I could say exactly what I meant, under stress, but none of this had not occurred to me. I believed that the world was benevolent, that I could manage whatever arose, and that a crisis would not occur.

Madame had also explained during our interview that she would not be able to get up with the baby during the night. She needed her sleep, she told me.

Ça va, I'd said, again, *d'accord*. I'd nodded as though this were my idea.

I didn't mind getting up with the baby, I told myself. How bad could it be? And anyway, what were my options? My husband, I knew, would not get up in the night with the baby. I would do it myself.

For a while I stayed at home, with my beautiful and irresistible baby. I didn't mind getting up in the night with her, since I could sleep all morning. Deep in my sleep I'd hear her sudden, distant wail on the intercom, like a cry from my own heart. I got up as though I were drawn on a tide, and I hurried upstairs. Each time, I couldn't wait to see her, so tiny and vital, so helpless and needy. I took her in my arms, in the darkened, silent house.

Much later, when I woke again, it was morning, and the sun came into our bedroom—for we were in the back, overlooking the gardens. Madame brought the baby in to me and then she stood nearby, smiling, her pale hands folded over her smock, waiting to take the baby away again when I wished. It was very civilized. The baby gained weight. My French improved. I don't remember who did the laundry.

Then the head of the Paintings Department called to say that our department had received a large and important collection. I was needed to help prepare the catalog. Would I be able, he asked, in his plummy English accent, to come back to work much sooner than I'd planned? Right away, actually?

I was flattered by the request—perhaps it meant that I was indispensable? And I had been planning on going back anyway. Moreover, I was incapable of saying no to anything.

Remember how I kept nodding and saying *bon, d'accord*?

I went back to work.

Each morning my adorable baby was brought in to me as soon as I woke up. She stayed with me until I was ready to leave, when I'd kiss her good-bye and set off for work. Each evening when I came home, she was presented, clean and smiling, in a fresh nightie, like a beautiful present. I had my wonderful job back, and I had my adorable baby as well. You see how well things were going? Though it's true that I was tired, increasingly tired, because my adorable baby was not yet sleeping through the night, and I could no longer sleep through the morning.

Then my friend Barbara came to stay. I loved Barbara, who was smart, candid, and warm. She was in New York on business, and during the day, between meetings, she was in the house while I was at work. In the evenings, we all had dinner together.

When she left, Barbara thanked me, and then said there was something she thought she should tell me. I stiffened: These are not words you ever want to hear.

"I thought I should tell you," Barbara said, "that your nanny doesn't take the baby outside. The baby never leaves her room. I thought you'd want to know."

I stared at her.

Surely Madame and I had discussed this? Someone had given us a grand English pram, navy blue with great chrome wheels. The baby was meant to go out in it every day. Surely that wasn't on the list of things Madame had explained to me that she wouldn't do?

"I'm sure she does," I said weakly.

Barbara shook her head firmly. "I've watched."

"Are you sure?"

She nodded.

I said nothing for a long moment.

I didn't know what I was going to say to Madame, later, and I also didn't know what I was going to say to Barbara, now. Almost worse than the fear that the nanny was delinquent was the shameful fact that my friend knew more than I did about my own child. Every day I left the house thinking that I was in charge, but this notion was perhaps pure folly. What if I were wrong about everything? I felt as though a thief had snuck into my life.

"I'll talk to Madame," I said to Barbara. "Thanks for telling me."

I really was grateful to Barbara for telling me—of course I'd rather know—but I also resented it. And I could not help resenting the source. For a long time, when I thought of Barbara it was with resentment, as though she had somehow damaged me.

This feeling was heightened by something else. One night Barbara had overheard a terrible fight between my husband and me. It had been really bad, frighteningly bad. She couldn't have helped but hear it. In the morning, when I saw her, I was ashamed and embarrassed, and did not know whether to mention it apologetically or to pretend it had not happened. Surely something like this was a part of married life, wasn't it? Didn't all marriages have these sinking black horrors in them? Or did they? Was ours worse than everyone else's? I didn't dare ask. I was afraid that ours was worse. How did you know what other people's marriages were like? Like the baby not leaving the room, the fight seemed shameful to me, another evidence of my inability to run my household—or my life—properly. I decided to say nothing at all about the fight to Barbara, but now that she had delivered this unwelcome information about the nanny, I couldn't help but feel that she was privy to the worst recesses of my life.

And I had no idea of how to speak to Madame.

I was in my early twenties, and I did not have an inkling of how to reprimand a sixty-year-old Frenchwoman. Moreover I had no wish to do so. It was Barbara's fault, it seemed, that Madame was no longer as responsible as she had seemed, my marriage no longer as solid. I wanted things to run smoothly, and I had no plans for what to do if they did not. What I did not want to do was start over. The thought of looking for a new nanny, now, was terrifying. The baby was no longer an abstraction, as she had been during my pregnancy. She was now a real person, the most valuable presence in my life. The idea of finding someone new, of allowing a new face into the household, someone to whom I could entrust the baby, made me nearly choke with fear. But I could see that I might have to start over, I began to feel that things were more precarious than I had imagined.

I spoke to Madame.

"I'd like to know," I said in French, "if you take the baby outside every day."

Madame smiled and blinked in astonishment, tilting her head.

But of course not, she said.

She seemed amazed that I should ask.

Certainly not. I come in and play with her, she is adorable, but carry her downstairs and outside, no, no.

Madame smiled kindly and shook her white curls, waiting for me to understand how absurd it was for me to ask.

I paused, uncertain. I looked at Madame, her thick middle, her narrow legs, her sensible—but still, high—heels. I thought about her carrying the baby down three flights of stairs, back up again. The question of physical capability hung in the air, unspoken, the sudden great fear of her falling.

Did this mean I would have to find another nanny?

Later, I said to my husband, "Actually, I'd rather not have her taking the baby up and down those stairs. It's too dangerous, three flights. I can take her out myself, on the weekends." My husband agreed.

It was winter then, and the days were raw and cold. The weather was not good for babies' outings. I wanted things to keep on as they were, without disruption. We had no more guests, so there were no more witnesses to the fights between my husband and me, which continued. Madame, who must certainly have been aware of them, was not exactly a friend, and thus was not exactly a witness. In some ways it seemed as though she was blind and deaf to our lives—or this was what I allowed myself to believe. She never hinted in any way that she was aware of disharmony. What I wanted, so deeply, was for things to go smoothly, in that pretty high-ceilinged house.

It was my husband who noticed the bottles in the little drinks cupboard, down in the back parlor, where we rarely went. They seemed to be losing their contents, the levels dropping steadily. When he told me this, we stared at each other.

"Are you sure?" I asked. He nodded. We didn't drink much ourselves, almost never during the week. We didn't keep any wine, just bottles for the bar—vodka, gin, whiskey. My husband drank Jack Daniels.

Could someone in our own household be drinking our liquor? It couldn't be true, we told each other. We didn't even hint at who the culprit might be.

My husband made tiny marks on the bottles, showing the levels. We waited. We told each other that it must have been the plumber who came in that time to fix the sink. We guessed that it was the meter man, or a bold delivery boy, ducking furtively into the back parlor on his way out.

What you fear, all the time, as a young mother, is that you are doing something wrong. That there is some error you are making, that you have already made, that might be irreversible, some terrible mistake that you will rue for the rest of your life. Most of the time this doesn't happen. Babies are tough, and they mostly survive falls, fevers, broken limbs. Still you worry, still you wake in the night, your throat tight with fear at a close call, a missed hint.

The levels in the bottles dropped steadily. Vodka, gin, bourbon—it didn't seem to matter. Still, for as long as I could, I put off the moment of reckoning. I was fearful of losing Madame, fearful of searching for someone new, fearful of finding someone worse, fearful of learning how bad things really were. My husband didn't press me; all this was my territory.

Finally I told Madame that my husband and I wanted to talk to her. This was serious business, and I needed him for moral support. Together we met with her in the high-ceilinged parlor, on the formal furniture, under the chandelier. We explained the situation.

The alcohol in the bottles is diminishing, my husband said. The bottles are being drained.

Madame looked at me, mildly surprised. I looked steadily back at her.

We are not happy, my husband said.

Madame looked at him and shook her head, raising her eyebrows.

It's simply that I have a terrible thirst, she said. She touched her pale throat with her long tapering fingers. "I drink all the time, anything, it doesn't matter to me whether it is alcoholic or not." She shrugged her shoulders. "It could be mineral water, soda water, quinine, or vodka. *Le Coca-Cola*! *Ça m'est egal*! It makes no difference." She shook her white curls and smiled confidently, her head high, waiting for us to reply.

Punctual, I thought.

For a moment, before we answered her, for that last moment, everything was still in place. Right then I had everything that I had wanted, everything that I had planned for and achieved: the beautiful house, the handsome husband, the enchanting baby, the exciting job, and the elegant French nanny.

THE NEXT NANNY was not from Paris but from Puerto Rico. She was younger than I, with a broad brown face, and narrow good-natured eyes. Her hair was thick and reddish-brown, and her accent was nearly impenetrable. At home she wore bare feet and clogs, faded T-shirts, and the shortest cut-off jeans I have ever seen. She was a perfectly wonderful nanny—kind, diligent, honest, and incredibly responsible. She took on all the housework as well as the baby, and she worked for me until I left the art world to start writing. Later I left New York, and moved to the country, and after that I never had a nanny.

My husband and I split up less than a year afterward. How could we not? We were never suited to one another, and this had become increasingly apparent to us both. We sold the pretty brick house, and we moved to different parts of the city, and then we each remarried. I forgave Barbara.

After Madame left, I found one of her navy wool skirts forgotten in the closet. I couldn't send it to her because she'd given us no forwarding address. No one ever called me to ask about a reference, so I could never tell anyone else how punctual she was. For a while I kept the skirt, thinking that somehow I'd get it back to her, but finally, during one of my moves, it vanished.

The house is still there, on West 4th Street, between 11th and

Bank, still a peaceful, shady block. My daughter is now married, and lives nearby. One evening I took her and her husband past the house, to show it to them. It was after dinner, and as we walked down the sidewalk, we heard our footsteps echo in the quiet street. The trees, of course, are bigger now.

I showed my daughter the tall windows where the front parlor was, and those on the next floor, where the dining room was, and then those smaller ones, on the top floor, where she and the French nanny lived, during those odd, disjointed months when I thought I had reached the pinnacle of my life.

THE LONG GOOD LULLABY

Alice Elliott Dark

ildie had to go. The question was when I'd get up the nerve to tell her. September passed.

When I woke up on the morning of October first, I vowed to do it—immediately. I was a grownup and a mother, after all, way too old to be such a wimp. I had a right to decide who was in my house—even if it was only a crummy apartment. I also had a right to send my child to pre-pre-preschool a few mornings a week, even if it meant making a new babysitting arrangement. Yes, it would be awkward, and maybe Tildie would even cry, but I'd make the separation as easy as possible, including giving her plenty of time to find another job. I could do this. I could do it today.

Yet as nine o'clock approached, my stomach was jumping. Maybe I should wait until tomorrow, when I'd surely be less nervous. Maybe it would make more sense to do it at the end of the week, when we'd both have the weekend afterward to recover and regroup. Maybe I should keep her one more month. . . .

These temptations sounded sensible. Too bad I couldn't convince myself of any of them. Nothing in my toolbox of anxiety-

reducing strategies was working for me anymore—not procrastina-
tion, not denial, not evasion, not even white lies. I'd used each of
these many times already to stick with Tildie for as long as I had.
They'd all become old and rusty, and were crumbling at the slight-
est touch.

Even reminding myself of everything that was good about having Tildie with us wasn't cutting it anymore. That list went under
the category of grasping at straws.

I had to get it over with, or risk reaching the point where I'd just
blow up, which I didn't want to do. I'd already made up my mind
that when I had the conversation, my speech would be simple and
direct, and that I'd leave all my recriminations toward her out of it.
What was the point of raising them now, when she'd be given no
opportunity to change? It wasn't her fault that I was too timid to address all but the worst things that happened on her watch. I'd let
the little things go. Like feeding him chicken and rice at a Latin
restaurant when we were raising him as a vegetarian. The fact that
although we purposely avoided taking him to stores—it seems absurd now that we imagined we could stave off consumerism by in-
troducing it late—he came home from his days with Tildie babbling
about the Gap and CVS. The call I'd received from an acquaintance
who said she saw Tildie slapping my son's hand at the playground in
Riverside Park. Not to mention Tildie's tardiness; she was late to
work often—some weeks it happened every day. I was working at
home so it didn't matter to anyone but me, but the aggravation
added up.

I kept quiet about it, though, except for indulging in some
passive-aggressive snippiness. I'd taken to heart the advice I'd
heard on the Penelope Leach shows I'd watched during my pregnancy. Penelope said to view your childcare helper not as a servant
but as an equal partner in raising your baby. I liked that; it afforded
a greater chance of a real bond between my child and his babysitter,
and it seemed humane all the way around. Adopting that point of

view, I thought I should cut my partner the same slack I'd want her to give me. If I were late, I wouldn't want to be scolded for it.

Along with Penelope Leach, I also had in my ear the voice of my best friend, who gave me a piece of advice shortly after my baby was born that somehow penetrated the fog of fear and fascination that dominated my thoughts at the time. "Don't think you are the only person who can take care of your child." Tildie did take care of my child well enough. What was the point of nitpicking over minor mistakes?

Yet the mistakes loomed as nine o'clock passed, and she was officially late again. It seemed the final ammunition I needed. My nerves settled as my purpose became clear. I was ready to do it. Today was the day.

The lock turned at about nine twenty-two. Before Tildie had a chance to settle in, and before the moment had a chance to fade, I approached her.

"I need to talk to you."

No one likes to hear those words. They never mean anything good is coming. She looked to the side.

"Okay. I know."

She had a strong voice, funneled through a light Jamaican accent. My son had picked up many of her phrases, and said "mon" at the end of his sentences.

Suddenly I realized what she'd said. She knew? How did she know we needed to talk? Did she realize I was on the verge of firing her? How? Or was this just another of her attempts to appease me? She was as nonconfrontational as I was. When I caught her hailing a taxi with my son perched on her arm, in complete violation of my buses-only policy (unless she had asked ahead of time and took the car seat), I actually had gotten angry. She had absorbed that anger placidly, showing no sign of a reactive irritation on her broad smooth face. When I finished, she simply said she was sorry. I chose to believe her, and that was that.

"I bin' wanting to tell you," she said.

Tell me? Tell me what? I was the one who had something to say. I wondered lately if she sensed it coming and had gone out of her way to give me excuses. She'd been arriving later than ever, and often took naps in the afternoon. I'd never discouraged this practice. She was my partner, after all, and as Penelope said not to assign housekeeping tasks to your childcare helper, I didn't ask her to do laundry or pick up the house while my son was asleep. Instead I thought it made sense for her to rest herself, to gird up for the next few hours. Lately, however, these naps were long, often lasting past the time my child woke up. I'd be in my room working at my desk and he'd come to my door, exactly what she was there to prevent. I'd have to play with him for a while and then go wake her. But she seemed just as dozy when she was awake, apt to nod off at any second. I'd considered the possibility that she'd taken a second job, but when I hinted around in that direction, she seemed bewildered. I hoped now that I'd been right about that. Maybe she'd been working up the courage to tell me she was leaving. I crossed my fingers. Nothing would make me happier at that moment than to sit back while she fired herself. Could I possibly be that lucky?

"Go ahead," I said.

She began to smile. That was odd. Then she ran her hands along the sides of her waist. Over her hips. Her jeans looked very tight. She was chunky to begin with, slow moving and placid, but now she was bursting out of her clothes. I'd seen her unbutton her jeans when she sat down. What did that have to do with anything, though? An answer to that question began to form in my mind. All the evidence came together, and I figured out the mystery just as she made her proclamation. Oh no. No, no, no, no, no.

"I'm pregnant," she said, bashful and pleased.

Of course she was. It all made sense—the naps, the weight, the smile. What could I do but smile back?

"Congratulations, Tildie." Part of me was able to hug her

warmly, because I'd recently learned how incredible it is to have a child. But another part of me, the part that had been working up to this for weeks, was shouting, *What the hell am I supposed to do now?*

MANY YEARS LATER, after we moved to New Jersey, I was waiting at the bus stop to go to New York when I fell into a conversation with a man I know who is an acting coach. I asked him about his work, and somewhere in his answer he made an offhand comment that was one of those bits of wisdom that, when grasped, completely rocks your world. "Your acting problems are your life problems," he said. Since then I've extrapolated that nugget to apply to every-thing; it doesn't take much to see that my nanny problems were my life problems. I tend to make big decisions impulsively, and then slowly pay the price for not thinking things through. That is an apt nutshell description of my relationship with Tildie. Her announce-ment of her pregnancy was just an upping of the price I was paying for making a poor decision to begin with. I wanted to blame her, but I couldn't quite get away with that. My fingerprints were all over the scene.

I hired Tildie impulsively, when I suddenly decided I needed to create saner hours for my work than simply when my child was asleep—especially as he was a famously nonsleeping baby. I heard about her through the grapevine in the park, and went down to meet her at the Jamaican nanny bench. She had an open, pleasant face, an easy laugh, and she connected with my son. Although I'd never hired a sitter even for a few hours, I was able to picture him with her for half the day. She knew all these other babysitters, so he'd have a social life beyond me, and spend hours in the park that I didn't have the patience for. I'd made a mental adjustment to the situation even before she came up to the apartment for an interview.

I know now what you are supposed to ask a prospective baby-sitter, and that you are meant to talk to many candidates before picking exactly the right one. In how many movies have a succession of creeps given alarming answers to the simplest of questions before a perfect Mrs. Doubtfire shows up? At the time, I felt that I was the one being picked, and that I had to appeal to Tildie, who might otherwise choose to work for someone else. My husband and I spent the interview selling her on us and our son. The questions I asked were mainly about Jamaica. I behaved more as if I were writing a travel piece than interviewing the person who'd be responsible for my child for one quarter of the day. Speaking of which: Tildie wanted a full-time job, whereas I'd envisioned hiring a part-time babysitter. Impulsively—here was a pattern at work, for sure—I decided that full-time was better after all. I could do that much more work if she were here all day. No problem!

It occurred to me that I needed to figure out how much to pay her. I was clueless, and had neglected to ask around. I was compelled to ask Tildie directly how much she charged. Eight dollars. An hour, I wondered? How could that be? That was half of what a dog-walker cost, for thirty minutes. I'd gotten five dollars an hour when I was fourteen, in the 1960s. I thought she must be making a mistake, but her English was perfect. She made eight dollars an hour, for doing a really hard job. I asked her if that was usual. She said it was more than what some other people she knew earned. Wow. What did that say about what society thought our children were worth, or the parents who raised them, for that matter? Who could live on such a low wage? Then I figured out how much it would cost us per week, and I had no idea how we were going to pay it. We were living very close to the bone. My husband had a part-time job and I was doing freelance proofreading on a very spotty basis. We both wanted to write, and were willing to live cheaply to afford the time. (Yes, that was still possible in Manhattan as recently as fifteen years ago.) The only way we could pay a babysitter was to cut deeply into our budget. No dinners out, no vacations except to parents' houses, no nothing.

The whole thing made no sense. I didn't want to spend the entire day apart from my child, or any time at all, for that matter. What had I been thinking? I could continue to work around him, just as I had been. Or I could get a job in a company that had a good day-care center in the building. This whole babysitter thing was for other people, not me.

"I'll give you a dollar an hour more than that, plus carfare," I said. "When can you start?"

THIS PREGNANCY WASN'T Tildie's first. After she'd been with us for about eight months, we were having a casual conversation when she told me that she had a six-year-old daughter in Jamaica.

I didn't know what to say. Every normal question seemed tasteless and intrusive. I finally asked whether she was planning to visit her while on vacation. I thought maybe I could pay for her ticket. I wanted to do something; I couldn't imagine being separated from my son like that. Tildie said it was too dangerous for her to go back. She didn't have a green card, and might not be allowed to leave again. The whole situation seemed desperate and awful, but Tildie was proud of herself for making money to send back to her mother for her child's needs. I had fantasies about getting Tildie a green card and bringing her daughter to the United States, then buying a house where we could all live and our children could grow up together. On the other hand, I already knew by then that I didn't want her with me forever, or much longer at all. I felt terrible for her, but there really wasn't much I could—or was willing—to do.

I thought of that faraway girl when Tildie told me her news. What would she think when she heard she had a brother or sister living with her mother? Would that bother her, or was Tildie such a shadowy figure to her that it wouldn't matter? Maybe she'd been told that Tildie was an aunt, and that the woman she lived with was her mother. Maybe, maybe, maybe. It really wasn't my life problem.

Knowing that, though, didn't stop me from thinking about it, and wishing life weren't so hard.

THE PRESENT PROBLEM of firing a pregnant woman was mine, however, and the question was, what to do? It was hard to think this through rationally, when I'd finally gotten up the courage to end the relationship. Just as I'd imagined Tildie in my life before I hired her, I was now living in a mental future in which she was gone. I wanted it over, now. But could I have what I wanted, in all good conscience?

My husband and I talked into the night. If we fired her now, she'd have to get another job. What would happen when someone called us for references? Could we legitimately withhold the information that she was pregnant, now that we knew it? According to her she was nearing the sixteen-week mark. A person who hadn't known her before might not notice the pregnancy, but she wouldn't be able to hide it for long. Should we even put her in a position where she'd be forced to obscure the truth about a condition that clearly affected her and whoever she'd work for? Would that be fair to anyone? How would we feel if someone did that to us—or if we hired a sitter who would have to leave, even if all went well, after only a few months? What about the child involved, bonding, et cetera? We couldn't not tell the truth, but if we did, we doubted anyone would hire Tildie.

No wonder there were federal laws protecting pregnant women. They needed protection. They didn't apply to Tildie, though. It was up to us to figure out what was right.

It was only a few more months, we decided. I suspected I'd count the days.

I DID, TOO; there wasn't a magical transformation because I'd acted out of the goodness of my heart. I resented having to be good, and her lateness still bothered me, but in other ways things were different between Tildie and me. Maybe it was because we were stuck with each other now, and had to make the best of it. There was definitely a feeling of commitment that I hadn't had before, when I was free to fantasize about her vanishing. I got up the courage to be more open about what I expected of her, and I cut her more slack. I was frank about the future, too; she'd have to look for a new job after the baby arrived. She had a boyfriend who'd help her after the birth, although she wasn't sure how long she wanted to be with him. I said we'd come to the wedding, but she didn't respond to that, and I wondered if she had a husband in Jamaica, too.

She worked until she was thirty-six weeks pregnant. James was born five weeks later, a healthy eight-pound boy. We took the subway to Brooklyn to see him—the first time we'd experienced the commute she made every day, twice. She was very proud of her beautiful baby who lay like a prince in an enormous satin-lined cradle. I agreed he was gorgeous. We left, proclaiming plans to get together again soon, but we never saw her again.

We did exchange Christmas cards for many years, and I was always interested to see James's growth and smile—so like Tildie's—but then one of us forgot one year, and we fell out of touch. That, too, is one of my life problems.

THE OTHER MOTHER

Anne Burt

get her machine again—as always. She won't pick up the phone but I know she's listening.

"If you ever loved my daughter," I begin this time, "please, please call and just talk to her. She misses you so much. It's been five months since you saw her. She talks about you all the time. Please, Carolina, please." My voice is a whisper by the end and when I hang up, my hands are shaking.

I no longer leave appropriate messages; since the calls are never returned I can talk as if into a void. The last message I left, a week earlier, was "Tessa thinks you're dead."

I'm the nightmare ex, the stalker who won't let go of the embers of a flame that blazed strong, then died a one-way death. Never before have I been so unhinged by a relationship; even the dissolution of my marriage didn't send me over the edge of reason. But Carolina—she was never supposed to betray me. She told me when my husband left that she would never leave me. She was my mother, my therapist, my guru, my heart.

Of course Carolina was none of these things: She was my daugh-

ter's nanny. Part-time nanny at that, until the nuclear-family structure that I had hired her to supplement broke into pieces, leaving
me an underemployed single mother with a preschooler. My husband moved out of our suburban New Jersey home and back to
New York City—a mere twelve miles on the map but with one of
the worst commuter routes in the country, it could take him as long
as two hours to reach Tessa. This rendered him useless in case of an
emergency. My mother lived too far away to help on a regular basis.
I scrambled to find a full-time job that would provide enough
money to live on; suddenly I, too, was a commuter who had to leave
our new apartment (still cluttered with boxes from the move out of
our former, spacious house) before the sun came up. Carolina gen-
erously agreed to arrive by six-thirty each morning and deliver
Tessa to preschool at noon, after years of more genteel working
hours. She rearranged her schedule of picking up her own grandchildren in the afternoons to bring Tessa home whenever Tessa's father couldn't make it back to New Jersey. With Carolina, Tessa was
much more than safe—she was secure. I could bury many of my
own feelings of powerlessness and fury at our precarious situation
because Carolina was there to pick up the role of stay-at-home parent that I had to surrender. And burying my feelings was exactly
what I needed to do at the time, or else I would have abandoned us
to the dark, tumultuous fears that knocked loudly whenever I
stopped moving, stopped working, stopped maintaining order day
after day, until I dropped, exhausted, into bed.

The morning I learned that Carolina was leaving, she was an
hour late to work. It was raining, so I didn't worry; she was such an
amazing babysitter that I ignored her iffy record in inclement
weather. I had just sold my first book, and used my good fortune to
end the grueling commute to New York and freelance again, spending more time with Tessa. Things were stabilizing, just a little, both
professionally and personally. Still, an array of deadlines loomed: a
proposal for an article; a finalized syllabus for the writing course I

would teach at a nearby university. And I was eager for Carolina to arrive. Tessa and I played Zoo on the kitchen floor surrounded by the piles of dirty laundry Carolina would wash that day. Out front, my trash cans lay scattered on the sidewalk after the garbage truck collected their contents; I left them there rather than go out in the rain to retrieve them because Carolina always brought them up to the house after she parked her car. My refrigerator was empty because on a rainy day, it was so much more efficient for me to go to the supermarket without dragging Tessa—we were even out of milk.

Nine A.M. passed, then nine-fifteen, then nine-thirty. I started to feel antsy about my work; much as I enjoyed my role in Zoo, pretending to be a lion, I was ready to leave the animal kingdom, or at least to shower and put on some clothes. I had bills to pay.

Then the phone rang: It was Carolina's twenty-two-year-old daughter, Lisa. Lisa called three or four times a morning for her mother, so I was unconcerned and answered blithely. Sometimes Lisa babysat for Tessa; when Lisa's engagement to her boyfriend, Miguel, fell apart, she practically moved into the house I owned before my husband left. Now she was happily employed at a company run by a close friend of mine where, I assured her, she would meet new men who would appreciate her brains as well as her beauty.

"Hey, Lisa, what's up?" I asked. "How was your vacation?" Lisa and Carolina had spent the week in Florida visiting Carolina's oldest daughter, Laura, and Laura's son, Marius. Laura often called here, too, usually when she had a dream about her mother that she thought was a portent of evil.

"Lisa! Lisa!" Tessa cried with delight. "Mommy, ask Lisa when she can babysit for me because I miss her so much!"

"Anne, I hate to tell you this with Tessa right there," said Lisa. Her voice sounded subdued. I immediately transferred into fight-or-flight mode—mind blank, body tensed, all five senses primed.

"My mother isn't going to come back."

"From Florida?" I asked.

"No, to work. She's going to retire."

No one died, but time stopped anyhow.

"When does she want to stop working?" I asked, still in shock but knowing that the first thing I needed was a time frame.

"She's not coming back at all. She's really sad because of her relationship with Tessa, but she can't see her. I don't know when she'll be home, but she won't come back."

I melted into tears. They wouldn't stop. Tessa looked at me and started crying.

"Mommy, why are you crying?"

I wanted Lisa to hear everything we were saying. I wanted her to suffer, too.

"Because Carolina isn't going to be your babysitter anymore."

Tessa started wailing. I cried even harder. The pair of us huddled in a clump on the kitchen floor in our pajamas, the cordless phone wedged between us, sobbing over our deep loss.

Finally, Tessa grabbed my arm there on the rug and asked, eyes fearful, "Mommy, can you be done crying now?" The best I could manage was to cry into my sleeve when her back was turned.

Why? Why? What had I done wrong? I pleaded with Lisa to tell me anything to explain Carolina's decision, but she refused to budge. Tell her how much we love her, I begged. Is it the money? I'll pay more, and more, I will. I knew it wasn't the money; Carolina's twenty-six-year-old son, Raymond, was making more than $200,000 a year as a mortgage broker, still lived in her house, and bought her a brand new Jeep just months earlier. When I owned a house, he put together a refinancing package for us. Carolina was more financially stable than I was, and had been from the time she started working for us. With Lisa graduating from college, Carolina missed children and had too much energy to stay home and do nothing. She was Argentinian, so couldn't take many jobs reserved for American citizens only. She still didn't trust her English.

Originally, I was happy that Carolina didn't need the money to survive—I told myself that it made the love she felt for Tessa that much more pure. She was willing to work three days a week instead of full-time. But, I realized now, that without financial incentive, Carolina had no reason to need me, while I had every reason to need her. She held all the cards and I lay in a puddle on the floor.

The next two weeks I found myself dissolving into tears several times a day. Attempts to communicate with Carolina or Lisa were futile. I was furious at Carolina's unprofessionalism. No notice? Refusing to tell me herself? What kind of employee ever treats a boss this way? At the same time, I was leaving frantic and unprofessional messages on her answering machine. I didn't fail to note with some irony that I pursued her and obsessed over her far more than I did my ex-husband. Since he left (and, I understood at this point, for quite some time before) Carolina and I were far more intimately involved in raising Tessa than he and I had been. I knew full well that in such an intimate relationship the lines between work and family are blurred; what I didn't know until Carolina left was how problematic the blurring could be.

DIVORCE CUTS HARD. I recently met a woman who decided to end her marriage, but her husband was still living in the basement of their house until he could find an apartment and she planned to use family money to buy him out of his half. All of this had transpired in the past couple of weeks. We were at a mutual friend's surprise fortieth-birthday party. She looked stunning, with her honey-blond hair blown out and her perfectly tanned skin smooth and soft. Her eyes betrayed her only if you knew her—they registered slightly glassy and just verging on fear. But she was flirting and drinking and looked like she was having a great old time.

"What's the difference if he stays or goes?" she laughed loudly over her beer. "I do everything around the house and for the kids already. Now I just won't have to deal with him!"

This is one of those early divorce statements that I've learned is a hundred percent guaranteed to unravel within two weeks, or, in this case, whenever her husband moves out of the basement and into his own place. The reason every divorcée, including myself, says such things is that we are thinking only about the emotional toll that the one-on-one relationship has taken. And that feeling is genuine— there is a true elation about those early days when the constant strain and stress of a bad marriage feels like it's simply gone. The adrenaline alone made me feel like I had the energy of two parents. But what crept in, what made the unraveling even more intense, was my realization that in the universe that was my home, I was now the only adult who knew the rules. When my husband lived there, I didn't have to question why these quirky rules through which we stumbled were ever established in the first place. And even more like the elated woman at the birthday party, I lost the person I used to resent when I stood in front of the kitchen sink at ten P.M. scrubbing the lasagna pan while wishing he was home taking out the trash instead of being out late, yet again. He took up conversation space in my head, even if it was an angry internal monologue that passed for conversation. Washing dishes in a fury is far more companionable than washing dishes with no one to resent. When my husband left and my own elation subsided, the loneliness rushed in, real and raw.

Enter the nanny. Carolina already knew the rhythm of our home. She would arrive for work and my loneliness would lighten. I didn't have to explain anything to her, and I felt then as if all I was doing was explaining myself and my choices to everyone I knew. I leaned on Carolina's kindness and loving presence. When she told me she would never leave me, I let myself believe her. With my husband gone, I needed someone who would never leave me more than I needed air.

WHEN CAROLINA DID LEAVE, I sobbed on the floor in my pajamas for a million reasons. I needed Carolina so I wouldn't be the only one washing the dishes. I needed her to ease my guilt about putting my daughter through her parents' divorce. I needed her to love my daughter and I needed to think that she loved me, too. And I sobbed because her disappearance, combined with my husband's, forced me to see that the only choice I had left was to finally, truly become the grownup in my family.

THE MORNING AFTER MY FINAL BEGGING, inappropriate phone call to Carolina, I was working at home while Tessa was at preschool when the doorbell rang. I came downstairs and there was Carolina, standing on the steps with a bag of Dunkin' Donuts' Munchkins, Tessa's favorite, in her hand.

"Don't ask me questions," she announced as she came in. As if I could—my crying started all over again, as pained and unstoppable as that rainy June morning five months earlier when Lisa lowered the boom. She sat down across from me, surprised, somehow, that Tessa was now old enough to be at school on a Friday morning at eleven A.M. When I was capable of again gasping "Why, why," a jumbled story came out despite Carolina's wish for privacy: Laura's son, Marius, had moved up from Florida to live with her; Raymond had a new baby and needed Carolina's help. She had a family that wasn't my family, no matter how many broken engagements I commiserated over and job hunts I helped with. Her family didn't want her to work outside the house anymore.

And yet, the next words out of her mouth were exactly what I longed to hear.

"I want to make babysitting for Tessa," Carolina said. "I want to help you."

It was as if the world—which had been careening off its axis through five months of cobbled-together part-time sitters, the goodwill of friends, and strips of my fingernails bitten off nightly as I obsessed over how my child would be cared for and my work would get done—stopped its crazy spinning and I could breathe again.

"No, no, you're too busy," I protested weakly, my tears starting to let up a bit. "It's too much. Your family needs you." But she insisted. What could I do? "Well, I know Tessa will be so happy," I said.

"I clean for you now," Carolina said. I noticed for the first time since she walked in how beautiful she looked in her immaculate white silk sweater and white pants. Her manicure was flawless, her hair a chic shorter cut than when I saw her last, with subtle red and light-brown highlights. She had just passed her sixtieth birthday. She stood up and went right to where she knew I kept the vacuum. She still knew everything about me, my daughter, my apartment.

"You go back upstairs and work. Go out, do something. I no want to get paid this time."

"Really?" I sniffled.

"My gift," she said with her beautiful smile. I hugged her, and returned to my computer.

If she had been an employee in a business I was running, I would have thanked her for all of her work for the past four years, told her that we were doing just wonderfully, and moved forward with my life while she moved forward with hers. But appropriateness simply did not apply in this situation. I was running a family, and running it with my heart, not my head. Yes, I was emotionally dependent on her for myself as well as for Tessa, and the reason was that with Carolina back in our lives, a fundamental piece of the otherwise unsolvable puzzle of childrearing was again in place. I pushed aside my anger at her for leaving because I had to. The job of being my daughter's nanny couldn't be filled by just anyone; it had to be filled by her.

Carolina was Tessa's other mother—and without another mother, another me, I was simply unequipped to do what I needed to do. Raising a child is a full-time commitment, and if I couldn't commit all of my time because I had to earn a salary, manage a divorce, and run a home, then I would twist and bend and contort in every possible way to keep Tessa's other mother in our lives. Between us, we could give her the love that she needed. If I wasn't divorced, maybe I would have had the luxury to be professional. But I was alone, and alone was not how I wanted to raise my child.

TODAY WE'RE IN A much happier situation. I've remarried, to a man with a daughter the same age as Tessa. We have the whole Ozzie and Harriet traditional-family thing going on now, albeit a postmodern version with two ex-spouses, multiple careers, five sets of grandparents, a couple of step-dogs, and four different last names. Tessa is in school full days; each morning as I watch her climb onto the yellow bus with her lunchbox and backpack I'm in awe that this confident girl is the same little toddler whose well-being I thought I had jeopardized through my overdependence on her nanny during a dark time in my life.

Carolina comes just one afternoon a week these days—as much for the sake of her friendship with Tessa as anything else. I no longer need her in the damaged, desperate way I did in the midst of my divorce, and she will never be part of the fabric of my new family the way she was of my old. This feels right. I trusted Carolina more than I trusted my first husband, which gave her a primacy in Tessa's life that's unnecessary now. I'm glad that she's still a part of our lives—when Carolina rings the doorbell (she used to have her own key; no more) Tessa's face lights up, and she careens into her with a gigantic bear hug. The five missing months of her relationship with Carolina are merely a blip on her radar now, and she falls into the same loving rapport that she and Carolina have always had. It's clear to me that the betrayal I felt was on my behalf, not Tessa's; Tessa feels nothing but love and gratitude each time they are together. Carolina is still Tessa's other mother. I no longer need her to be mine.

TINA

Katharine Weber

hen she came to work for us, there was only one chair in our entire house on which Tina dared to sit, a big green stuffed armchair in which she spent hours with Lucy, our tiny newborn daughter, perched on her vast bosom.

Tina weighed close to four hundred pounds. She was a black woman in her thirties, and she lived in a grim New Haven housing project with her family. The first time I saw her, I was stunned, and then I was embarrassed at how stunned I was, but I had never seen anyone so large. Tina was very matter-of-fact about being "big," yet her eating was enough of a pride issue that it took her months before she relaxed enough to eat anything at all during her days at our house.

Tina had four children of her own, two boys and two girls. Lisa, the oldest, had been born when she was fourteen. The youngest one was named Deejay—Dee for David Earl, her husband, and Jay for Justine, which turned out to be Tina's actual name. David Earl was a rather taciturn man who worked long hours at a local hardware factory, making doorknobs and lock sets.

Tina drove out to our rural location in an ancient, scorched-looking gold ragtop Buick that had no suspension whatsoever. Her arrival was heralded by the scraping sound of the Buick transmission bottoming out in the driveway. Soon enough, that big green stuffed armchair where Tina spent so much time with Lucy during those first months (a year and a half later, Lucy's sister Charlotte would also spend some of her first weeks perched on that ample bosom) had developed a similarly spring-shot suspension.

Tina had a wonderful smile, a sweet, mellifluous voice, and a big deep laugh. She loved to laugh, and was very easily amused not only by Lucy or Charlotte's every adorable gesture or scowl, but she was also genuinely intrigued by Weber family stories. "Say what?" she would exclaim over some improbable tale of my father's shady business ventures. "For real?" she would ask between chuckles over some childhood escapade of my husband, Nick. "He did that? My, my, my. And then what did your mother say?"

Tina was unflappable without ever being vague or careless. In my experience, most people as sweet and calm as Tina are also usually a little bit out to lunch, but within her serenity she possessed a remarkable intuitive alertness when it came to the needs of our babies, from infancy through toddlerhood and into their elementary-school years. I think she pitied us a little bit, too—prosperous white people who had to pay someone to love their babies because they didn't have sisters and aunts and grandmothers handy and eager to do it. Her own family was vast, with dozens of aunts and uncles and cousins of all ages, and dozens of children, scattered from New Haven to New York to South Carolina.

Tina's uncle was the minister at the Glorified Deliverance Baptist Church on Dixwell Avenue in New Haven, which was the center of her family life. Her widowed mother, Essie Mae, kept house for her preacher brother and lived next door to the church in the parish house. Countless numbers of Tina's relatives attended this small, storefront church, where Cousin Stella sang every Sunday in a joyful, molasses voice. Stella's daughter Mook played with Lucy and Charlotte in the summers.

Is this unbearably clichéd: the liberal white people feeling good about their children having a black friend? Were we somehow using Mook, who surely had another name I don't recall, a little black child imported from a grimy city for some fresh air and sunshine and wholesome food, so we could congratulate ourselves about our virtue and generosity and how marvelous it was that Lucy and Charlotte played so naturally with her and probably didn't even notice any differences? I can only say it didn't feel as forced or contrived at the time as it does now, in the telling. On the other hand, why did I fail to mention the fact that Stella cleaned our house on some of those days? It's an impossible bind for the guilty white liberal, always trying to find the balance, always trying to get it right.

When Lucy and Charlotte began to attend a private school in a leafy neighborhood of New Haven just blocks from the Yale campus, sometimes Tina took them to visit Essie Mae after she picked them up after school, only a few blocks but a world away. Those visits with Essie Mae impressed my children. Her house was cleaner than ours, they said, though she lived on the edge of a poverty-blighted part of New Haven that was unsafe after dark, and not so safe in daylight. The warmth and devotion that the members of Tina's extended family all felt about one another was joyful, and Lucy and Charlotte were swept right into the middle of it, the only white faces among all the children of varying ages brought along by the inevitable visiting cousins and aunts from around Connecticut, or up from New York City, or South Carolina.

Tina and her mother had lived in a house in another New Haven neighborhood when she was growing up, and for several years certain members of the Black Panthers had lived upstairs. Many other Black Panthers came to stay with them, Tina told me, and she had met a lot of them, among them Joanne Chesimard. She herself had no interest in Black Panther politics, though she did think it was a shame Fred Hampton got shot like that by the police. Years later, when I was idly perusing an FBI Most Wanted bulletin board at my post office while waiting to buy stamps, I was struck by Joanne Chesimard's list of aliases, which included "Justine Henderson," which was remarkably similar to Tina's full name.

Tina herself, meanwhile, never voted and had no curiosity about world events or local politics. She didn't know about the Holocaust, or where Europe was, or the difference between Republicans and Democrats. "The Democrats are the party of compassion! The Republicans want to see the rich get richer and the poor get poorer!" I would propagandize, and she would just smile and say, "For real?"

I never could get her to register to vote, though she was fascinated that I was able to make some calls to her congresswoman, whom I had met at a fundraiser, and get a broken streetlight at her housing project fixed very quickly, although her ordinary requests through housing authority channels had been ignored for weeks, despite the increase in crime and muggings that were made possible by the darkness. This experience expanded her sense of how the world worked far better than had my political fulminating, but she still wouldn't vote, saying she felt too ignorant to know how to make a choice.

The plain facts of the Holocaust did trouble her when I told her about it. Tina never seemed perturbed that we were sort of Jewish; she mostly seemed disappointed that we didn't do more about it, whatever it was. I am not certain that she ever really understood that we didn't accept the divinity of Christ. If she had ever been told that Jews were wicked, Christ-killing heathens headed straight to hell, she had the good taste not to bring it up. Our Chanukah candles were a fascination, but the puzzle, for Tina, was that our devotion to spiritual matters was very small, while her devotion to spiritual matters was very large. One of her many graces was that she never attempted to impose her religiosity on our daughters. (We had a teenaged occasional babysitter who did just that, which

dawned on me the day I drove by a church and Charlotte blurted
out, "St. Agnes! That's Gail's favorite saint!")

Tina had never known a white family so well and our Jewishness,
limited as it was, probably seemed to her to be part of our other-
ness. We had never known a black family so well, and her family's
devotion to the church was, for us, similarly defining. In fundamental ways, for better or worse, naive as this may sound, each family
became representative to the other of whiteness and blackness.

FOR EIGHT YEARS, Tina was in our family life several days a week.
She was endlessly patient with Lucy and Charlotte—far more patient than I might have been at certain times. Her serenity soothed
not only my children but also my husband and me. She was fond of
my mother, and while she listened sympathetically to my rants
about my mother's failings, Tina's kinder viewpoint offered me a
useful perspective. Tina was uneducated, having left high school at
fourteen when she had Lisa, but when it came to emotional intelli-
gence, I think it is reasonable to say she was a genius.

We helped Tina's family move out of the housing project and
into their own house through a HUD urban homesteading program.
We bought her a used station wagon, after the Buick broke down.
When my mother moved from a house in New York, we gave them
their pick of furniture and household items, including closets full of
castoff clothing which they took for distribution at church. Is it too
smug and PC to mention these things? Wouldn't leaving them out
be a significant omission of certain elements in the relationship?

Tina was extraordinarily graceful about being grateful without
being *too* grateful for our various kindnesses and generosities over
the years. The effusive gratitude was reserved for the occasion when
I helped her sister Pat out of a tricky situation in which she had
been falsely accused of child abuse by prosperous white people,
people we once considered to be good friends, who lied about the

circumstances of their baby's broken leg. They had used their whiteness and her blackness to misdirect the authorities, and I used my own whiteness to turn the investigations in a more fruitful direction. I did the right thing in a difficult situation, which should never have been necessary to do it in the first place.

At Thanksgiving I roasted ducks and made quarts of cranberry sauce for Tina's family, because she had discovered both things at our house, and loved them—the morning Thanksgiving delivery to her house was an annual tradition. Every summer we had a big cookout for Tina's family; some fifty people, half of them children, would attend. It seemed a natural thing to offer, as we often hosted all-school nursery school family picnics, and it was easy enough to do. I suppose there was something mildly self-congratulatory in our efforts, as well, given certain racist neighbors up the street in our white-bread Connecticut town. I did sincerely hope they would drive by just as our guests were arriving. So, yes, I suppose these events did satisfy some of our white liberal sanctimoniousness, but the picnics were fun, and there was nothing forced or staged about the warmth and joy of those afternoons.

Like Tina, most of her relatives were large people. "Big" was the word they used to describe the familial obesity. Some of the men were massive. It was at once completely comfortable and yet also almost surreal to be one of the four comparatively small white people surrounded by this enormous family gathering. Once, when a newcomer from out of town arrived with some sausages for the grill and Tina told him to give them to Nick, and he asked, "Which one is Nick?" and I replied, "He's the skinny white guy over at the grill," Tina thought that was about the funniest thing I had ever said.

I HAVE ATTENDED the Glorified Deliverance Baptist Church on Dixwell Avenue only twice. Once was when Tina's nephew Ray-Ray was shot and killed in a drive-by shooting at age nineteen. He was laid out in a suit that seemed oddly familiar; I am pretty sure it was one of my father's. The other time was for Tina's funeral. Ray-Ray's death brought the dangers of Tina's ghetto neighborhood, home ownership or not, into sharp focus. We began to have more concern about our children's safety when they went to her house. Tina had those concerns as well and it was at this time that she acquired a white German shepherd who patrolled the fenced-in yard.

When you're that heavy, your body will fail. Tina had developed diabetes, asthma, blood pressure, and heart problems, which was why she had to stop working for us. It was no longer safe for her to drive. And the truth was, as the girls had grown up, we had begun to outgrow Tina. Not only did we need her fewer hours each week, but also her level of literacy was too low for her to be able to provide practical homework support for second- and third-graders, and her physical limitations had become increasingly problematic. It was awkward that Lucy could read more fluently than Tina, that Charlotte's writing was better. It wasn't right that Tina's education had been so limited, and that was our explanation to the girls, when they questioned Tina's borderline illiteracy, which was unique among the adults in their orbit. Tina herself was, as always, graceful and matter-of-fact about her lack of ability to read and write at a higher level.

Over the next few years there were some wonderful visits, and then some sad ones, and then there was an emergency requiring some financial assistance when Tina was hospitalized in South Carolina on the brink of death. This was followed by a miraculous recovery, some more wonderful visits, and then came the final rapid decline, culminating in the loss of her legs, which made me think inanely of Ella Fitzgerald as I sat beside Tina's comatose form in the intensive care unit at St. Raphael's Hospital in New Haven.

Tina rallied for a few weeks, and then, somehow, despite a prolonged absence, she reinhabited her body briefly and seemed herself again (asking for Lucy and Charlotte, asking for news of our problematic brother-in-law), the way people can on their deathbeds. The last time I saw her, still in the hospital, was a few days before she died. She was fifty-one.

It was wrong that she had died so young, so unfortunate that she had left school at fourteen to have a baby, so unfair that she never got a better education or a better job, so tragic that her health was so bad, that she had eaten herself to death because of poverty and lack of education and everything that is wrong with our culture. It was infuriating that no benefits had been available for a medically supervised weight-loss program, although her final illness and hospitalizations must have cost hundreds of thousands of tax dollars.

We had always paid Tina in cash, at her request, knowing as we did that we were not contributing to her Social Security benefits, that we were part of the problem, not part of the solution, knowing that it was wrong, but it was what she preferred, and it was the simplest choice. We had paid her well, we had been generous according to just about any standard by which generosity can be measured—and yet it never felt like enough. Should we have funded her stay in an in-patient weight-loss program? I had even looked into these programs, but they cost thousands of dollars we really didn't have, and after I had argued her case to no avail on the telephone with her health insurance provider, which came through David Earl's factory job, the subject was dropped.

I had taught Tina to broil and roast chickens instead of frying them, I had introduced her to steamed vegetables, but those things had been for my own family's benefit primarily, though she did adapt some of our recipes for her own family. At a certain point, frightened by the major illness in South Carolina, she had gone on a strict regime for about a year, eating a great deal of salad, which she laughingly called "rabbit food." And she had lost some fifty pounds, but it was too little, too late.

The funeral was a glorious thing. Nick, Charlotte, and I (Lucy was away at school) were the only white people among the packed congregation, an echo of the summer cookouts. People greeted me by name, and I was embarrassed that I couldn't put a name to every face, though some of the elegant young women had been toddlers when I had last seen them scampering for another turn on the Slip 'n Slide or lining up for ice cream cones on one of those boundless summer afternoons. The funeral service was a living, breathing thing—"Our Lord has called our beloved Justine home," said the minister—with much spontaneous congregation response—"Yes he has! Praise Jesus!" "Yes he has, he's called her home!" There was singing and a little dancing in the aisles. I wept several times, as did most of the people around me.

If I was ever going to believe in the divinity of Christ, it was there and then. I think I came as close as I ever will. I could feel myself being lifted up by the spirit of the service and the people all gathered there, everyone moved by the spirit that had been our beloved Tina. It was a powerful force surrounding us, and that day, for that hour, I felt that I had been given a glimpse of the grace that had sustained Tina through all her days.

ACKNOWLEDGMENTS

We are deeply grateful to the contributors to *Searching for Mary Poppins* for their enthusiasm and for writing about their nanny experiences with such clarity, candor, and grace. They made our editorial work a pleasure.

This anthology would not exist without the intrepid faith of our agents, Amy Rennert and Beth Vesel, and of our publisher and editor, Laureen Rowland. These three women believed in this project when it was just a wisp of an idea and they each helped will it into reality. We're thankful as well to Danielle Friedman, Sara Loubriel, Liz Keenan, and Marie Coolman at Hudson Street Press, as well as to Abigail Powers and Norina Frabotta at Penguin, to our copy editor, John Morrone, and to attorney Jessica Friedman. Our sincere thanks to our children's nannies, Carol Johnson and Mirta Zuniga.

Lastly, we offer our eternal gratitude and love to our Sewanee sister, Anne Burt; to our mothers, Edwina Davis and Leigh Hyams; and to our husbands, Paul Bogas and Dave Barrett.

Susan Davis and Gina Hyams

ABOUT THE CONTRIBUTORS

 **JANE MEREDITH ADAMS** is the coauthor of the Lambda Literary Award–winning memoir, *The Last Time I Wore a Dress* (Riverhead/Putnam, 1997). A former staff reporter for the *Boston Globe*, her humorous essays have been broadcast on National Public Radio's *Morning Edition* and have appeared in many national magazines, including *O: the Oprah Magazine*, *Organic Style*, and *Health*.

 **SUZANNE BERNE** is the author of two novels, *A Perfect Arrangement* (Algonquin Books of Chapel Hill, 2001) and *A Crime in the Neighborhood* (Algonquin Books of Chapel Hill, 1997), which won Great Britain's Orange Prize. She currently teaches fiction writing in the English Department at Harvard University and lives outside of Boston.

MELISSA BLOCK is cohost of National Public Radio's evening newsmagazine, *All Things Considered*. She joined NPR in 1985, and worked as a producer, editor, director, and a New York–based correspondent before being named host in 2003. She lives in Washington, D.C., with her husband, writer Stefan Fatsis, and their daughter, Chloe.

MARINA BUDHOS has published two novels, *The Professor of Light* (Putnam, 1999) and *House of Waiting* (Global City Press, 1995), and a nonfiction book, *Remix: Conversations with Immigrant Teenagers* (Henry Holt, 1999). In 2006, she published her first young adult novel, *Ask Me No Questions* (Atheneum/Simon & Schuster). She has received a Fulbright Scholarship to India and the Rona Jaffe Award for Women Writers. She is an assistant professor of English at William Paterson University.

ANNE BURT is the editor of *My Father Married Your Mother: Writers Talk about Stepparents, Stepchildren, and Everyone in Between* (W. W. Norton, 2006). Her essays have appeared on National Public Radio's *All Things Considered* and in publications including *Salon*, the *Christian Science Monitor*, and *Working Mother*. She received *Meridian* literary magazine's 2002 Editor's Prize for Fiction and is working on a novel.

SUSAN CHEEVER is the bestselling author of twelve books, including five novels and the memoirs *As Good as I Could Be: A Memoir of Raising Wonderful Children in Difficult Times* (Simon & Schuster, 2002), *Note Found in a Bottle* (Simon & Schuster, 1999), and *Home Before Dark* (Houghton Mifflin, 1984). Her work has been nominated for the National Book Critics Circle Award and won the *Boston Globe*'s Winship Medal. She is a Guggenheim fellow, a member of the Corporation of Yaddo, and a member of the Author's Guild Council. She writes a biweekly column for *Newsday* and teaches in the Bennington College M.F.A. program. She lives in New York City with her family.

MEG WAITE CLAYTON is the author of the novel *The Language of Light* (St. Martin's Press, 2003), which was a finalist for the Bellwether Prize. Her stories have appeared in numerous literary magazines, including *Shenandoah*, *Other Voices*, *The Literary Review*, and *Chelsea*, and her personal essays have appeared in *The Virginia Quarterly Review* and *Runner's World*. She has also been a Tennessee Williams Scholar at the Sewanee Writer's Conference and an Emerging Voices Author at BookExpo 2004. A graduate of the University of Michigan Law School and former big-firm lawyer, she now lives in Palo Alto, California, with her husband and their two sons.

ALICE ELLIOTT DARK is the author of one novel, *Think of England* (Simon & Schuster, 2002), and two collections of short stories, *Naked to the Waist* (Houghton Mifflin, 1991) and *In the Gloaming* (Simon & Schuster, 2001). The title story of the latter collection was included in *Best American Stories of the Century*, edited by John Updike, and made into an HBO movie starring Glenn Close and directed by Christopher Reeve. She is working on a new novel called *The Poor Relation*.

MARISA DE LOS SANTOS is a poet, essayist, and novelist. Her first novel, *Love Walked In*, was published by Dutton in 2006. Her poetry collection, *From the Bones Out*, was part of the James Dickey poetry series from the University of South Carolina Press. Her poems have appeared in many distinguished journals, including *Prairie Schooner* and *Poetry*. Her essays have appeared on *Nerve.com* and in the anthology *The May Queen*. Film rights to her novel were recently aquired by Paramount, with Sarah Jessica Parker attached to star and coproduce with Michael London (producer of *Sideways*). She lives with her husband and two children in Wilmington, Delaware.

ELIZABETH GRAVER is the author of three novels: *Awake* (Henry Holt, 2004), *The Honey Thief* (Henry Holt, 1999), and *Unravelling* (Hyperion, 1997). Her short story collection, *Have You Seen Me?* (University of Pittsburgh Press), was awarded the 1991 Drue Heinz Literature Prize, judged by Richard Ford. Her stories and essays have been anthologized in *Best American Short Stories*, *Prize Stories: The O. Henry Awards*, *Best American Essays*, and *Pushcart Prize: Best of the Small Presses*. The recipient of fellowships from the National Endowment for the Arts and the Guggenheim Foundation, she is a professor of English at Boston College. She lives in Lincoln, Massachusetts, and is the mother of two young daughters.

ANN HOOD is the author most recently of a collection of short stories, *An Ornithologist's Guide to Life* (W. W. Norton, 2004), and of seven novels, including *Somewhere Off the Coast of Maine* (Judy Piatkus Publishers, 1988) and *Ruby* (Picador, 1998), and a memoir, *Do Not Go Gentle: My Search for Miracles in a Cynical Time* (Picador, 2000). Her short stories and essays have appeared in *Glimmer Train*, *Tin House*, *Condé Nast Traveler*, *Bon Appetit*, *More*, the *New York Times*, the *Washington Post,* the *Paris Review*, and many other publications. She is the recipient of a Pushcart Prize, a Best American Spiritual Writing Award, and the Paul Bowles Prize for Short Fiction.

PAMELA KRUGER has written about family, work, and women's issues for the *New York Times*, *Child*, *Parenting*, *Redbook*, the *International Herald Tribune*, *Fast Company*, and many others. She has been a contributing editor of *Fast Company*, consulting editor to Lifetime Television Online, and contributing editor to *Fortune Small Business*. Currently a contributing editor to *Child*, she coedited and was a contributor to the anthology *A Love Like No Other: Stories from Adoptive Parents* (Riverhead/Penguin, 2005). She is an adjunct professor of journalism at New York University, and lives with her husband and their two daughters in New Jersey.

CAROLINE LEAVITT is the award-winning author of eight novels, including *Girls in Trouble* (St. Martin's Press, 2004). The recipient of a New York Foundation for the Arts Award in fiction and a National Magazine Award nominee for personal essay, she was also a finalist in the Nickelodeon Screenwriting Fellowship Awards. A book columnist for the *Boston Globe* and *Imagine Magazine*, her work has appeared in *Salon*, *Parenting*, *Parents*, *Redbook*, the *Chicago Tribune*, the *Washington Post*, and more.

JOYCE MAYNARD has been a magazine journalist, a reporter with the *New York Times*, a syndicated newspaper columnist ("Domestic Affairs"), contributor to National Public Radio's *All Things Considered*, and a writer of fiction for both young adult and adult readers. Her novels include *To Die For* (Dutton, 1992), *The Cloud Chamber* (Atheneum/Anne Schwartz Books, 2005), and *The Usual Rules* (St. Martin's Press, 2003), the latter named a best book for young adults by the American Library Association. Her bestselling memoir *At Home in the World* (Picador, 1998) has been translated into nine languages. Mother of three grown children, Maynard, a New Hampshire native, now makes her home in northern California.

DAPHNE MERKIN is the author of the collection of essays *Dreaming of Hitler: Passions & Provocations* (Harvest/HBJ, 1999) and the novel *Enchantment* (Harcourt, 1986). She is a regular contributor to the *New York Times Book Review*, the *New York Times Magazine*, *The New Yorker*, and many other magazines.

JACQUELYN MITCHARD is the author of seven novels, including the *New York Times* bestsellers *The Deep End of the Ocean* (Viking Press, 1996), the first novel chosen for the Oprah Winfrey Book Club, and *Twelve Times Blessed* (HarperCollins, 2003). Her first children's novel, *Starring Prima! The Mouse of the Ballet Jolie*, was published in 2004 by HarperCollins. A longtime journalist, Mitchard writes a syndicated column ("The Rest of Us") that appears in 100 newspapers nationwide. She lives near Madison, Wisconsin, with her husband and their seven children.

ANDREA NAKAYAMA works as the production director for the New York book packager, Melcher Media. She works and writes from her home in Portland, Oregon, where she lives with her son, Gilbert.

JESSICA NEELY's work has appeared in *The Best American Short Stories*, the anthology *American Fiction*, *The Unfeigned Word: Fifteen Years of The New England Review*, and other literary journals and magazines. She lives and works in Washington, D.C.

KYMBERLY N. PINDER is an associate professor in Art History, Theory, and Criticism at the School of the Art Institute of Chicago. She teaches, writes, lectures, and curates exhibitions about representations of race, religion, and history in American art. Her work has appeared in the *Art Bulletin*, the *African American Review*, and *Third*

Text. She is the editor of *Race-ing Art History: Critical Essays in Race and Art History* (Routledge, 2002). Currently, she is researching murals in African American churches in Chicago, where she lives with her husband and three young children.

ROXANA ROBINSON is the author of seven books, including the novels *Sweetwater* (Random House, 2003) and *This Is My Daughter* (Random House, 1998), the short story collections *A Perfect Stranger* (Random House, 2005) and *Asking for Love* (Random House, 1996), and the biography *Georgia O'Keeffe: A Life* (HarperCollins, 1989). Her stories have appeared in *The New Yorker*, *Harper's*, *The Atlantic Monthly*, and other magazines, and several have been selected for *Best American Short Stories* anthologies. Her honors include a nomination for the National Book Critics Circle Award and fellowships from the National Endowment for the Arts and the John S. Guggenheim Foundation. She has taught fiction writing at the New School, Wesleyan University, and the University of Houston.

ELISSA SCHAPPELL is the author of the novel *Use Me* (William Morrow, 2001) and coeditor of the anthology *The Friend Who Got Away* (Doubleday, 2005), as well as a contributing editor to *Vanity Fair*, a cofounder of *Tin House*, and a former senior editor at the *Paris Review*. She is a frequent contributor to the *New York Times Book Review*, and her work has appeared in magazines such as *GQ*, *Vogue*, and *SPIN*, as well as *The KGB Bar Reader*, *The Mrs. Dalloway Reader*, and *The Bitch in the House*.

KAREN SHEPARD is a Chinese American who was born and raised in New York City. She has a BA from Williams College and an MFA from the University of Houston. She is the author of numerous short stories and essays as well as three novels: *An Empire of Women* (Putnam, 2000), *The Bad Boy's Wife* (St. Martin's Press, 2004), and *Don't I Know You?* (William Morrow, 2006). She teaches at Williams College and lives in Williamstown, Massachusetts, with her husband, writer Jim Shepard, their three children, and their two very strange dogs.

LAUREN SLATER is the author of six books, most recently a collection of short fiction, *Blue Beyond Blue* (W. W. Norton, 2005), and *Opening Skinner's Box* (W. W. Norton, 2004), which was nominated for a *Los Angeles Times* Book Award, Science Category, in 2005. Her work has appeared several times in *Best American Essays*. She was a 2003 National Endowment for the Arts honoree in nonfiction. She has a Master's degree in psychology from Harvard University and a doctorate from Boston University. She is a practicing psychologist in the Boston area.

REBECCA WALKER was named by *Time* magazine as one of fifty influential American leaders under forty. She is the author of the award-winning, international bestseller *Black, White and Jewish: Autobiography of a Shifting Self* (Riverhead/Putnam, 2001) and the editor of two groundbreaking anthologies, *What Makes a Man: 22 Writers Imagine the Future* (Riverhead/Penguin, 2004) and *To Be Real: Telling the Truth and Changing the Face of Feminism* (Anchor/

Doubleday, 1995). She has written for many publications, including *Vibe*, *Essence*, *Harper's*, *SPIN*, and *Glamour*, and her work is widely anthologized. Her memoir about becoming a mother will be published in 2006 by Riverhead/Putnam. She divides her time between New York City and northern California.

 **KATHARINE WEBER** is the author of the forthcoming novel *Triangle* (Farrar, Straus and Giroux, 2006) and *The Little Women* (Farrar, Straus and Giroux, 2003), *The Music Lesson* (Crown, 1998), and *Objects in Mirror Are Closer Than They Appear* (Crown, 1995), all three named *New York Times* Notable Books. Her short fiction has appeared in, among other publications, *The New Yorker*, *Story*, *Redbook*, and *Southwest Review*. Named by *Granta* as a regional finalist in their Best Young American Novelist Competition in 1996, she has taught fiction writing at Yale, Connecticut College, and in the Paris Writers Workshop. She is the Kratz Writer in Residence at Goucher College in 2006.

About the Editors

SUSAN DAVIS has worked in public radio for more than a decade and currently is a senior producer at North Carolina Public Radio/WUNC. She's a graduate of Reed College and has an MFA in poetry from the University of Houston. The author of a book of poetry, *Gathering Sound* (Fairweather Books), she lives in Chapel Hill, North Carolina, with her husband and two children.

GINA HYAMS is the author of several books on travel and the arts, including *Pacific Spas* and *In a Mexican Garden*, both published by Chronicle Books. Her work has also appeared in *San Francisco* magazine, *Newsweek*, and *Salon*. She lives in western Massachusetts with her husband and daughter.

Photo Credits

Photo of Jane Meredith Adams by Karin Evans
Photo of Suzanne Berne by Jerry Bauer
Photo of Melissa Block © 2004 NPR, by Steve Barrett
Photo of Marina Budhos by Claudine Ohayon
Photo of Anne Burt by Claudine Moore
Photo of Susan Cheevers by Sigrid Estrada
Photo of Meg Waite Clayton by Daniel Heron
Photo of Alice Elliot Dark by H. Durston Saylor
Photo of Marisa De Los Santos by Luigi Ciuffetelli
Photo of Elizabeth Graver by Debi Milligan
Photo of Andrea Nakayama by Jessica Clement
Photo of Ann Hood by Sarah Thacher
Photo of Pamela Kruger by David Rosenzweig
Photo of Caroline Leavitt by Jeff Tamarkin
Photo of Joyce Maynard by David Bartolomi
Photo of Daphne Merkin by David Vaughn
Photo of Jacquelyn Mitchard by Michelle Allen
Photo of Jessica Neely by Lee Phan
Photo of Kymberly N. Pinder by Mark Caughey
Photo of Roxana Robinson by Ellen Warner
Photo of Elissa Schappell by Emily Tobey
Photo of Karen Shepard by Barry Goldstein
Photo of Lauren Slater by Roswitha Hecke
Photo of Rebecca Walker by Marion Ettlinger
Photo of Katharine Weber by Marion Ettlinger